# Pro Ajax and Java™ Frameworks

Nathaniel T. Schutta and
Ryan Asleson

Apress®

**Pro Ajax and Java™ Frameworks**

**Copyright © 2006 by Nathaniel T. Schutta and Ryan Asleson**

ISBN-13 (pbk): 978-1-59059-677-7

ISBN-10 (pbk): 1-59059-677-3

Printed and bound in the United States of America 9 8 7 6 5 4 3 2 1

Trademarked names may appear in this book. Rather than use a trademark symbol with every occurrence of a trademarked name, we use the names only in an editorial fashion and to the benefit of the trademark owner, with no intention of infringement of the trademark.

Java and all Java-based marks are trademarks or registered trademarks of Sun Microsystems, Inc., in the U.S. and other countries.

Apress, Inc., is not affiliated with Sun Microsystems, Inc., and this book was written without endorsement from Sun Microsystems, Inc.

Lead Editor: Chris Mills
Technical Reviewer: John R. Fallows
Editorial Board: Steve Anglin, Ewan Buckingham, Gary Cornell, Jason Gilmore, Jonathan Gennick,
    Jonathan Hassell, James Huddleston, Chris Mills, Matthew Moodie, Dominic Shakeshaft, Jim Sumser,
    Keir Thomas, Matt Wade
Project Manager: Richard Dal Porto
Copy Edit Manager: Nicole LeClerc
Copy Editor: Hastings Hart
Assistant Production Director: Kari Brooks-Copony
Production Editor: Laura Esterman
Compositor: Susan Glinert
Proofreader: April Eddy
Indexer: Lucie Haskins
Artist: Susan Glinert
Cover Designer: Kurt Krames
Manufacturing Director: Tom Debolski

Distributed to the book trade worldwide by Springer-Verlag New York, Inc., 233 Spring Street, 6th Floor, New York, NY 10013. Phone 1-800-SPRINGER, fax 201-348-4505, e-mail orders-ny@springer-sbm.com, or visit http://www.springeronline.com.

For information on translations, please contact Apress directly at 2560 Ninth Street, Suite 219, Berkeley, CA 94710. Phone 510-549-5930, fax 510-549-5939, e-mail info@apress.com, or visit http://www.apress.com.

The source code for this book is available to readers at http://www.apress.com in the Source Code section.

*To Christine, for always believing.*
*—Nathaniel T. Schutta*

*For Sara, the love of my life, and Adam, my favorite playmate.*
*—Ryan Asleson*

# Contents at a Glance

About the Authors . . . . . . . . . . . . . . . . . . . . . . . . . . . . . . . . . . . . . . . . . . . . . . . . . . . . . . .xi

About the Technical Reviewer . . . . . . . . . . . . . . . . . . . . . . . . . . . . . . . . . . . . . . . . . . . . . xiii

Acknowledgments . . . . . . . . . . . . . . . . . . . . . . . . . . . . . . . . . . . . . . . . . . . . . . . . . . . . . xv

Introduction . . . . . . . . . . . . . . . . . . . . . . . . . . . . . . . . . . . . . . . . . . . . . . . . . . . . . . . . . . xvii

## PART 1 ■■■ Introducing Ajax

■CHAPTER 1    What Is Ajax? . . . . . . . . . . . . . . . . . . . . . . . . . . . . . . . . . . . . . . . . . . . . 3

■CHAPTER 2    Development Tools . . . . . . . . . . . . . . . . . . . . . . . . . . . . . . . . . . . . . . 27

## PART 2 ■■■ Libraries and Toolkits

■CHAPTER 3    Java-Agnostic Toolkits . . . . . . . . . . . . . . . . . . . . . . . . . . . . . . . . . . 75

■CHAPTER 4    Java-Specific Frameworks . . . . . . . . . . . . . . . . . . . . . . . . . . . . . . . 117

## PART 3 ■■■ Web Frameworks

■CHAPTER 5    Struts and Ajax . . . . . . . . . . . . . . . . . . . . . . . . . . . . . . . . . . . . . . . . 153

■CHAPTER 6    Tapestry . . . . . . . . . . . . . . . . . . . . . . . . . . . . . . . . . . . . . . . . . . . . . . 183

■CHAPTER 7    Spring and Ajax . . . . . . . . . . . . . . . . . . . . . . . . . . . . . . . . . . . . . . . 219

■CHAPTER 8    JavaServer Faces . . . . . . . . . . . . . . . . . . . . . . . . . . . . . . . . . . . . . . 263

■INDEX . . . . . . . . . . . . . . . . . . . . . . . . . . . . . . . . . . . . . . . . . . . . . . . . . . . . . . . . . 297

# Contents

About the Authors ............................................................. xi

About the Technical Reviewer ............................................. xiii

Acknowledgments ........................................................... xv

Introduction ................................................................ xvii

## PART 1 ▪▪▪ Introducing Ajax

▪CHAPTER 1    **What Is Ajax?** .............................................. 3

The Rise of the Web Application ..................................... 3

And Then There Was Ajax .......................................... 5

The XMLHttpRequest Object ........................................ 9

Methods and Properties ............................................ 12

An Example Interaction ............................................ 13

Avoiding Common Gotchas ......................................... 16

Ajax Patterns ..................................................... 20

    The Fade Anything Technique (FAT)......................... 21

    Auto Refresh .............................................. 22

    Partial Page Paint ........................................ 22

    Draggable DOM............................................ 23

Summary ......................................................... 25

▪CHAPTER 2    **Development Tools** ....................................... 27

JavaScript Source Code Editor ..................................... 27

    JSEclipse ................................................. 28

    NetBeans JavaScript Plug-in................................ 32

JavaScript Compression and Obfuscation ........................... 35

    The Dojo Toolkit's JavaScript Compressor .................. 37

Inspecting a DOM Structure ........................................ 38

    Mouseover DOM Inspector ................................. 39

Debugging Ajax Requests .......................................... 40

    NetBeans HTTP Monitor.................................... 41

    Firefox FireBug Extension ................................. 43

JavaScript Logging ............................................... 45
　　Log4JS................................................... 46
　　Lumberjack .............................................. 49
JavaScript Debugging Tools ....................................... 52
　　Using Venkman ........................................... 52
Testing Tools .................................................. 56
　　JsUnit................................................... 57
　　Selenium ................................................ 58
Summary .................................................... 71

# PART 2 ■■■ **Libraries and Toolkits**

■CHAPTER 3　**Java-Agnostic Toolkits** ............................. 75

Prototype .................................................... 75
　　$() ..................................................... 76
　　Working with Forms ....................................... 77
　　Manipulating the DOM ..................................... 78
　　Try: Simplified Browser Detection .......................... 84
　　Ajax Support ............................................. 86
script.aculo.us ................................................ 90
　　Effect ................................................... 90
　　Autocomplete ............................................ 98
Dojo Toolkit .................................................. 102
　　Animations............................................... 103
　　Effects .................................................. 105
　　dojo.io.bind .............................................. 107
Taconite ..................................................... 110
　　Taconite on the Client Side ................................ 111
　　Taconite on the Server..................................... 112
　　Getting Started with Taconite .............................. 113
Summary .................................................... 116

■CHAPTER 4　**Java-Specific Frameworks** .......................... 117

DWR ........................................................ 117
　　Installation............................................... 118
　　Installation Verification.................................... 120
　　JavaScript Templates....................................... 137

AjaxTags ................................................ 141
    The Ajax "Killer Application" ............................. 142
    AjaxTags Autocomplete Component....................... 142
Other Options .......................................... 149
Summary .............................................. 149

# PART 3 ■■■ Web Frameworks

■CHAPTER 5    **Struts and Ajax** ................................... 153

Struts Design ........................................... 153
Ajax Validation ......................................... 155
Struts Validation........................................ 156
Struts and Ajax Integration .............................. 157
    Ajax-Powered Validation .............................. 161
    Implementing Struts .................................. 163
    Struts and Ajax Design Considerations .................. 179
The Future of Struts...................................... 180
    Struts 1.3 and Beyond ................................ 181
    Struts Shale......................................... 181
    Struts Ti ............................................ 182
Summary .............................................. 182

■CHAPTER 6    **Tapestry** ........................................ 183

What Is Tapestry? ...................................... 183
Getting Started ........................................ 185
Calling the Server ...................................... 188
Tapestry Forms ........................................ 193
Tapestry Exceptions .................................... 203
Tapestry and Ajax ...................................... 204
    Tacos Components.................................... 205
    Setting Up Tacos..................................... 206
    Using a Component .................................. 206
    Enabling Debug Information ........................... 211
    Modifying the Form Example........................... 212
Summary .............................................. 217

■CHAPTER 7    **Spring and Ajax** ........................................... 219

What Is Spring? ............................................. 219
    Just Another Framework? ................................. 220
    Aspect-Oriented Programming and Dependency Injection ...... 220
Getting Started with Spring ................................... 225
    Ajax and Spring ........................................... 234
    The Inventory Control Application .......................... 234
Summary .................................................. 261

■CHAPTER 8    **JavaServer Faces** ........................................ 263

What Is JSF? ............................................... 263
Getting Started with JSF .................................... 264
Dynamic Navigation ........................................ 269
JSF Taglibs ............................................... 270
Validating and Converting ................................... 274
Developing JSF Applications with an IDE ........................ 280
Other JSF Technologies ..................................... 282
    Apache Tomahawk ........................................ 282
    Facelets ................................................ 282
    Shale .................................................. 283
    Seam .................................................. 283
The JSF Life Cycle ......................................... 283
    Restore View ........................................... 284
    Apply Request Values .................................... 284
    Process Validation ...................................... 285
    Update Model .......................................... 285
    Invoke Application ...................................... 285
    Render Response ........................................ 285
JSF and Ajax ............................................. 285
JSF Ajax Components ...................................... 292
Summary .................................................. 295

■INDEX .................................................... 297

# About the Authors

**NATHANIEL T. SCHUTTA** is a senior software engineer and author in the Twin Cities area of Minnesota with extensive experience developing Java Enterprise Edition–based web applications. He has a degree in Computer Science from St. John's University (MN) and a master's of science degree in software engineering from the University of Minnesota. For the last several years, Nathaniel has focused on user interface design, contributed to corporate interface guidelines, and consulted on a variety of web-based applications. A longtime member of the Association for Computing Machinery's Computer-Human Interaction Special Interest Group and a Sun-certified web component developer, Nathaniel believes that if the user can't figure out your application, then you've done something wrong. Along with his user interface work, Nathaniel is the cocreator of the open-source Taconite framework (`http://taconite.sf.net`), and has contributed to two corporate Java frameworks, developed training material, and led several study groups. During the brief moments of warm weather found in his home state of Minnesota, he spends as much time on the golf course as his wife will tolerate. He's currently exploring Ruby, Rails, and Mac OS X. For more of his random thoughts, check out his blog at `www.ntschutta.com/jat`.

**RYAN ASLESON** is a software developer who lives and works in the Twin Cities area of Minnesota. Ryan has been building web applications since 1998 and has extensive experience with JavaScript and web development tools. He helped his organization make the transition from servlet-based content creation to JavaServer Pages and has also maintained a corporate web application framework based on Java Enterprise Edition. He is the cocreator of the open-source Taconite framework (`http://taconite.sf.net`), which greatly simplifies Ajax development. His interests include performance tuning and standards-based development. When not working, Ryan enjoys spending time with his family and doing outdoor activities such as fishing, hunting, and water sports.

# About the Technical Reviewer

**JOHN R. FALLOWS** is a Java architect at TXE Systems. Originally from Northern Ireland, John graduated from Cambridge University in the United Kingdom and has worked in the software industry for more than ten years.

Prior to joining TXE Systems, John worked as a JavaServer Faces technology architect at Oracle. John played a leading role in the Oracle ADF Faces team to influence the architecture of the JavaServer Faces standard and to extend the standard to provide Ajax functionality in the ADF Faces project.

John is a popular speaker at international conferences such as JavaOne and JavaPolis, and he has written numerous articles for leading IT magazines such as *Java Developer's Journal*.

John is the author of the recently published book *Pro JSF and Ajax: Building Rich Internet Components* (Apress, 2006).

# Acknowledgments

A huge thanks to the team at Apress for providing us with another opportunity to express our passion about Ajax! Thanks to Chris Mills for helping us refine our rough ideas into the finished product you see before you. Hats off to Richard Dal Porto for keeping us focused and on schedule. Gregg Bollinger and John Fallows provided valuable feedback that helped make this a better book. Hastings Hart had the misfortune of fixing our multiple spelling and grammatical mistakes, and for this we are forever grateful. We thank Laura Esterman for guiding us through the final production process, and we were thrilled to see our work transformed from words in a word processor to a formatted book. We appreciate the support that our agent, Laura Lewin, and the staff at Studio B gave us throughout this adventure.

Nathaniel T. Schutta and Ryan Asleson

First and foremost to my coauthor, Ryan—I can't thank you enough for your tireless effort on this book; I don't know how you did it! I'm proud and honored to have you as a friend and partner. Thanks to Sara and Adam for your support in this adventure, it was good of you to share Ryan (again). I can't thank my wife enough for putting up with me throughout this book. I couldn't have done it without your love and patience. During this entire experience you've never lost your head (even when I did), and your faith in me kept me grounded. Often life only makes sense backwards—but for that one project, I'd have never met Nathan Good, who gave me the inspiration to write in the first place.

I owe a huge debt to my parents, one that can never be repaid. Without their foresight, I probably wouldn't even be in this field. Thanks for seeing the future and making sure I had the latest hardware. You fueled a passion for reading that has evolved into this new adventure of writing. Thanks, Mom and Dad—I don't say it enough! A big thanks to Brent Ashley for all his support and advice over the last year; his counsel means a lot to me. Special thanks to Jeff Jensen of the Twin Cities Java User Group, John Collins of the University of Minnesota, Kasi Periyasamy of the University of Wisconsin at La Crosse, Jim Schnepf and Mike Heroux of St. John's University, and Aleh Matus of OTUG for providing us forums to spread the word on Ajax. We are deeply appreciative for all your help. I know I've left some very deserving people off this list and for that my heartfelt apologies—I only have so much space! Thanks again to everyone mentioned here and all those who I keep in my heart.

Nathaniel T. Schutta

I have to thank my friend and coauthor, Nate, for making the authoring process as enjoyable as it has been. I can't thank you enough! I couldn't ask for a better teammate. Thank you for your hard work and unmatched dedication to this book. Christine, thanks for letting Nate work with me on another project.

Words cannot describe the love and appreciation I have for my wife, Sara, who has graciously supported me during the sometimes grueling authoring process. I could not have done it without your unwavering support and understanding. My son, Adam, provided me with hours and hours of much needed fun and joy away from the computer.

I also extend my thanks to those important people in my life who helped shape me into the person I am today. I can't list all of those people here, but certainly you know who you are! Finally, I thank Mom and Dad for everything they have done for me over the years; without their love and encouragement, none of this would be possible.

Ryan Asleson

# Introduction

**W**e thought we had found the Holy Grail of software development when we started building web applications several years ago. Previously we had been developing thick client applications that required a lengthy installation process every time a new version of the company's application was released. The application was deployed to several hundred users scattered across the country, and much to our dismay we had to watch as the complex and error-prone installation process continually caused headaches and angst for developers and users alike.

Deploying an application through a browser seemed like a much more palatable option because it would eliminate the need to install software on the client computer. So, like many others, our organization moved swiftly to deploying applications to the web.

Despite the relative ease of deployment, web applications still had their share of issues. Most notable from a user's perspective was the significant loss of rich interactivity provided by the user interface. Web applications were constrained to the basic set of widgets provided by HTML. Worse yet, interacting with the server required a complete refresh of the page, which was disconcerting to users who were familiar with rich client/server applications.

We always considered this constant need to refresh the page a serious liability of web applications and often experimented with ways to avoid a page refresh whenever possible. We even at one point considered writing a Java applet that would handle the communication between the browser and the server. However, it soon became apparent that as more web applications were deployed, users simply got used to the constant page refreshes, and our zeal for finding alternatives slowly faded.

Fast-forward five years. Even before the term *Ajax* was coined, asynchronous communication between the browser and server using the XMLHttpRequest object was creating a buzz within the developer community thanks to applications such as Google Suggest and Gmail. The XMLHttpRequest object had been available in Internet Explorer for several years, but now that it was being supported by other browsers, it was poised for a breakthrough. We added Ajax functionality to an existing Java application we happened to be working on at the time, and we were so impressed with the results that we thought, "Hey, somebody should write a book about this." Thus, the seeds for this book were sown.

# An Overview of This Book

*Pro Ajax and Java™ Frameworks* is written to give you, the Java developer, all the tools you need to add Ajax techniques to your existing or future applications. Our motto while writing this book was, "Everything you need to know; nothing you don't." We assume that as a reader of this book, you are already an experienced web application developer. Because of this, we focus on the topics that are most likely new to you: Ajax and its associated tools and techniques.

Chapter 1 is a whirlwind tour of Ajax. We cover the basics of the XMLHttpRequest object along with some of the common gotchas of Ajax development. We also cover some of the common patterns you'll see in Ajax development.

Chapter 2 provides an overview of the tools that will make developing Ajax applications easier. We touch on JavaScript editors, formatters, and obfuscators. Debugging can be a real pain, which is why we've shown you a wealth of tools that treat JavaScript like the first-class citizen that it is. For starters, we'll show you how to log without using alerts. Of course you'll also want to test your code, which is why we review JsUnit and Selenium, proving that testing isn't just for server-side code.

Although Ajax certainly isn't rocket science, that doesn't mean you want to do all the heavy lifting yourself. In Chapter 3 we take a look at a variety of frameworks and toolkits that you'll want to leverage to make developing Ajax applications a snap. We'll review Dojo, Prototype, script.aculo.us, Taconite, and the Yahoo! library.

Chapter 4 continues our look at libraries, focusing on those that are of particular interest to the Java developer. We'll review DWR and AjaxTags, giving you an idea of the strengths of each library.

The second half of the book shows you how to integrate Ajax techniques into four of the leading Java frameworks. Chapter 5 discusses the wildly popular Struts framework. We'll show you how to take advantage of Struts validation, and we also discuss design considerations with Struts and Ajax.

Chapter 6 covers the component-based Tapestry framework. After an overview of Tapestry, we show you how to leverage the Ajaxified Tacos components to spiff up your applications.

You can hardly turn around these days without running into a Spring-based application, and in Chapter 7, we show you how to leverage Ajax in the Spring space. We show you how using DWR makes developing Ajaxified Spring applications a snap.

Of course no discussion of Java web frameworks would be complete without a look at JavaServer Faces. After showing you the basics of JSF, we show you how you can write your own Ajax components, and we also introduce you to prebuilt Ajax components.

# Obtaining This Book's Source Code

All the examples in this book are freely available from the Source Code section of the Apress website. Point your browser to www.apress.com, click the Source Code link, and find *Pro Ajax and Java™ Frameworks* in the list. From this book's home page you can download the source code as a ZIP file. The source code is organized by chapter.

# Obtaining Updates for This Book

Despite our best efforts, you may find an occasional error or two scattered throughout the book—although we hope not! We apologize for any errors that may be present in the text or source code. A current errata list is available from this book's home page on the Apress website (www.apress.com) along with information about how to notify us of any errors you may find.

# Contacting Us

We value your questions and comments regarding this book's content and source code examples. Please direct all questions and comments to proajaxandjava@gmail.com. We'll reply to your inquiries as soon as we can; please remember, we (like you!) may not be able to respond immediately.

Thank you for buying this book! We hope you find it a valuable resource and enjoy reading it as much as we enjoyed writing it.

Best regards,
Nathaniel T. Schutta and Ryan Asleson

# PART 1

■ ■ ■

# Introducing Ajax

In the recent past, the word "Ajax" conjured up a popular cleaner, an Amsterdam football club, perhaps even a Greek hero. Today "Ajax" has taken on yet another meaning—it is one of the most talked-about technologies on the web. Google Maps, Basecamp, ESPN—all of these sites take advantage of Ajax techniques to improve their user experiences, and although the first uses of Ajax may have originated at leading technology companies, by the time you finish reading this book, your users will have encountered an Ajaxified website. In case you haven't noticed, their expectations for a web application are rising. Despite what some contend, Ajax is not rocket science; in fact, most of you probably already know more than enough to take advantage of this mix of technologies. In this section, we'll give you a refresher on the basics of Ajax and discuss some tools that will make adding Ajax to your application simpler.

# CHAPTER 1

■ ■ ■

# What Is Ajax?

The Internet as we know it is a very different beast than when it began. Although many find it second nature to buy the latest DVD or plan their next vacation online, in the beginning there was only text; today we have video podcasts and can easily share photos of the cats with anyone in the world. What began as a mechanism to enable greater collaboration in the research community has morphed into not only a significant sales channel but also one of the primary delivery mechanisms for modern applications.

## The Rise of the Web Application

In the early days, web pages were simple static text, which worked fine for posting your latest paper or a class schedule. However, it didn't take long for people to want a dynamic experience. As the web browser became a nearly ubiquitous aspect of everyone's operating system, people started developing web-based applications. Considering the rather poor user experience possible within early browsers, this may have seemed like an odd choice, but there are three major benefits to the thin client, at least for the developers.

The barrier of entry for using a web application is very low—a prospective user doesn't need to install any software. If you don't think this matters, ask a decent-sized group how many have used Google Maps (a web-based mapping program); chances are nearly every hand will go up. Ask the same audience how many have used Google Earth (a desktop application that combines satellite imagery with maps that allows people to virtually fly over the earth). Odds are the former will have more takers (especially if you're talking to a group of Mac users—until recently, Google Earth worked only on a PC.) Think of it this way: are you more likely to try an application that involves little more than a click or one that requires you to download and run an executable?

The ubiquity of the browser is closely related to a lower barrier of entry. Unlike most installed applications, a web application will work on any operating system that has a browser written for it. Although this issue is largely mitigated in the Java space, just ask the folks maintaining the Standard Widget Toolkit (SWT) how much fun it is to work with five code bases. A browser-based application allows developers to reach an extremely large audience.

Compared to thick clients, a web app is much easier to maintain. If you've ever worked on a traditional thick app, you know how much fun it is to manage dependencies. Maybe your latest upgrade relies on version 1.2.3 of Spiffy Library but your user only has the 1.2 model. Sure, you can update that as part of your install, but what happens when their other critical application relies on 1.2 and just can't seem to function right with 1.2.3? Of course your users get the rich experience that an installed application provides, but the cost of managing upgrades can be huge. With a browser-based application, we control the servers, so rolling out a fix is (usually) easy. If we need a newer library, we can just add it because we control the deployment environment. This also allows us to make changes more frequently—just push the new code to the servers, and your customers get the latest version.

Despite the advantages, the web has a major downside as an application medium. First, no one would confuse the average web application with Word or Quicken. Sure, if you're moving from the mainframe to the browser, you might not mind, but if your previous app had all the power of the thick client, they might be a tad upset when you take that rich experience away from them. Still, the pros usually outweigh the cons, and a good number of software engineers have spent the last several years building web applications.

Still, users weren't entirely satisfied with the thin client. We may have convinced them to just accept it, but truth be told, the differences between the average web app and a dumb terminal connected to the mainframe are mostly cosmetic.[1] Over the years, we've evolved from using CGI bin scripts to JSPs, and more recently, we have a host of XML-based languages such as XML User Interface Language (XUL) and Extensible Application Markup Language (XAML) that aim to provide a near desktop–like look and feel. Of course Flash has been used to create some fantastic interfaces, but it requires expensive tools and browser plug-ins.

But to reach the widest possible audience, we've been forced to stick pretty close to the browser, meaning that our applications have been tied directly to the synchronous nature of the request/response underpinnings of the Internet. Although request/response makes perfect sense for publishing an article, repainting the entire page even if only a couple of things have changed is not the most usable (or performant) approach. If only we could send a request asynchronously and update just what changed....

---

1. When a former employer first ventured into the land of web applications in 1998, our CIO was fond of calling our new web apps "lipstick on a pig."

# And Then There Was Ajax

Today we have another tool to create truly rich browser-based applications: Ajax. Before you ask, Ajax is more of a technique than a specific technology, though JavaScript is a primary component. We know you're saying, "JavaScript is not worth it," but application and testing frameworks are easing the burden on developers because of the resurgent interest in the language because of Ajax and better tool support. With the introduction of Atlas, Microsoft is throwing its weight firmly behind Ajax, and the infamous Rails web framework comes prebuilt with outstanding Ajax support. In the Java space, Sun has added several Ajax components to its BluePrints Solutions Catalog, and any web framework worth its salt has announced at least minimal support for Ajax.

To be honest though, Ajax isn't anything new. In fact, the "newest" technology related to the term—the XMLHttpRequest object (XHR)—has been around since Internet Explorer 5 (released in the spring of 1999) as an ActiveX control. What is new is the level of browser support. Originally, the XMLHttpRequest object was supported in only Internet Explorer (thus limiting its use), but starting with Mozilla/Firefox 1.0, Opera 7.6, and Safari 1.2, support is widespread. The little-used object and the basic concepts are even covered in a W3C standard: the DOM Level 3 Load and Save Specification. At this point, especially as applications such as Google Maps, Google Suggest, Gmail, Flickr, Netflix, and A9 proliferate, XHR is becoming a de facto standard.

Unlike many of the approaches used before, Ajax works in most modern browsers and doesn't require any proprietary software or hardware. In fact, one of the real strengths of this approach is that developers don't need to learn some new language or scrap their existing investment in server-side technology. Ajax is a client-side approach and can interact with J2EE, .NET, PHP, Ruby, and CGI scripts—it really is server-agnostic. Short of a few minor security restrictions, you can start using Ajax right now, leveraging what you already know.

Who is using Ajax? As mentioned, Google is clearly one of the leading early adopters with several examples of the technology including Google Maps, Google Suggest, and Gmail, to name just a few applications. Yahoo! is beginning to introduce Ajax controls, and Amazon has been adding a number of interesting features of late. One example involves product categories. Amazon has clearly grown beyond its roots as a purveyor of books, and although their tab metaphor has worked for a while, after Amazon created a certain number of stores, it proved impractical. Enter their new design shown in Figure 1-1. Simply hover over the Product Categories tab to display a list of all the different Amazon stores, allowing you to quickly select the one you wish to explore.

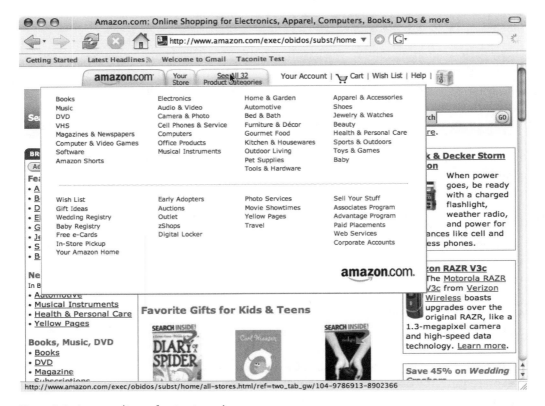

**Figure 1-1.** *Amazon's product categories*

Another site that takes advantage of a number of Ajax techniques is the DVD rental company Netflix. When a customer hovers over the graphic for a movie, the movie ID is sent back to their central servers, and a bubble appears that provides more details about the movie (see Figure 1-2). Again, the page is not refreshed, and the specifics for each movie aren't found in hidden form fields. This approach allows Netflix to provide more information about its movies without cluttering up its pages. It also makes browsing easier for their customers. They don't have to click the movie and then click back to the list (known as pogo-sticking in the usability community); they simply have to hover over a movie.

**Figure 1-2.** *The Netflix browse feature*

We want to stress that Ajax isn't limited to "dot-com" darlings; corporate developers are starting to scratch the surface as well, with many using Ajax to solve particularly ugly validation situations or to retrieve data on the fly. Heck, one of our local papers, the *Star Tribune* (`www.startribune.com`) recently added a useful Ajax feature. Although most news sites show related articles, there is only so much real estate that can be taken up with these links. Rather than deny their readers these other links, the *Star Tribune* site shows additional related links when a user hovers their mouse over a "See more related items" link (see Figure 1-3).

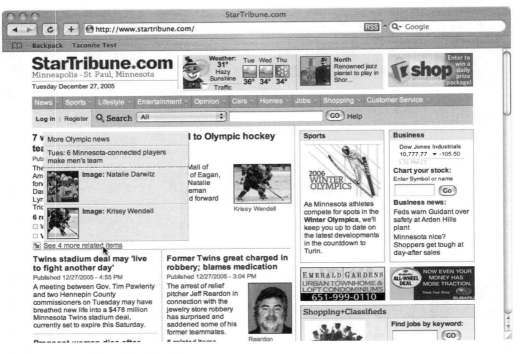

**Figure 1-3.** StarTribune's *related items*

Although it isn't exactly new, the *approach* that is the meat of Ajax is an important shift in the Internet's default request/response paradigm. Web application developers are now free to interact with the server asynchronously, meaning they can perform many tasks that before were limited to thick clients. For example, when a user enters a ZIP code, you can validate it and populate other parts of the form with the city and state; or, when they select "United States", you can populate a state drop-down list. We've been able to mimic these approaches before, but it's much simpler to do with Ajax.

So who invented Ajax? The exact origin involved is a subject of debate; however, Jesse James Garrett of Adaptive Path first coined the term in February 2005. In his essay "Ajax: A New Approach to Web Applications" (www.adaptivepath.com/publications/essays/archives/000385.php), Garrett discusses how the gap is closing between thick client, or desktop, applications and thin client, or web, applications. Of course, Google really gave the techniques a high profile when it released Google Maps and Google Suggest in Google Labs; also, there have been numerous articles on the subject. But Garrett gave us a term that wasn't quite as wordy as Asynchronous, XMLHttpRequest, JavaScript, CSS, the DOM, and so on. Though originally considered an acronym for Asynchronous JavaScript + XML, the term is now used simply to encompass all the technologies that allow a browser to communicate with the server without refreshing the current page.

We can hear you saying, "So what's the big deal?" Well, using XHR and the fact that you can now work asynchronously with the server lets you create web applications that are far more dynamic. For example, say you have a drop-down list that is filled based on the input in some other field or drop-down list. Ordinarily, you would have to send all the data down to the client when the page first loaded and use JavaScript to populate your drop-down list based on the input. It's not hard to do, but it does bloat the size of your page, and depending on just how dynamic that drop-down list is, size could be an issue. With Ajax, when the trigger field changes or the focus is lost, you can make a simple request to the server for only the information you need to update your drop-down list.

Imagine the possibilities for validation alone. How many times have you written some JavaScript validation logic? Although the edit might be simple in Java or C#, the lack of decent debuggers, combined with JavaScript's weak typing, can make writing them in JavaScript a real pain and error prone to boot. How often do these client-side validation rules duplicate edits on the server? Using XHR, you can make a call to the server and fire *one* set of validation rules. These rules can be far richer and more complex than anything you would write in client-side JavaScript, and you have the full power of debuggers and integrated development environments.

We can hear some of you now saying, "I've been doing that for years with IFRAMES or hidden frames. We've even used this particular technique as a way to post or refresh parts of a page instead of the entire browser, and truth be told, it works." A fair point possibly, but many would consider this approach a hack to get around XHR's original lack of cross-browser support. The XHR object that is the heart of Ajax is truly designed to allow asynchronous retrieval of arbitrary data from the server.

As we've discussed, traditional web applications follow a request/response paradigm. Without Ajax, the entire page (or with IFRAMEs, parts of the page) is reloaded with each request. The previously viewed page is reflected in the browser's history stack (though if IFRAMEs are used, clicking the Back button doesn't always result in what the user expects). However, requests made with XHR are *not* recorded in the browser's history. This too can pose an issue if your users are used to using the Back button to navigate within your web application.

# The XMLHttpRequest Object

Although Ajax is more of a technique than a technology, without widespread support for XMLHttpRequest, Google Suggest and Ta-da List wouldn't exist as we currently know them. And you wouldn't be reading this book! Chances are pretty good that you won't spend much time working directly with XHR (unless you decide to write your own library), but for much the same reason that introductory programming courses typically use text editors and the command line, this section strips away the fluff to show you what's under the hood.

XMLHttpRequest was originally implemented in Internet Explorer 5 as an ActiveX component, meaning that most developers shied away from using XMLHttpRequest until its recent adoption as a de facto standard in Mozilla 1.0 and Safari 1.2. It's important to note that XMLHttpRequest is *not* a W3C standard, though much of the functionality is covered in a new proposal: the *Document Object Model (DOM) Level 3 Load and Save Specification* (www.w3.org/TR/2004/REC-DOM-Level-3-LS-20040407). Because it is not a standard, its behavior may differ slightly from browser to browser, though most methods and properties are widely supported. Currently, Firefox, Safari, Opera, Konqueror, and Internet Explorer all implement the behavior of the XMLHttpRequest object similarly.

That said, if a significant number of your users still access your site or application with older browsers, you will need to consider your options. If you are going to use Ajax techniques, you will need to either develop an alternative site or allow your application to degrade gracefully. With most usage statistics[2] indicating that only a small fraction of browsers in use today lack XMLHttpRequest support, the chances of this being a problem are slim. However, you will need to check your web logs and determine what clients your customers are using to access your sites.

You must first create an XMLHttpRequest object using JavaScript before you can use it to send requests and process responses. Since XMLHttpRequest is not a W3C standard, creating an instance of XMLHttpRequest object requires a browser check. Internet Explorer implements XMLHttpRequest as an ActiveX object,[3] and other browsers such as Firefox, Safari, and Opera implement it as a native JavaScript object. Because of these differences, the JavaScript code must contain logic to create an instance of XMLHttpRequest using the ActiveX technique or using the native JavaScript object technique.

The previous statement might send shivers down the spines of those who remember the days when the implementation of JavaScript and the DOM varied widely among browsers. Fortunately, in this case you don't need elaborate code to identify the browser type to know how to create an instance of the XMLHttpRequest object. All you need to do is check the browser's support of ActiveX objects. If the browser supports ActiveX objects, then you create the XMLHttpRequest object using ActiveX. Otherwise, you create it using the native JavaScript object technique. Listing 1-1 demonstrates the simplicity of creating cross-browser JavaScript code that creates an instance of the XMLHttpRequest object.

---

2. www.w3schools.com/browsers/browsers_stats.asp
3. In IE 7, XHR will be implemented as a native object, which means all of our checks for ActiveX will, after a while, be the 20 percent case instead of the 80 percent.

**Listing 1-1.** *Creating an Instance of the XMLHttpRequest Object*

```
var xmlHttp;
function createXMLHttpRequest() {
    if (window.ActiveXObject) {
        xmlHttp = new ActiveXObject("Microsoft.XMLHTTP");
    }
    else if (window.XMLHttpRequest) {
        xmlHttp = new XMLHttpRequest();
    }
}
```

As you can see, creating the XMLHttpRequest object is rather trivial. First, you create a globally scoped variable named xmlHttp to hold the reference to the object. The createXMLHttpRequest method does the work of actually creating an instance of XMLHttpRequest. The method contains simple branching logic that determines how to go about creating the object. The call to window.ActiveXObject will return an object or null, which is evaluated by the if statement as true or false, thus indicating whether the browser supports ActiveX controls and thus is Internet Explorer. If so, then the XMLHttpRequest object is created by instantiating a new instance of ActiveXObject, passing a string indicating the type of ActiveX object you want to create. In this instance, you provide Microsoft.XMLHTTP to the constructor, indicating your desire to create an instance of XMLHttpRequest.

If the call to window.ActiveXObject fails, then the JavaScript branches to the else statement, which determines whether the browser implements XMLHttpRequest as a native JavaScript object. If window.XMLHttpRequest exists, then an instance of XMLHttpRequest is created, and on the off chance that your user isn't using a modern browser, well, the variable will be undefined.

Thanks to JavaScript's dynamically typed nature and to the fact that XMLHttpRequest implementations are compatible across various browsers, you can access the properties and methods of an instance of XMLHttpRequest identically, regardless of the method used to create the instance. This greatly simplifies the development process and keeps the JavaScript free of browser-specific logic.

# Methods and Properties

Table 1-1 shows some typical methods on the XMLHttpRequest object. Don't worry; we'll talk about these methods in greater detail shortly.

**Table 1-1.** *Standard XMLHttpRequest Operations*

| Method | Description |
|---|---|
| abort() | Stops the current request. |
| getAllResponseHeaders() | Returns all the response headers for the HTTP request as key/value pairs. |
| getResponseHeader("header") | Returns the string value of the specified header. |
| open("method", "url") | Sets the stage for a call to the server. The method argument can be GET, POST, or PUT. The url argument can be relative or absolute. This method includes three optional arguments. |
| send(content) | Sends the request to the server. |
| setRequestHeader("header", "value") | Sets the specified header to the supplied value. open must be called before attempting to set any headers. |

Let's take a closer look at these methods.

void open(string method, string url, boolean asynch, string username, string password): This method sets up your call to the server. This method is meant to be the script-only method of initializing a request. It has two required arguments and three optional arguments. You are required to supply the specific method you are invoking (GET, POST, or PUT) and the URL of the resource you are calling. You may optionally pass a Boolean indicating whether this call is meant to be asynchronous. The default is true, which means the request is asynchronous in nature. If you pass a false, processing waits until the response returns from the server. Since making calls asynchronously is one of the main benefits of using Ajax, setting this parameter to false somewhat defeats the purpose of using the XMLHttpRequest object. That said, you may find it useful in certain circumstances such as validating user input before allowing the page to be persisted. The last two parameters are self-explanatory, allowing you to include a specific username and password.

void send(content): This method actually makes the request to the server. If the request was declared as asynchronous, this method returns immediately, otherwise it waits until the response is received. The optional argument can be an instance of a DOM object, an input stream, or a string. The content passed to this method is sent as part of the request body.

void setRequestHeader(string header, string value): This method sets a value for a given header value in the HTTP request. It takes a string representing the header to set and a string representing the value to place in the header. Note that it must be called after a call to open(…).

void abort(): This method is really quite self-explanatory; it stops the request.

string getAllResponseHeaders(): The core functionality of this method should be familiar to web application developers. It returns a string containing response headers from the HTTP request. Headers include Content-Length, Date, and URI.

string getResponseHeader(string header): This method is a companion to getAllResponseHeaders() except it takes an argument representing the specific header value you want, returning this value as a string.

Of all these methods, the two you will use the most are open(…) and send(…). The XMLHttpRequest object has a number of properties that prove themselves quite useful while designing Ajax interactions.

In addition to these standard methods, the XMLHttpRequest object exposes the properties listed in Table 1-2. You'll use these properties extensively when working with XMLHttpRequest.

**Table 1-2.** *Standard XMLHttpRequest Properties*

| Property | Description |
|---|---|
| onreadystatechange | The event handler that fires at every state change (every time the readyState attribute changes); typically a call to a JavaScript function |
| readyState | The state of the request. The five possible values are 0 = uninitialized, 1 = loading, 2 = loaded, 3 = interactive, and 4 = complete |
| responseText | The response from the server as a string |
| responseXML | The response from the server as XML; can be parsed and examined as a DOM object |
| status | The HTTP status code from the server (200 for OK, 404 for Not Found, etc.) |
| statusText | The text version of the HTTP status code (OK or Not Found, etc.) |

# An Example Interaction

At this point, you might be wondering what a typical Ajax interaction looks like. Figure 1-4 shows the standard interaction paradigm in an Ajax application.

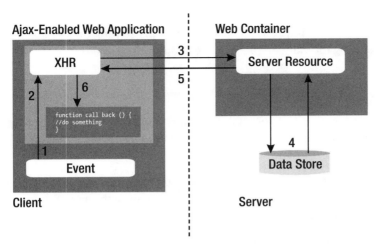

**Figure 1-4.** *Standard Ajax interaction*

Unlike the standard request/response approach found in a standard web client, an Ajax application does things a little bit differently.

1. A client-side event triggers an Ajax event. Any number of things can trigger this, from a simple onchange event to some specific user action. You might have code like this:

   ```
   <input type="text" d="email" name="email" onblur="validateEmail()";>
   ```

2. An instance of the XMLHttpRequest object is created. Using the open method, the call is set up. The URL is set along with the desired HTTP method, typically GET or POST. The request is actually triggered via a call to the send method. This code might look something like this:

   ```
   var xmlHttp;
   function validateEmail() {
     var email = document.getElementById("email");
     var url = "validate?email=" + escape(email.value);
     if (window.ActiveXObject) {
       xmlHttp = new ActiveXObject("Microsoft.XMLHTTP");
     }
     else if (window.XMLHttpRequest) {
       xmlHttp = new XMLHttpRequest();
     }
   xmlHttp.open("GET", url);
   xmlHttp.onreadystatechange = callback;
   xmlHttp.send(null);
   }
   ```

3. A request is made to the server. This might be a call to a servlet, a CGI script, or any server-side script (written in, say, PHP or ASP.NET).

4. The server can do anything you can think of, including access a data store or even another system (say, the billing system or the HR system).

5. The request is returned to the browser. The Content-Type is set to "text/xml"—the XMLHttpRequest object can process results only of the "text/html" type. In more complex instances, the response might be quite involved and include JavaScript, DOM manipulation, or other related technologies. Note that you also need to set the headers so that the browser will not cache the results locally. You do this with the following code:

```
response.setHeader("Cache-Control", "no-cache");
response.setHeader("Pragma", "no-cache");4
```

6. In this example, you configure the XMLHttpRequest object to call the function callback() when the processing returns. This function checks the readyState property on the XMLHttpRequest object and then looks at the status code returned from the server. Provided everything is as expected, the callback() function does something interesting on the client. A typical callback method looks something like this:

```
function callback() {
  if (xmlHttp.readyState == 4) {
    if (xmlHttp.status == 200) {
        //do something interesting here
    }
  }
}
```

As you can see, this is different from the normal request/response paradigm but not in a way that is foreign to web developers. Obviously, you have a bit more going on when you create and set up an XMLHttpRequest object and when the "callback" has some checks for states and statuses. Typically, you will wrap these standard calls into a library that you will use throughout your application, or you will use one that is available on the web. This arena is new, but a considerable amount of activity is happening in the open source community.

In general, the various frameworks and toolkits available on the web take care of the basic wiring and the browser abstractions, but others add user interface components. Some are purely client-based; others require work on the server. Many of these frameworks

---

4. Don't Pragma and Cache-Control do the same thing? Yes, they do, but Pragma is defined for backward compatibility.

have just begun development or are in the early phases of release; the landscape is constantly changing, with new libraries and versions coming out regularly. As the field matures, the best ones will become apparent. Some of the more mature libraries include Prototype, script.aculo.us, Dojo Toolkit, Direct Web Remoting (DWR), Taconite, and Rico. This is a dynamic space, so keep your RSS aggregator tuned to those sites dedicated to posting about all things Ajax!

### WILL AJAX MAKE MY APPLICATION WEB 2.0?

Since Tim O'Reilly[5] first coined the term, some people have been trying to rebrand their web applications as Web 2.0. What it means to be Web 2.0 is somewhat fluid though. In general, it signals applications that encourage a different style of user participation than those of the past. Web 2.0 is characterized by applications such as Wikipedia and Flickr and activities such as blogging and tagging.

Not everyone is convinced that Web 2.0 is a valuable concept, and some pundits have gone so far as to promise to never use the word again.[6] Although some of the criticism is valid (and some of the hype reminiscent of the late 1990s), many current web applications have characteristics that distinguish them from their older brethren. Many modern applications are more open and participative—note the many mashups (combining web services to create something new) that have been created off of Google Maps such as HousingMaps.[7] In fact, the Google Maps Mania[8] blog has sprung up to track the various applications built on top of Google Maps.

Many of these new-breed applications do indeed use Ajax to some extent, and it is an important component of Web 2.0; however, simply adding some fancy UI widgets doesn't necessarily equate to a Web 2.0 app. Although the boundaries are fuzzy, Web 2.0 is distinguished by using the intelligence in crowds (like Amazon's suggest functionality), software as service (such as Google and Salesforce.com), lightweight development (think deploying daily ... or more frequently), along with similar characteristics. Although Ajax is certainly a key component of delivering a richer user experience, it alone is not Web 2.0.

# Avoiding Common Gotchas

Ajax really does have the ability to drastically improve the user experience. However, there are a few gotchas that you need to look out for. You may not run into more than a couple of these issues, but before you start using Ajax everywhere, you should keep the following in mind:

---

5. www.oreillynet.com/pub/a/oreilly/tim/news/2005/09/30/what-is-web-20.html
6. www.joelonsoftware.com/items/2005/10/21.html
7. www.housingmaps.com/
8. http://googlemapsmania.blogspot.com/

*Unlinkable pages*: You may have noticed that in most of the figures we've shown you, the address bar doesn't change even when the page does. When you use the XMLHttpRequest object to communicate with the server, you never need to modify the URL displayed in the address bar. Although this may actually be a plus in some web applications, it also means your users cannot bookmark your page or send the URL to their friends (think about maps or driving directions). This isn't insurmountable; in fact, Google Maps now includes a "Link to this page" link (see Figure 1-5). If links are key to your application or site, be aware that Ajax makes this a bit of a challenge (some frameworks, such as Dojo, provide solutions to this issue).

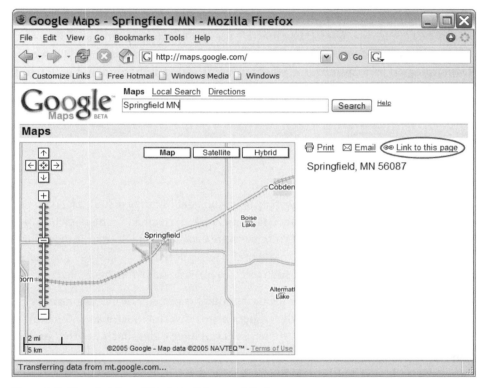

**Figure 1-5.** *Google Maps "Link to this page" link*

*Asynchronous changes*: Talking to the server asynchronously is one of the real steps forward with Ajax; however, it isn't without its issues. We've talked about this a few times, but it's worth discussing again: users have been trained to expect the entire page to be repainted anytime things change, so they may not notice when you update just parts of the page. Just because you can reload parts of the page doesn't mean this is the right approach for your entire application—use this approach judiciously. Be careful too that you don't have multiple overlapping asynchronous requests to the server. If you haven't properly coded your client, you may get some pretty odd responses if the server response isn't exactly what you expect (or got during testing).

*Lack of visual cues*: Since the entire page doesn't repaint, users may not perceive that anything has changed. Ultimately, this is why the Fade Anything Technique (FAT, discussed later in this chapter) was created, but you do have other options. For instance, Gmail uses a "Loading" icon to indicate that it is doing some work (see Figure 1-6). Depending on your application, you may have to add some sort of indication so your users know what is happening.

**Figure 1-6.** *Gmail's "Loading" icon*

*The broken Back button*: Some web applications deliberately disable the browser's Back button, but few websites do. Of course, with Ajax, clicking the Back button isn't going to do much of anything. If your users are expecting the Back button to work and you're using Ajax to manipulate parts of the page, you may have some problems to solve. (Once again, frameworks such as Dojo provide relief for this issue.)

*Code bloat*: Never forget that the JavaScript that powers Ajax applications runs locally on your client. Although many developers have powerful machines with reams of random access memory (RAM), some users still have older machines that just don't offer this horsepower. If you put too much JavaScript into your application, you may find sluggish response times on the client side. Even if the JavaScript runs fine, more JavaScript means larger and larger pages, which means longer download times. Until we all have broadband and dual-processor computers, keep JavaScript to a minimum.

*Death by a thousand cuts*: With the ease of making asynchronous calls, Ajax applications can get a bit chatty. (Remember the early days of entity beans?) You shouldn't add Ajax simply for the sake of adding Ajax. You need to think about each call you make to the server. Making a large number of fine-grain calls can have rather interesting impacts on your server architecture, so you'll want to spend some quality time with your favorite load-testing tool. Autocomplete (see Figure 1-7), although one of the most compelling Ajax widgets, has the potential to be very chatty. Use with caution.

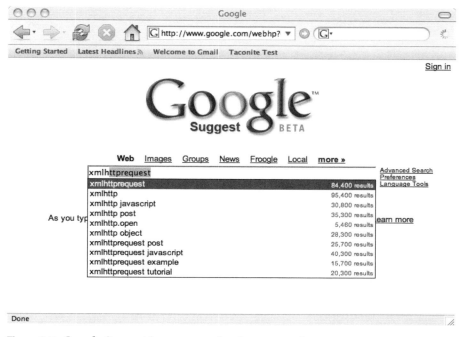

**Figure 1-7.** *Google Suggest is an example of autocomplete.*

*Exposing the business layer:* Never forget that your JavaScript is transmitted to the client, and although you can certainly obfuscate the code, if someone really wants to see what you did, they will. With that in mind, be very careful with what you show in your JavaScript. Exposing details about how your server works can open you up to those with ill intent.

*Forgetting about security:* Despite some arguments to the contrary, Ajax doesn't present any new security vulnerabilities. However, that doesn't mean you can just forget about it. All the standard security issues present in a regular web application still exist in an Ajaxified application.

*Breaking established UI conventions:* Ajax lets developers create far richer web applications than they've created in the past. However, this doesn't obviate the need to follow normal user interface guidelines. Just because you can do something doesn't mean you should. Also, your snappy new Ajax feature may not be obvious to your users, so don't be afraid to offer a tip like Netflix does with their movie queue (see Figure 1-8). The user can simply drag and drop movies to change their order, but after years of conditioning on web applications, many users might never have realized they could.

**Figure 1-8.** *The Netflix queue*[9]

How will you know if you've run afoul of any of these gotchas? We can't stress this enough: test your design with representative users. Before you roll out some snappy new Ajax feature, do some paper mock-ups, and run them by a few users before you spend the time and effort developing it. An hour or two of testing can save you from dealing with larger issues later.

# Ajax Patterns

Like any good technology, Ajax already has a slew of patterns. For a detailed look at Ajax patterns, please take a look at *Ajax Patterns and Best Practices* by Christian Gross (Apress, 2006) and the website Ajax Patterns (`http://ajaxpatterns.org/wiki/index.php?title=Main_Page`).

---

9. `http://ajaxian.com/archives/drag-and-drop-ajaxian-indicators`

# The Fade Anything Technique (FAT)

One of the really slick things about Ajax is that you can modify just part of a web page. Rather than repaint the entire view, you can update just the part that changes. Although this is a handy technique, it may confuse users who are expecting a full-page refresh. With this in mind, 37signals uses the Yellow Fade Technique (YFT) in its products like Basecamp (www.basecamphq.com) and Backpack (www.backpackit.com) as a way of subtly indicating to the user what has changed. YFT does just what it suggests: the part of the page that changed is repainted in yellow, and it slowly fades back to the original background color (see Figure 1-9).

The Fade Anything Technique (FAT) pattern is similar in nature. In essence, the only real change is the color you use to fade; after all, yellow might not be the best option for you. Implementing this technique is not terribly difficult; you can find sample code using your favorite search engine or, better yet, just use one of the libraries that makes this simple, such as script.aculo.us.[10]

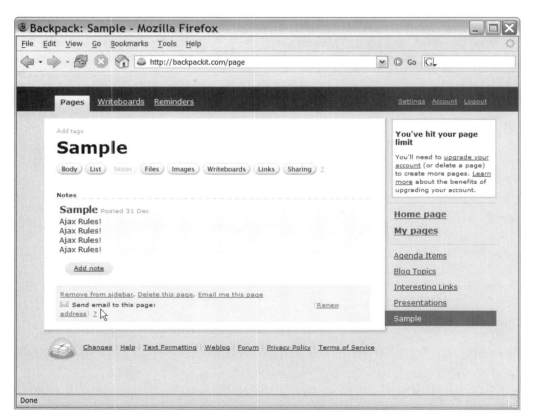

**Figure 1-9.** *Yellow Fade Technique as seen in 37signals' Backpack*

---

10. http://script.aculo.us/

## Auto Refresh

Being able to refresh parts of the page automatically is useful. With weather, news, or other information streams that change over time, repainting just the parts that change makes a lot more sense than refreshing the entire page for a few minor changes. Of course, this might not be terribly obvious to users who are trained to click the Refresh button, which is why the Auto Refresh pattern is so often paired with FAT.

Auto Refresh offers a significant benefit beyond less work for your user: it also reduces the load on your server. Rather than having thousands of users constantly clicking the Refresh button, you can set a specific polling period that should spread out the requests more evenly. Digg (www.digg.com) is a news site catering to the technology community that uses social bookmarking and community editorial control to publicize interesting stories. The content is user-driven and changes frequently, making it a perfect place to use Auto Refresh (see Figure 1-10).

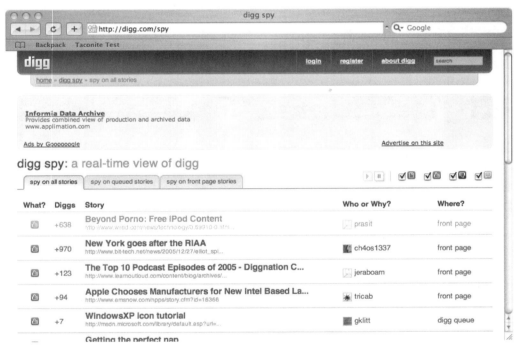

**Figure 1-10.** *Auto Refresh at work—new stories appear on the site while you watch!*

## Partial Page Paint

We've talked about this point quite a bit, but one of the real strengths of Ajax is that you no longer need to repaint the entire page; instead, you can just modify what has changed.

Clearly, you can use this in conjunction with FAT or Auto Refresh. In fact, this can be helpful for web applications.

Many of the existing frameworks will help you modify part of the page, and thanks to solid DOM support in modern browsers, this approach is much easier than you think. Figure 1-11 shows A9's BlockView (`http://maps.a9.com`) feature, an example of the Partial Page Paint pattern. When you select a different part of the map on the left, the corresponding pictures of the street automatically change to reflect where your map is pointing (assuming pictures exist).

**Figure 1-11.** *A9's BlockView feature*

## Draggable DOM

Portals were supposed to be the solution to all our problems. Corporate intranet sites were designed to be one-stop shopping for employees to have all the information they needed at their fingertips. Your most frequently used applications, links to your key reports, industry news—a customized portal was supposed to be the answer. Unfortunately, corporate intranets never really took off, but at least part of the reason had to do with clumsy interfaces for adding new sections and moving existing ones. Typically, you had to go to a separate administration page to make your changes (a full-page refresh), save your changes, and return to your home page (another page refresh). Although this approach worked, it certainly wasn't ideal.

Portals are given a new life with Ajax, especially using the Draggable DOM pattern. With this approach, the individual sections are editable right on the main page, and to customize the page, you simply grab them with your mouse and drag them to their new location. Several sites, including the personalized Google (www.google.com/ig), have used this pattern, as shown in Figure 1-12.

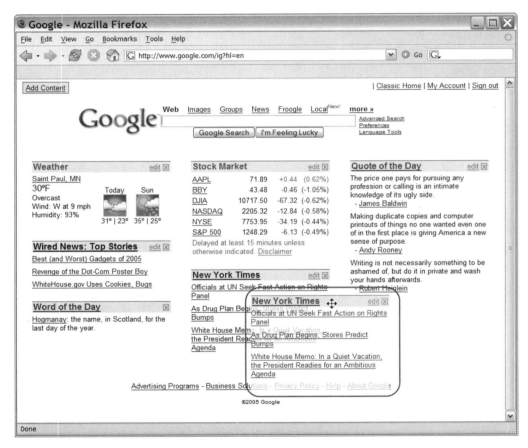

**Figure 1-12.** *Personalized Google uses Draggable DOM.*

# Summary

The Internet has certainly evolved from its early origins as a way for researchers to connect and share information. Though the Internet began with simple textual browsers and static pages, it is now hard to find a company that doesn't have a polished website. In its early days, who could have possibly imagined that people would one day flock to the Internet to research that new car or buy the latest Stephen King novel?

Developers fed up with the difficulty of deploying thick client applications to thousands of users looked to the web to ease their burden. Several web application technologies have been developed over the years, some proprietary, others requiring significant programming abilities. Though some provided a richer user experience than others, no one would confuse a thin client application with its desktop-based cousin. Still, the ease of deployment, the ability to reach a wider customer base, and the lower cost of maintenance means that despite the limitations of browsers, they are still the target platform of choice for many applications.

Developers have used hacks to circumvent some of the most troublesome restrictions the Internet places on developers. Various remote scripting options and HTML elements let developers work asynchronously with the server, but it wasn't until the major browsers added support for the `XMLHttpRequest` object that a true cross-browser method was possible. With companies such as Google, Yahoo!, and Amazon leading the way, we are finally seeing browser-based applications that rival thick clients. With Ajax, you get the best of both worlds. Your code sits on a server that you control, and any customer with a browser can access an application that provides a full, rich user experience.

■ ■ ■

# CHAPTER 2

# Development Tools

It's no secret: developing software can be rather difficult. Unlike other disciplines, software development doesn't produce a concrete, three-dimensional product that we can hold, touch, and inspect. Regardless of how much time we may spend drawing class diagrams or designing flowcharts, ultimately we're expected to write code. Reams and reams of source code are necessary to produce today's software systems. Even though we may have designed the software ourselves, and in most cases even written the source code ourselves, it doesn't take long before the amount of source code simply becomes overwhelming. Let's face it: we need help.

Fortunately, improving development tools are greatly easing the life of the software developer. Source code editors, debugging tools, and others are making it easier to build and debug today's large-scale software systems.

In this chapter we'll investigate some of the tools that can make Ajax development easier. Fortunately we'll be able to leverage a lot of the tools and techniques that you may already use in your normal day-to-day Java development.

## JavaScript Source Code Editor

Many of us use some type of integrated development environment (IDE) to write Java. Yes, it is possible to write Java using a simple text editor and the command-line compiler. However, most of us benefit from the productivity gains afforded by today's modern IDEs.

If you're reading this book, you obviously write web applications using Java. Java-based web applications are made up of more than just Java source code files. Web applications built using the Java EE platform are made up of Java source code files, HTML and XHTML files, XML files, and even plain text files. Modern IDEs are capable of managing all of these files, which reduces the number of applications we need to use (and learn!) to build Java EE applications.

How many of us like having to read reams and reams of source code? Worse yet, what if it's source code that we didn't write, and thus we're not familiar with it? One handy feature of an intelligent source code editor is reserved word highlighting. It's a feature that you probably find handy but rarely think about. Reading source code in an editor that highlights the language's reserved words is much more pleasant to the eye.

Object-oriented development would be nearly impossible without today's modern IDEs. Imagine the scenario where you're writing a class that exists within an object hierarchy. You want to write a method, but you're not sure whether any of the parent classes have already defined such a method. How do you find out? The most time-consuming option is to open the source file for the parent class. You may find that the method you have in mind doesn't exist in the parent class. But does it exist in the parent class's parent? You could continually open the source files for each class in the object hierarchy. This is tedious and time-consuming.

Worse yet, what if you don't have the source code to all the classes in the object hierarchy? Suddenly you can't just browse the source code files. How about checking the Javadocs? Browsing Javadocs can be slow, too, and that's assuming that Javadocs are available.

The single greatest productivity improvement in the history of software development is arguably the intelligent code completion that is standard on nearly every Java IDE available today. If you don't know what methods or properties are available on a class, simply invoke the IDE's code-completion feature, and a list of the available methods and properties will pop up, allowing you to choose the desired one. Better yet, many editors even provide a list of all available objects and classes as part of the code completion list. Not only does this intelligent code completion reduce the amount of time spent searching through source code, but it also reduces the amount of typing we do, which in turn reduces the number of typing mistakes you're likely to make, which in turns reduces the number of failed compilations.

So why all this talk about Java IDEs? The truth is that you have likely experienced large gains in productivity by using an intelligent IDE for editing Java source code. Now that Ajax is becoming a part of your developer's toolbox, you'll likely be writing more JavaScript than you have in the past. This, of course, begs the question: are there intelligent code editors available for JavaScript?

In short, the answer is yes. JavaScript editors are not as advanced as Java editors, although they will continue to get better as Ajax and JavaScript development matures. Many editors already offer simple features like reserved word highlighting.

Today's most popular Java IDEs—Eclipse, NetBeans, and IntelliJ IDEA—all offer support for editing JavaScript source code files. At the time of this writing, IDEA supports JavaScript source files right out of the box, although JavaScript support is available as plug-ins for Eclipse and NetBeans. In this section you'll see how to install and configure the JavaScript plug-ins for Eclipse and NetBeans.

## JSEclipse

One of the most advanced JavaScript editors available is JSEclipse offered by InterAKT. JSEclipse is a free plug-in for the Eclipse development environment. It offers features such as code completion, an outline window, error reporting, and code wrapping.

Installing JSEclipse is easy thanks to Eclipse's plug-in architecture. Open Eclipse's plug-in installation wizard by selecting Help ➤ Software Updates ➤ Find and Install. Select "Search for new features to install" and click Next.

The Install window should now be showing. Click the New Remote Site button and enter "InterAKT Online" into the Name field and "http://www.interaktonline.com/" into the URL field, then click OK. At this point the Install window should look something like Figure 2-1, with InterAKT Online appearing in the list.

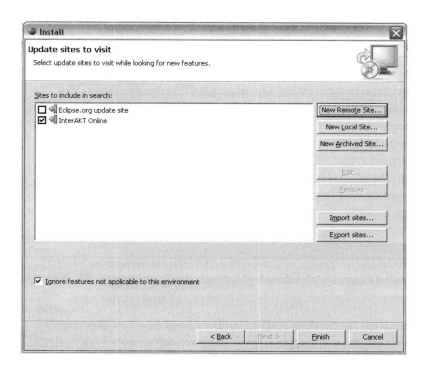

**Figure 2-1.** *Eclipse's Install window after adding InterAKT Online as a remote site*

Note that JSEclipse requires Java 1.5 or later. Click through the rest of the installation to finish installing JSEclipse. Restart Eclipse to ensure that the plug-in is installed completely.

With JSEclipse installed, you can now start writing JavaScript. JSEclipse identifies all files with the .js extension as JavaScript source files. Create a new JavaScript source file by choosing File ➤ New ➤ File and enter a file name that ends with the .js extension. With a new JavaScript source file now created, you're ready to start writing JavaScript.

The first thing you'll notice when editing JavaScript in JSEclipse is that it provides syntax highlighting of JavaScript keywords. Also notice that the Outline view includes an outline of the JavaScript source, showing the methods that exist on the objects defined within the source file.

Figure 2-2 shows a JavaScript source file open in JSEclipse. There are two JavaScript files in the project named `Department.js` and `Employee.js`. The `Employee.js` file is opened in the source editor. The JavaScript files have their own icons in the Navigator panel on the left side of the window, and the outline of the currently opened source file is displayed in the Outline panel on the right side of the window.

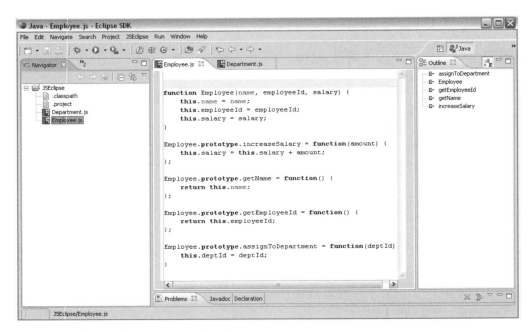

**Figure 2-2.** *The JSEclipse source code editor*

That's not all that JSEclipse will do. As discussed earlier, one of the greatest productivity tools of all time is intelligent code completion. JSEclipse provides intelligent code completion for user-defined JavaScript objects. Figure 2-3 demonstrates the code-completion functionality. A simple function in the `Department.js` file creates an instance of an `Employee` object. Then, the object's methods are accessed via dot notation. JSEclipse automatically shows the code completion window when the dot is typed.

JSEclipse also provides code completion for built-in JavaScript objects such as `Date`, `String`, `document`, and `window`.

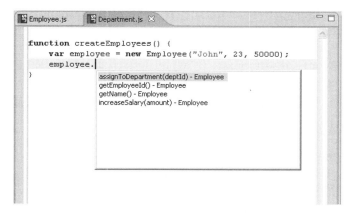

**Figure 2-3.** *JSEclipse provides code completion for JavaScript objects.*

JSEclipse also provides a way to extend the native code-completion functionality. You can write a simple XML file that defines the code-completion list that should appear for objects of a certain type. In fact, the default JSEclipse distribution defines the code completion for built-in JavaScript objects using XML files. Listing 2-1 lists the contents of the object.xml file, which defines the code completion for a base JavaScript object.

**Listing 2-1.** *object.xml Defines the Code Completion for a Basic JavaScript Object*

```
<?xml version="1.0" encoding="UTF-8"?>
<completion prefix="Object">
    <item repl="constructor" display="constructor Function" />
    <item repl="prototype" display="prototype" />
    <item repl="eval()" display="eval(String expresion)" />
    <item repl="toSource()" display="toSource() String" />
    <item repl="toString()" display="toString() String" />
    <item repl="unwatch()" display="unwatch(String prop)" />
    <item repl="valueOf()" display="valueOf() #primitive value#" />
    <item repl="watch()" display="watch(String prop, Function handler)" />
</completion>
```

The object.xml file is located in the library directory of JSEclipse's installation directory. In this directory you'll find other XML files that define the code completion for various JavaScript objects. You can modify these files to fit your needs. Better yet, you can create your own XML files that describe JavaScript files you've already built. You could build a set of XML files that provide code completion functionality for JavaScript files that are shared across your organization. The JSEclipse Help system provides a nice tutorial for creating your own code-completion libraries. You can access the tutorial by opening Eclipse's

Help menu and searching for the "JSEclipse extending the code completion" section and selecting the appropriate result.

JSEclipse is a powerful JavaScript editor that is sure to simplify your JavaScript development tasks. Development tools will continue to improve as Ajax and JavaScript usage become more mainstream, but for now, JSEclipse is a fine choice for your JavaScript editor.

## NetBeans JavaScript Plug-in

At the time of this writing the current version of NetBeans, version 5.0, does not provide native support for JavaScript source files. However, NetBeans user and contributor Nicolas Désy built a plug-in for NetBeans that supports editing of JavaScript source files.

The plug-in's home page is www.liguorien.com/jseditor. From here you can read more about the plug-in's features and download the plug-in itself.

Nicolas warns that this plug-in is only meant to be a stopgap remedy until NetBeans natively supports JavaScript source files and that there will be no further development on this plug-in. Nevertheless, this plug-in provides a nice set of features for those who work in the NetBeans environment.

### Installation

There are two ways to install the NetBeans JavaScript plug-in. The first way is to register the plug-in home page as a NetBeans update center and install the plug-in from there. The second way is to manually download and install the plug-in module. The two methods are similar, and here we'll demonstrate the installation using the manually downloaded files.

Visit the plug-in home page and click on the link that points to the NetBeans JavaScript Editor binaries. This will initiate the download of the plug-in module, which has a .nbm file extension.

After you download the plug-in module, open NetBeans and select the Update Center menu option from the Tools menu. This opens the Update Center Wizard that will guide you through the process of installing the plug-in. Select the Install Manually Downloaded Modules radio button and click Next. In the following window, click the Add button and navigate to and select the .nbm file you downloaded. Click the Next button.

The next window, shown in Figure 2-4, shows the modules that will be installed. The JavaScript editor should already be selected as shown in Figure 2-4.

Click the Next button and accept the license agreement, then click Next on the download screen. On the final screen, check the Include check box and click the Finish button to complete the installation. The JavaScript editor becomes fully operational after restarting NetBeans.

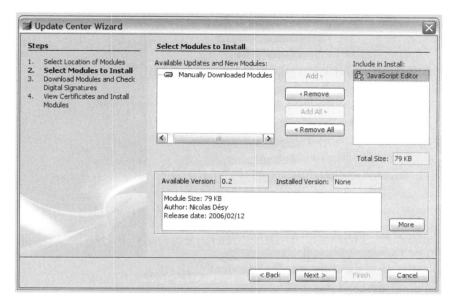

**Figure 2-4.** *Installing the NetBeans JavaScript Edtior plug-in*

## Features and Usage

The NetBeans JavaScript Editor recognizes all files with a `.js` file extension as JavaScript source code files. You can create a new JavaScript source file by selecting New File item from the File menu and then selecting the JavaScript category. The editor provides syntax highlighting for all JavaScript keywords, highlighting of matching opening and closing curly braces and parentheses, and basic code completion for the standard DOM objects such as `document` and `window`. Code completion can be invoked with the Ctrl+Space key combination.

One of the nicest features of the JavaScript editor is that it will format JavaScript source files. How many times have you inherited a lengthy JavaScript source code file that was difficult to read due to incredibly poor formatting and indentation? With the NetBeans JavaScript Editor you can reformat an entire JavaScript source file using the Ctrl+Shift+F key combination.

How well does it work? Figure 2-5 shows a simple JavaScript file that suffers from poor form and indentation. Even with its small size the file is difficult to read and prone to errors should it ever need to be updated. Figure 2-6 shows the same file after the JavaScript editor's formatting function was invoked using the Ctrl+Shift+F key combination.

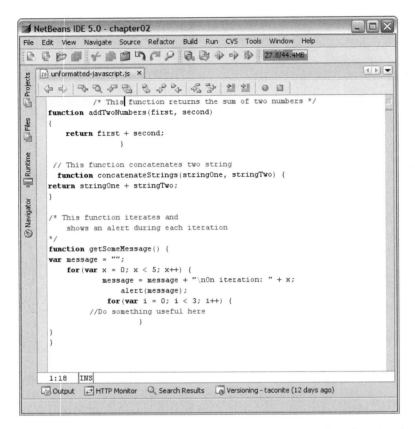

**Figure 2-5.** *Poorly formatted JavaScript is difficult to read and maintain.*

The NetBeans JavaScript Editor plug-in is a handy tool for those who use NetBeans for Java development. The plug-in is easy to install and possesses a nice set of features. NetBeans support for JavaScript development is sure to improve once JavaScript editing support becomes part of the standard NetBeans distribution.

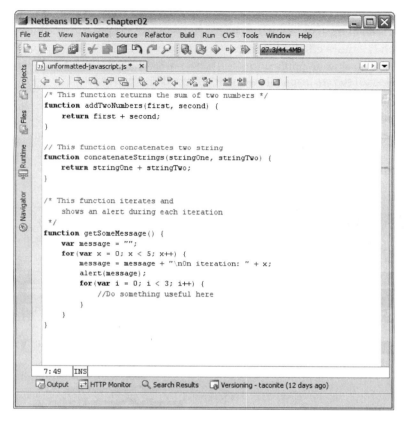

**Figure 2-6.** *Nicely formatted JavaScript, thanks to the NetBeans JavaScript Editor*

# JavaScript Compression and Obfuscation

We all know that JavaScript is an interpreted language that executes within the client's browser. JavaScript is downloaded as plain text to the browser, which then executes the JavaScript code as needed.

JavaScript source code can always be read by the user by using the browser's View Source functionality, which displays the complete HTML markup of the page, including any JavaScript blocks. Even if the JavaScript source is placed in an external file and referenced with the `script` tag's `src` attribute, it can still be downloaded and read by the user. Because the JavaScript source is always available to anybody viewing the page, proprietary or sensitive logic algorithms should not be placed in JavaScript. Such logic is best left on the server where it is more secure.

as JavaScript usage grows in Ajax-based
avaScript is never compiled to machine-
format for executable code. A large
own as it needs to download the source
ted. In addition, a large set of JavaScript
commented.
vaScript's lack of a binary executable
nloads. Is there a way around these

d a number of tools that can help solve
simply strip JavaScript source of all
educe the size of the source code down-
characters can reduce the size of a
n the situation. Note that the JavaScript
a semicolon before it can be compressed
s or unintended behavior.

Remember that although JavaScript statements should always end with a semicolon, most browsers are very forgiving and allow the trailing semicolon to be absent as long as there is a line break where the semicolon should be. Many compressors eliminate line breaks, which can cause unintended results on JavaScript source files where the statements aren't properly terminated with a semicolon. JavaScript does not have a compiler to catch these sorts of issues, so instead, you should use a JavaScript verifier that ensures that all lines end with semicolons and that all statement blocks use curly braces. One fine JavaScript verifier is JSLint, found at `www.jslint.com`. Always use a JavaScript verifier such as JSLint before compressing JavaScript as it will help prevent errors caused by compressing and obfuscating noncompliant JavaScript.

Other tools go one step further by offering obfuscation services. Obfuscation is the process of scanning through source code and changing field and function names from their original names to coded, nonsensical names in an effort to prevent others from learning the intent and inner workings of the source code. Obfuscation is typically not needed for languages like C++ that are compiled to machine-level binary instructions. Even modern languages like Java and C#, which are compiled to intermediate bytecodes rather than binary instructions, require obfuscation tools for maximum security.

Building a JavaScript obfuscation tool is challenging because of JavaScript's inter-preted nature. JavaScript obfuscation tools can have trouble ascertaining the scope and visibility of function names, function variables, and global variables, and as a result, the compressed source code often doesn't function correctly. The best rule of thumb is to simply avoid exposing sensitive or secret algorithms in JavaScript, instead keeping them on the server where they are safely under wraps. If you insist on using a JavaScript obfus-cator, be sure to thoroughly test the obfuscated JavaScript to ensure that it still functions as expected.

# The Dojo Toolkit's JavaScript Compressor

One of the most impressive JavaScript compressor and obfuscator tools available today is provided by the Dojo toolkit available at `www.dojotoolkit.org/docs/compressor_system.html`. Like many JavaScript compressors, Dojo's compressor shrinks JavaScript source files by removing comments, removing spaces around operators, and replacing variable names with shorter names. But wait—replacing function and variable names sounds a lot like obfuscation. Didn't we just say that obfuscation should be avoided due to the problems it presents?

What sets the Dojo compressor apart from its peers is *how* it goes about compressing and obfuscating the JavaScript source code. Many JavaScript compressors use regular expressions to remove spaces and comment lines. Regular expressions can easily break, and they also have no context by which to determine the scope of a variable name. The Dojo compressor uses the Rhino JavaScript engine provided by the Mozilla Foundation.

Using Rhino gives the Dojo compressor the ability to determine the context and scope of a variable name. Since Rhino is a real live JavaScript interpreter, the Dojo compressor can determine the scope of a variable name and safely shorten the variable name without worry.

The main goal of the Dojo compressor is to maintain public API compatibility and ensure that the compressed script functions identically to the uncompressed script. Even though the Dojo compressor shortens variable names, it does so for the sake of size reduction, not obfuscation. The Dojo compressor's creators believe that JavaScript obfuscation is not a useful goal, but size reduction definitely is. As such, the Dojo compressor attempts to strike a nice balance between size reduction while still maintaining some readability and debuggability.

## Using the Dojo Compressor

The Dojo compressor is packaged as a single JAR file named `custom_rhino.jar` that can be downloaded from the Dojo website. The Dojo compressor can be easily invoked from the command line by specifying the name of the JavaScript file to be compressed and the name of the compressed file:

```
java -jar custom_rhino.jar -c uncompressed.js > compressed.js
```

In that line, `uncompressed.js` is the name of the JavaScript file to be compressed and `compressed.js` is the name of the compressed file.

As a Java developer you probably use Ant to automate your build process, and you're probably not too keen on having to manually compress your JavaScript files each time you perform a build. Fortunately the Dojo compressor can also be used within an Ant task as shown in Listing 2-2.

**Listing 2-2.** *The Dojo JavaScript Compressor Used Within an Ant Task*

```
<target name="dojo-compress-javascript">
    <java jar="${basedir}/lib/custom_rhino.jar"
                    fork="true" output="compressed-javascript.js">
        <arg value="-c" />
        <arg value="uncompressed-javascript" />
    </java>
</target>
```

When using the JavaScript compressor within an Ant task, be sure to provide the correct path to `custom_rhino.jar`. You must also ensure that the Rhino `.jar` file is included in Ant's classpath.

By how much will the Dojo compressor reduce the size of a JavaScript source file? Using the Dojo compressor, a JavaScript source file from a leading Ajax framework was compressed. Figure 2-7 shows the size of the file before compression (left) and after compression (right).

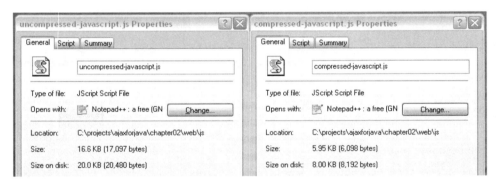

**Figure 2-7.** *The size of the uncompressed script (left) and the compressed script (right)*

As you can see in Figure 2-7, the uncompressed JavaScript source was 16.6KB in size. The compressed file, created using the Dojo compressor, is 5.95KB in size. That's a 64 percent reduction in size!

# Inspecting a DOM Structure

Implementing Ajax in your web applications means that you'll likely have to write some JavaScript to update the DOM after making an Ajax request. You'll have to use DOM methods and properties such as `getElementById` and `childNodes` to traverse the DOM. In today's development environment it's unlikely that a single web page is built from a single HTML or JSP page. Instead, behind the scenes, there are likely several JSPs and other include files that are brought together at runtime to generate a single web page. Although this practice increases maintainability and reusability, it makes it more difficult for the developer to conceptualize the DOM structure of the resulting web page.

You can always use your browser's View Source feature to view the resulting page's DOM structure, but this lists the page's entire source, which may not be well formatted for easy reading. There's got to be a better way to inspect the DOM structure of a web page.

## Mouseover DOM Inspector

The Mouseover DOM Inspector solves this problem by providing a convenient way to inspect the DOM structure of a web page. The Inspector is implemented as a favelet (or "bookmarklet") that allows the user to inspect and modify a web page's DOM by simply mousing over the document. The Inspector can be installed by visiting `www.slayeroffice.com/tools/modi/v2.0/modi_help.html`. The Mouseover DOM Inspector supports Firefox, Mozilla, Netscape 8, Opera 7.5 and above, and Internet Explorer 6 and above.

You activate the Inspector by clicking on the Inspector's bookmark. Once activated, moving the mouse over the web page will open the Inspector window, as shown in Figure 2-8.

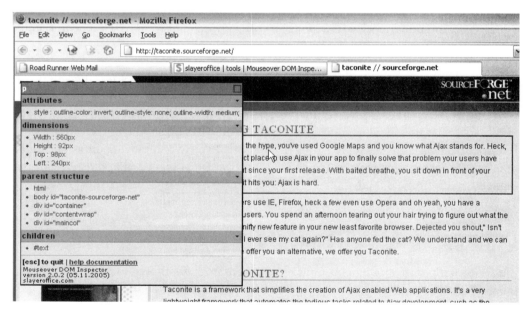

**Figure 2-8.** *Inspecting the DOM using the Mouseover DOM Inspector*

Figure 2-8 shows the Mouseover DOM Inspector in action. In this example, the mouse is hovering over a paragraph on the page, indicated by the solid red outline. The Inspector window is shown in the upper-left corner of the screen. The window indicates that you're looking at a `<p>` element by displaying the tag name at the top of the window.

The first section lists all of the node's attributes; in this case, the `style` attribute is listed. In this particular instance, the XHTML source for this node doesn't explicitly define a `style` attribute. Instead, the style is applied from an external style sheet. Knowing the styles that are being applied to a node from an external style sheet is an extremely powerful tool that can aid in debugging or otherwise understanding the DOM structure. The second section lists the dimensions of the current node.

The third and fourth sections are key to understanding the structure of the DOM relative to the currently selected node. These sections, respectively, list the parent nodes and child nodes of the currently selected node. The Inspector lists all of the parent nodes, starting with the root `<html>` node and working down to the current node's direct parent. In this example, the only child of the current node is the paragraph text.

The Mouseover DOM Inspector provides basic DOM manipulation functionality through a combination of the mouse and keyboard. Pressing the A key while hovering over a node clones the node, then hovering over a different node and pressing S appends it to the node. The H key hides the current node, and J shows all elements hidden using the H command. Nodes are removed using the R key. Finally, the T key starts at the top node of the document and steps through each node in the DOM, including nondisplay elements such as `<meta>`. Use the Esc key to close the Mouseover DOM Inspector window. Other commands can be found on the Inspector's home page.

What good are these DOM manipulation methods, other than for having some fun? One potential use of these methods is rapid prototyping. Consider, for instance, that you're halfway through a development iteration and you're showing your latest work to your business customer. Your customer sees a page you've built and decides that a certain section of text is no longer necessary and that another section should be moved to the bottom of the page. Instead of recoding the JSP (or JSPs) and redeploying the application, you can simply modify the page using the Mouseover DOM Inspector and receive immediate feedback from your customer.

# Debugging Ajax Requests

Ajax is, by definition, an asynchronous request sent from the browser to the server. This means that as soon as the Ajax request is initiated, the browser continues evaluating the script that initiated the Ajax request. The script does not block and wait for the server's response before continuing to execute. Doing so prevents the browser from locking up and allows it to continue responding to user input while the browser waits for the server to respond. The upshot of all this is that the application feels much faster and more responsive to the user.

The downside of the asynchronous nature of Ajax is that it makes debugging more difficult. Consider the scenario where you're building a form that takes user input, such as a name and telephone number. The user clicks a button to submit the form elements to the server via Ajax, and the response is displayed at the bottom of the page.

You've built the page, written the JavaScript, built a servlet to handle the Ajax request, and deployed the application for testing. You fill in the form, click the button, and … nothing happens. What went wrong? Did the servlet fail to process the request properly? Did the JavaScript fail somewhere along the way? Was the request even sent in the first place?

As Java EE developers we're used to having powerful tools and IDEs at our disposal. We can use our favorite IDE to start the application in debug mode and step through the servlet to see if any errors occur there. However, that works only if we know that the request was sent in the first place. Furthermore, how do we know that the correct query parameters were sent? Once an error condition is found, wouldn't it be nice to be able to replay the scenario to verify that the error has been fixed?

A convenient tool would be to use some sort of HTTP sniffer. Such a tool would monitor all of the HTTP traffic to and from a specific port. A sniffer would allow us to inspect the communication between the browser and the server and determine whether there are any errors.

## NetBeans HTTP Monitor

A handy tool for debugging Ajax requests is the NetBeans HTTP Monitor. NetBeans IDE is a full-featured Java IDE available from www.netbeans.org. An HTTP sniffer called the HTTP Monitor comes standard with every installation of NetBeans. The HTTP Monitor is integrated into NetBeans and the Apache Tomcat servlet container that ships with NetBeans. HTTP Monitor can be installed on any servlet container such as JBoss or Jetty, and the instructions to do so can be found in NetBean's built-in help system.

HTTP Monitor, when enabled, automatically records all of the requests that are handled by the servlet container. It records information such as request parameters, cookies, session attributes, and HTTP headers. The information is saved until explicitly deleted by the user or until the IDE closes. A powerful feature is that saved requests can be reopened, modified, and resubmitted to the servlet container. Figure 2-9 shows the HTTP Monitor main panel.

As you can see in Figure 2-9, the left side of the HTTP Monitor main window displays the recorded requests. You can right-click on a record and select Save to permanently store a record. You can select a record to display its information in a series of tabs on the right side of the panel. The tabs are self-explanatory; for example, the Request tab displays data about the request and any query string parameters, and the Cookies tab lists data about any cookies that were sent as part of the request or returned along with the response.

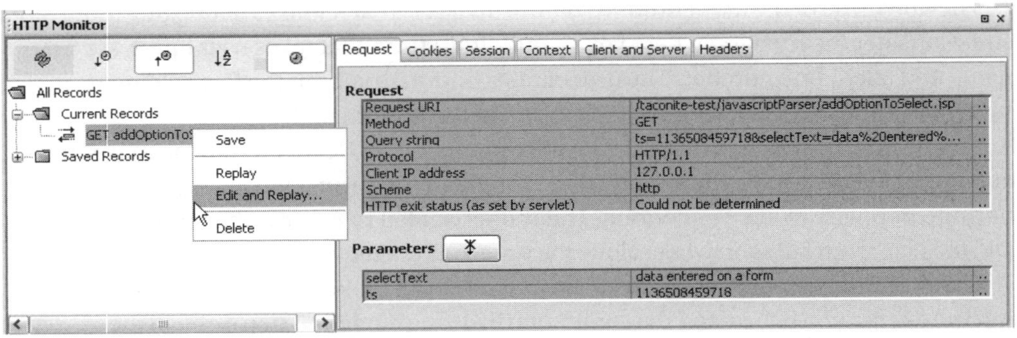

**Figure 2-9.** *HTTP Monitor main panel*

As you inspect the information on the tabs, you'll see how useful this tool could potentially be when debugging Ajax requests. The Parameters section on the Request tab contains the most useful information. Here you can verify that the correct parameters were sent from the browser to the server without having to debug through the servlet.

The most powerful and unique feature of the HTTP Monitor is the ability to modify a stored request and resubmit the request to the server. Right-click on the desired record and select Edit and Replay. This will open the Edit and Replay window, shown in Figure 2-10.

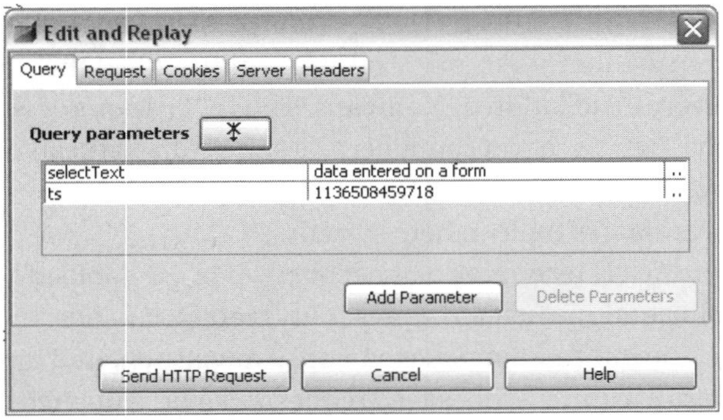

**Figure 2-10.** *Edit and Replay window*

The Edit and Replay window allows you to modify the information making up a stored HTTP request and resubmit the data to the web container. As shown in Figure 2-10, you can add, modify, and delete query parameters. You can also add or remove cookies to be sent along with the request and modify the HTTP headers that are part of the request. You can then click the Send HTTP Request button to submit the request to the server. NetBeans will open your system's web browser to display the server's response.

The NetBeans HTTP Monitor is a powerful tool that can aid in debugging Ajax requests (or any kind of HTTP request, for that matter). It is integrated into the NetBeans IDE and can be installed on any servlet container. With it, you can record the requests sent to the container, inspect the properties and data of the request, and even edit the request and resubmit it to the servlet container. Consider adding it to your developer toolbox.

## Firefox FireBug Extension

FireBug is an extension for Firefox described by its developer as a combination of the JavaScript console, DOM Inspector, and a command-line JavaScript interpreter. Better yet, FireBug includes a feature called XMLHttpRequest Spy that allows you to see the requests and responses used by the XMLHttpRequest object. In this section you'll get a quick introduction to FireBug's most useful features. FireBug's home page is located at https://addons.mozilla.org/extensions/moreinfo.php?id=1843&application=firefox.

After installing FireBug and restarting Firefox, the first thing you'll notice is that FireBug opens as a window pane at the bottom of the Firefox window. The FireBug pane's visibility can be toggled using the F12 key.

The top of the FireBug window is the menu bar from which you can access FireBug's functionality. The first button on the menu bar is the Inspect Element button. Like the Mouseover DOM Inspector, this tool displays various DOM information about the selected element. To use it, just click the Inspect Element button and then click on the desired element in the browser window. Once selected, you'll be able to view the XML markup that defines the element, the CSS rules that apply to the element, the CSS box model attributes of the element, and the JavaScript properties and methods that apply to the element. Figure 2-11 shows the CSS box model information supplied by FireBug for the Firefox icon that appears in the upper-right corner of the page.

The standard Firefox error console is a useful web development tool. The error console shows all JavaScript and CSS errors that occur on a page, and most of the JavaScript error messages are descriptive and helpful. The downside is that the error console logs *all* JavaScript and CSS errors in one place, which can cause the console window to become cluttered and difficult to read.

Fortunately FireBug solves this problem by extending the standard error console's functionality to include the ability to filter errors by type and by the originating domain. The third button on FireBug's menu bar is the Errors button. Clicking the Errors button shows a drop-down list from which you can toggle the various filters. The available filters are shown in Figure 2-12.

**Figure 2-11.** *The Inspect Element feature provides a host of information about any element on the page.*

**Figure 2-12.** *FireBug lets you filter the errors by type and originating domain.*

The most useful feature of FireBug for Ajax developers is the XMLHttpRequest Spy feature. This feature inspects all Ajax requests and the associated server responses. XMLHttpRequest is disabled by default and must be enabled by clicking the Options button and toggling the Show XMLHttpRequests item.

Once you've enabled XMLHttpRequest Spy, every Ajax request made using XMLHttpRequest is logged by FireBug. You can click the Post button to view any POST parameters that were sent as part of the Ajax request. This can be useful when you need to ensure that the correct information was sent to the server as part of the Ajax request.

Clicking the Response button will display the Ajax response that the server sent. FireBug will show the text of the response regardless of whether it's plain text, XML, or even JavaScript Object Notation (JSON). An example of the server response captured by FireBug is shown in Figure 2-13.

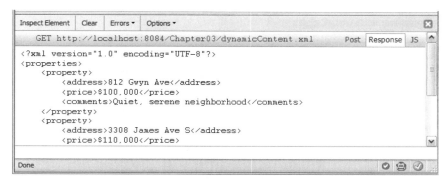

**Figure 2-13.** *FireBug captures the server response from an Ajax request.*

The last option provided by XMLHttpRequest Spy is the JavaScript option, which you can access by clicking the JS button. Here you will see the JavaScript method and property values of the XMLHttpRequest object that sent the Ajax request.

FireBug is a powerful addition to your web development toolbox that can help you rapidly diagnose problems or better understand the structure and CSS rules of a web page. The best feature of FireBug is its ability to capture the request, response, and JavaScript information pertaining to an Ajax request made using the XMLHttpRequest object.

# JavaScript Logging

As a Java developer you're almost surely familiar with a tool called log4j. Log4j is a logging utility available from the Apache Foundation at http://logging.apache.org/log4j/docs. Log4j's goal is to be a powerful, easy-to-use, and unobtrusive logging facility that allows developers to instrument their code with logging statements. The logging is configurable via an external XML file allowing changes to the logging configuration without changing the application binary. Logging provides detailed context information for application failures, which can aid in debugging, as it is sometimes difficult or impossible to debug distributed, remote, or multithreaded applications. Logging can also be used for auditing purposes.

JavaScript development has long been hampered by its lack of quality development tools and libraries. How many of us have debugged JavaScript by peppering the code with alert statements? Certainly this gets the job done, but the problem with alert statements is that they must be removed before the application is released to the general public. Adding a host of alert statements only to have to remove them later can be tedious and error-prone.

New tools are becoming available that bring log4j-like capabilities to JavaScript. The next few sections review these tools and give a brief overview of their use.

## Log4JS

Log4JS is, as described on its website, a JavaScript logging class similar in spirit to Apache's log4j. Log4JS writes logging output to a customizable logging class. Log4JS can be found at http://log4js.sourceforge.net.

Four logging classes are available: alert, write, popup, and console. The alert class pops up logging messages in an alert box. The write logger writes to a new page in the browser. The popup logger writes messages to a separate browser window, which is convenient for keeping track of the log messages. Finally, the console logger writes to Safari's console or to a pop-up window if the browser is not Safari.

Log4JS is similar to log4j in that it defines different logging thresholds. The logging thresholds for Log4JS are, in increasing order, DEBUG, INFO, WARN, ERROR, FATAL, and NONE. A logger will only log messages that are of equal or greater value to the logger's threshold. For example, if a logger is created with a threshold of WARN, then logging a message with the info() method will produce no output, but logging a message with the warn(), error(), or fatal() method will output the message.

If you've ever used log4j then using Log4JS will be rather easy. Figure 2-14 shows the simple test used to demonstrate Log4JS. It's a simple page that uses JavaScript to calculate the sum of two integers. Log4JS is used to log messages during the execution of the script. The page's source code is shown in Listing 2-3.

**Listing 2-3.** *log4jExample.js*

```
<!DOCTYPE html PUBLIC "-//W3C//DTD XHTML 1.0 Strict//EN"
                       "http://www.w3.org/TR/xhtml1/DTD/xhtml1-strict.dtd">
<html xmlns="http://www.w3.org/1999/xhtml">
    <head>
        <title>Log4js Example</title>
        <script type="text/javascript" src="js/log4js.js"></script>
        <script type="text/javascript" src="js/log4jsExample.js"></script>
    </head>
    <body>
        <p>
            Add Two Integers:
            <input type="text" id="addOne" size="4"/>
            +
            <input type="text" id="addTwo" size="4"/>
            =
            <input type="text" id="result" size="10" disabled="disabled"/>
            <button value="Calculate" onclick="calculateSum();">
                Calculate
            </button>
        </p>
    </body>
</html>
```

**Figure 2-14.** *Simple page for calculating the sum of two numbers*

The JavaScript that calculates the sum of the two integers is shown in Listing 2-4. The script starts by creating two global loggers, one with a logging threshold of info and the other with a threshold of error. The calculateSum function starts by retrieving the input values from the input boxes. Log4JS is used to log the input values to the pop-up logger. The script continues by attempting to convert the input values to integers. If one or both of the values is not a valid integer, then errors stating so are written to the pop-up logger and the function exits. Finally, the two integers are summed and the result is displayed on the page.

**Listing 2-4.** *log4jsExample.js*

```
/* Create Log objects */
var logger = new Log(Log.INFO, Log.popupLogger);
var errorLogger = new Log(Log.ERROR, Log.popupLogger);
function calculateSum() {
    /* Retrieve the user's input from the text boxes */
    var inputOne = document.getElementById("addOne").value;
    var inputTwo = document.getElementById("addTwo").value;
    /* Log the user's input */
    logger.info("first input: " + inputOne
                                + "\nsecond input: " + inputTwo);
    /* Attempt to convert the user's input values to integers */
    var firstNumber = parseInt(inputOne);
    var secondNumber = parseInt(inputTwo);
    /* Log an error if either of the values is not an integer */
    if(isNaN(firstNumber)) {
        errorLogger.error("firstNumber is not a number: " + inputOne);
        clearResult();
        return;
    }
    if(isNaN(secondNumber)) {
        errorLogger.error("secondNumber is not a number: " + inputTwo);
        clearResult();
        return;
    }
    /* Calculate the sum and display on the page */
    var sum = firstNumber + secondNumber;
    document.getElementById("result").value = sum;
}
function clearResult() {
    document.getElementById("result").value = "";
}
```

The logging messages from this example were written to the popup logger, shown in Figure 2-15. The messages are appended to the list, so as long as you don't close the messages window you'll be able see the entire history of logged messages. This can be useful if you've made some changes to the script and want to see how the behavior of the script has changed as a result of the edits.

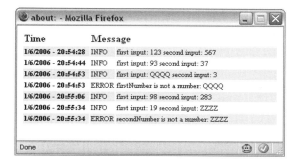

**Figure 2-15.** *Log messages written to the pop-up logger*

Log4JS also includes a facility for logging the properties of objects, which can be useful in debugging. The Log class exposes a static function called dumpObject that writes a string representation of an object to the logger:

```
logger.debug(Log.dumpObject(new Array('red','white','yellow','blue')));
```

Remember that logging can be disabled by setting a logger's logging threshold to NONE. One way to deploy Log4JS in your production application might be to define all of the application's loggers in a separate JavaScript file that is used across all pages. When deploying the application to the production environment, you could simply update that simple JavaScript file to disable all logging. Taking it one step further, you might also employ Ant's replace task to set the logging thresholds depending on the type of build being performed: development, testing, or production.

## Lumberjack

Lumberjack is another JavaScript-based logging utility found at http://gleepglop.com/javascripts/logger. Like Log4JS, Lumberjack draws inspiration from Apache's log4j.

Lumberjack distinguishes itself from other JavaScript logging frameworks by the way that it displays the logged information. Lumberjack writes all the logging information to a special window whose display can be toggled by pressing Alt+D (or Cmd+D on Mac OS X). The output window is a floating window that appears at the bottom of the web page, even when the page is scrolled up and down. The output window even includes a regular expression-based filter so that only errors of the desired type are displayed. It also includes a JavaScript command-line area into which JavaScript commands can be entered.

---

### IMPORTANT—LUMBERJACK REQUIRES THE PROTOTYPE LIBRARY

Lumberjack is dependent on the Prototype JavaScript library, which can be found at `http://prototype.conio.net`. Because of this dependency, Prototype must be listed before Lumberjack when including their respective JavaScript files onto an HTML page using the `<script>` tag. Browsers read and evaluate JavaScript in these files in the order in which they are listed on the HTML page. If Lumberjack is listed before Prototype, then errors will occur when the browser attempts to evaluate the Lumberjack script, because values from the yet unevaluated Prototype script are not found.

---

Instead of creating separate logging classes as you do for Log4JS, Lumberjack exposes logging methods as static methods on a `Logger` class. The `Logger` class exposes four logging methods: `info`, `debug`, `warning`, and `error`. Each method takes a single string parameter representing the message to be logged. The `Logger` class also exposes a `log` method that takes two parameters: a string representing the message to be logged and string representing a custom logging level.

Let's reuse the previous example from Log4JS to demonstrate the usage of Lumberjack. As you can see from Listing 2-5, the JavaScript is nearly identical to the script from the Log4JS example. In this instance there are no longer two globally defined loggers at the top of the script. In addition, each logging statement now uses static methods on the `Logger` class to write log messages to the output. Note how static methods of the `Logger` class are used to write log messages.

**Listing 2-5.** *lumberjackExample.js*

```
function calculateSum() {
    /* Retrieve the user's input from the text boxes */
    var inputOne = document.getElementById("addOne").value;
    var inputTwo = document.getElementById("addTwo").value;
    /* Log the user's input */
    Logger.info("first input: " + inputOne
                                    + "\nsecond input: " + inputTwo);
    /* Attempt to convert the user's input values to integers */
    var firstNumber = parseInt(inputOne);
    var secondNumber = parseInt(inputTwo);
    /* Log an error if either of the values is not an integer */
    if(isNaN(firstNumber)) {
        Logger.error("firstNumber is not a number: " + inputOne);
        clearResult();
        return;
    }
```

```
    if(isNaN(secondNumber)) {
        Logger.error("secondNumber is not a number: " + inputTwo);
        clearResult();
        return;
    }
    /* Calculate the sum and display on the page */
    var sum = firstNumber + secondNumber;
    document.getElementById("result").value = sum;
}
function clearResult() {
    document.getElementById("result").value = "";
}
```

Figure 2-16 shows the Lumberjack output window. Remember that the output window's view is toggled using Alt+D (or Cmd+D for Mac OS X). The same log messages written to the output window and the messages are color-coded by type, with errors being red and informational messages being white. At the top of the output window is the input box for filtering the messages. You can type "error" into the box to see only the error messages, or type "error|warning" to see only errors and warnings.

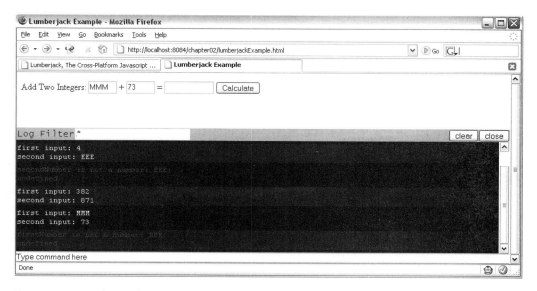

**Figure 2-16.** *Lumberjack writes logging messages to a floating window at the bottom of the page.*

Lumberjack provides a convenient method for inspecting JavaScript objects. The object's properties are written to the output window. To inspect a JavaScript object, open the Lumberjack output window, enter something like the following, and press Enter:

```
inspect(document.body)
```

Alternatively, you could pass a string to the inspect method that represents the ID of a DOM object on the page. For example, if you wanted to view the properties of the first input box that appears on the page in Figure 2-16, you would enter the following into Lumberjack's command line interface and press Enter:

```
inspect("addOne")
```

This will print all of the input box's properties to the output window.

# JavaScript Debugging Tools

Java development has long been enhanced by a debugging architecture that makes it easy to debug through application source code step by step. Many of today's Java IDEs have fabulous debugging environments that allow you to debug standard Java SE applications, applications deployed on a local Java EE application server, and even applications deployed on a remote Java EE application server.

Traditionally JavaScript has been more difficult to debug than Java because JavaScript lacked a high-quality debugging environment. This has now changed. The Venkman JavaScript debugger is an extension for Mozilla-based browsers such as Firefox that provides a full-featured JavaScript debugging environment.

The following is meant to be a quick introduction to Venkman and its features. A more complete tutorial can be found online at `www.svendtofte.com/code/learning_venkman`.

## Using Venkman

Venkman is available from `www.mozilla.org/projects/venkman/`. Venkman development started in April 2001 by Robert Ginda. Venkman is based on the Mozilla JavaScript debugging API known as js/jsd. The js/jsd API formed the basis of the Netscape JavaScript Debugger 1.1 that was available for the 4.x series of Netscape browsers.

Once you've installed it, you can start Venkman from the Tools ➤ JavaScript Debugger menu item from within Firefox. Figure 2-17 shows the default layout for Venkman.

Venkman offers a plethora of information, divided into eight panes. The default layout consists of a large pane showing the selected source code. Smaller panes are arranged vertically on the left side of the window. Venkman's command-line interface resides on the bottom of the window under the Source Code pane.

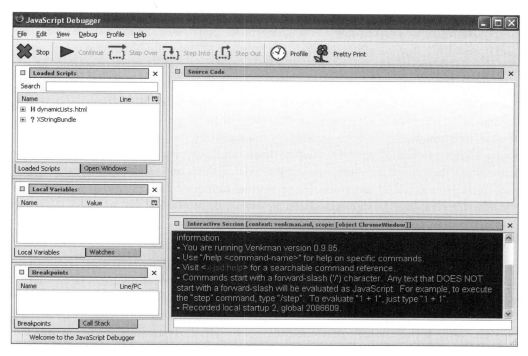

**Figure 2-17.** *Default window layout of Venkman*

You can drag each pane with the mouse and dock them at other locations within the main window. You can also add each pane as a separate tab to an existing pane. For example, referring to Figure 2-17, to make the Loaded Scripts tab exist within the Local Variables pane, drag and drop the Loaded Scripts tab to the Local Variables tab. You can also undock the panes from the main window by clicking the docking button located on the left side of the pane's title bar. Docking the pane back to the main window is as easy as clicking the docking button again.

As you work with Venkman, you'll get a feel for the panes that you use most often. Close the panes you don't often use by clicking the X button on the right side of the pane's title bar. You can reopen panes by selecting View ➤ Show/Hide. If at any time you want to return the pane layout to the default setting, enter "/restore-layout factory" at the command-line interface in the Interactive Session pane.

### Viewing Loaded Scripts

When Venkman is open, it recognizes all the JavaScript that is available to the page currently open in the browser window. Venkman recognizes JavaScript that is embedded within the HTML page using `<script>` tags and also recognizes external JavaScript files that are included in the HTML page using `<script src="js_file.js">` tags.

Venkman displays the currently available JavaScript in the Loaded Scripts pane. Clicking the plus sign next to each file opens a list under the file that details all the available JavaScript functions within that file along with the line number at which the function occurs within the file. Optionally, it displays the number of lines of code the function encompasses. Double-clicking a file within the Loaded Scripts pane opens the file in the Source Code pane and also scrolls directly to the function within the Source Code pane.

Right-clicking a file in the Loaded Scripts pane displays a number of options for both the file itself and the JavaScript functions contained within the file. For the file, this pop-up menu allows you to perform tasks such as disabling the debugging of eval and timeout statements, disabling the debugging of contained functions, and disabling the performance monitoring of contained functions. For individual functions, the context menu provides facilities for disabling the debugging and performance profiling.

## Source Code

The Source Code pane lists the source code for the currently open file. The file could be an HTML file, XHTML file, or JavaScript file. The Source Code pane implements a tabbed theme so multiple files can be opened at once with each file residing in its own tab. The code has some simple colorization that improves readability. JavaScript keywords such as `function` and `var` have bold formatting, and string literals have a different colored font. On the left side of the pane is the line numbering for the file. The far-left side of the Source Code pane is the gutter on which debugging breakpoints can be set.

## Breakpoints

Venkman supports two kinds of breakpoints, a *hard* breakpoint and a *future* breakpoint. This is a departure from most debugging environments, so we'll discuss the difference between the two.

A hard breakpoint is the type of breakpoint you're used to seeing in modern programming languages such as Java. It instructs Venkman to suspend processing at the breakpoint. Execution cannot continue until the user instructs it to do so. In Venkman, a hard breakpoint always exists *within the body of a function*.

A future breakpoint is similar to a hard breakpoint in that it instructs Venkman to suspend execution of the JavaScript at the breakpoint. The difference between the two is that a future breakpoint is set on lines that *do not exist within the body of a function*. These lines of code are executed as soon as they are loaded by the browser. By contrast, code that resides within the body of a function is not executed until the function is executed in response to some action or event.

For the most part you can simply ignore the differences between hard and future breakpoints. You'll likely use hard breakpoints in most of your work, and they should function identically to breakpoints in other debugging environments.

Venkman provides a window that lists all the currently set breakpoints. This can come in handy when you're debugging a page that has multiple breakpoints set in multiple files.

Each file in which a breakpoint is set is listed in the Breakpoints pane, and listed under each file are all that file's breakpoints.

### Stepping Through Code

With breakpoints set, you're now ready to start actually debugging code. Venkman will automatically suspend execution once a breakpoint is encountered. At that point you're in control of the script's execution. You can inspect variable values, modify variable values, and continue the script execution, either by looking at one step at a time or by restarting execution and letting it run to completion.

Venkman offers developers a few options for stepping through code once a breakpoint has been encountered. Once a breakpoint has been encountered, you can choose Continue, Step Over, Step Into, or Step Out.

The Continue option restarts script execution. Execution will not end until either another breakpoint is encountered or the script completes. The Continue option is useful when you need to track down the location of a problem. You can set breakpoints at points along the execution chain and, each time a breakpoint is encountered, inspect variable values to see whether the problem has cropped up yet. Once the problem appears, you know the error occurred somewhere between the current breakpoint and the previous breakpoint, and you can narrow it down further from there. The Continue option is also useful when debugging an iteration. You can set a breakpoint at one point within the iteration and use the Continue option to speed through the iterated code, checking each time execution suspends to see whether any problems have occurred.

The Step Over function is useful when you want to avoid stepping through a function that is called by the current function. The called function may be a function that has been extensively debugged and you *just know* the problem isn't there, or you may just want to avoid stepping through its code because you're concerned about only the current function. Keep in mind that stepping over a function does not prevent it from being executed; it merely means you're not going to step through it line by line.

The Step Into option is the opposite of the Step Over function. Step Into will step into a called function so you can debug the called function. Step Over and Step Into work well together when you're trying to track down the exact location of an error.

### Local Variables List

The Local Variables pane allows you to inspect and even modify variable values during script execution. The Local Variables pane always displays all the variables within scope whenever a breakpoint is encountered and execution of the script is suspended.

The Local Variables pane always has two top-level items, Scope and This. Scope refers to all the variables within the nearest current scope of execution. Because most JavaScript is written as a function, the nearest scope is usually *function* scope. For example, if a breakpoint within a function is encountered, then the Scope item within the Local Variables window will refer to all variables that are within that function's scope—namely, any variable defined with the keyword var within that function. Variables defined in the global scope (those defined outside any function body) are technically accessible within functions, but they are not shown within the current variable scope.

The second top-level item displayed in the Local Variables pane is the This item. The This item refers to whichever object the keyword this refers to. If the breakpoint occurs within a function that is part of an object, then this refers to the current object instance. The normal reference for this is the browser's window object. Note that any variables defined within the global scope will appear under the this item.

The Local Variables list also allows you to change the value of variables during runtime. This can be extremely powerful when you want to test the effects of different variable values on the script's output. It's also useful when you *think* you've found where a problem is occurring and want to see whether changing a variable value fixes the problem.

Right-click the variable value you want to change, and select Change Value from the context menu. This opens a small prompt window in which you can modify the variable's value. You can enter any valid JavaScript expression into the prompt, including expressions such as new Object(). Be sure that any string literals are enclosed in either double or single quotes. Remember that in the prompt window you can also reference other variables by using the variable name.

# Testing Tools

As a Java developer you're almost certainly familiar with development methodologies like test-driven development (TDD) and unit testing tools like JUnit, and you may even use these techniques and tools in your daily work routine. If you use JUnit, there has probably been at least one instance where a unit test has saved your hide by uncovering a previously unknown bug, or it's allowed you to comfortably refactor a class knowing that as long as all the tests pass, you've managed to refactor without breaking any functionality.

Wouldn't it be great to be able to apply TDD and other automated testing techniques to JavaScript and, more specifically, Ajax development? Now you can. New tools are popping up every day that allow you to develop JavaScript and Ajax-enabled applications that have complete test coverage. In this section we'll explore a couple of testing tools that allow you create automated tests for your JavaScript code and Ajax-enabled web applications.

# JsUnit

In 2001, Edward Hieatt began work on a "port" of JUnit, the popular Java unit testing framework (www.junit.org), for use in testing JavaScript in the browser—JsUnit. Since then, JsUnit (found at www.jsunit.net) has had nearly 10,000 downloads and counts almost 300 people as members of its newsgroup. JsUnit supports the common xUnit functions and is written entirely in JavaScript. If you're comfortable with JUnit (or similar xUnit frameworks), you'll find JsUnit pretty intuitive.

The usual suspects are present: setUp() and tearDown() are there, though as functions instead of methods; test functions (instead of test methods) are grouped into test pages (instead of test cases); and JsUnit comes with its own HTML-based test runners. Table 2-1 compares the two frameworks.

**Table 2-1.** *JUnit vs. JsUnit*

| JUnit | JsUnit |
| --- | --- |
| Test class extends TestCase | Test page includes jsUnitCore.js |
| Test methods | Test functions |
| Test classes | HTML-based test pages |
| TestSuite classes | HTML-based test suites |
| Various test runners | HTML/JavaScript-based test runner |
| setUp() and tearDown() methods | setUp() and tearDown() functions |
| Runs in the virtual machine | Runs in a browser |
| Written in Java | Written in JavaScript |

JsUnit tests are written much like JUnit tests. A test case is an HTML page that includes some JavaScript you want to test. You then write test methods much like you do in JUnit and use various assert methods to verify expected outcomes. Like JUnit, test cases can be grouped together as test suites. JsUnit's Test Runner (Figure 2-18) is an HTML page through which test cases and test suites can be executed within a browser, allowing fast code-test-repeat cycles.

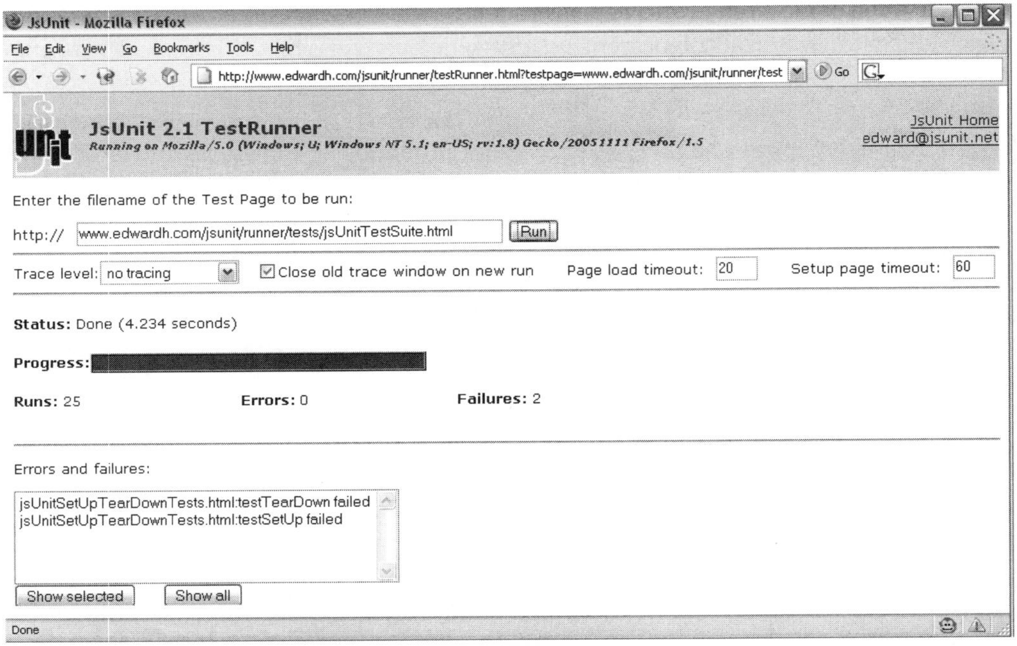

**Figure 2-18.** *Example Test Runner from JsUnit's home page*

This text won't discuss the nitty-gritty details of installing and using JsUnit. The JsUnit home page at jsunit.net has plenty of examples demonstrating how to use JsUnit.

## Selenium

Selenium, found at www.openqa.org/selenium, is a test tool for web applications. Selenium runs completely within the browser, just like real users do. It runs on all major browsers on all major platforms and serves two major purposes: browser compatibility testing and system functional testing. Since Selenium runs on all major browsers on all major platforms, you can use it to verify that your application works correctly across browsers and platforms. System functional testing is achieved by the creation of Selenium regression tests that verify application functionality and user acceptance.

Like JsUnit, Selenium can be used to test JavaScript and Ajax requests. The difference between the two is that JsUnit is more of a unit testing framework, and Selenium is more of an acceptance testing framework.[1] Because of this, JsUnit and Selenium complement each other. JsUnit can only be used to unit test JavaScript code, but Selenium can test

---

1. Unit tests are written by developers and test a single class or a small group of classes. Acceptance tests are written by the application's user community and test the functionality of the entire application.

JavaScript code at the application level, in addition to testing non-JavaScript aspects of a web application.

A Selenium test case is written as a simple HTML file containing a table with three columns. The three columns represent a *command*, *target*, and *value*. Not all commands require a value, in which case the table cell can be left blank. Since test cases are written as simple HTML files, not JavaScript functions as in JsUnit, it's possible that nontechnical personnel could create the test cases.

A command simply tells Selenium to do something. Commands come in two varieties: actions and assertions. Actions are generally tasks that change the state of the application, such as "click this button" or "enter text into a text field." Assertions verify the state of the application. Examples include "verify this text appears on a page" or "the current URL is this." All assertions can be one of two modes, *assert* or *verify*. They are identical except that when an assert fails, the test stops. Table 2-2 lists some of the most common commands. For a complete list, visit Selenium's home page.

**Table 2-2.** *Common Selenium Action and Assertion Commands*

| Command | Description |
| --- | --- |
| open(url) | Opens the specified URL; accepts both relative and absolute URLs |
| click(element) | Clicks a button, link, radio button, or check box |
| clickAndWait(element) | Same as click, except waits for the new page that is loaded in response to the click; typically used on links and submit buttons |
| type(element, value) | Sets the value of an input field as if it was typed in |
| pause(interval) | Waits the specified number of milliseconds; useful for Ajax requests |
| assertValue(element, pattern) | Asserts that the value of an input field matches the specified pattern |
| verifyTextPresent(text) | Verifies that the specified text appears somewhere on the page |

A target is the DOM object on which the specified command is to operate. All commands must have a specified target. If the clickAndWait command is specified then a target object for the click must be specified—in this case, probably a button or a link. Selenium supports several strategies for specifying the desired target. The most common and likely the easiest to use is to specify the DOM object's id attribute. Selenium can also locate DOM objects by searching on the object's name attribute, by evaluating a given JavaScript or XPath expression, or by specifying a link's text.

Like JUnit, Selenium test cases are grouped together as test suites. Like test cases, test suites are written as simple HTML files with tables. The test suite's table consists of multiple table rows that have a single table column. Each table cell contains an anchor tag whose href attribute points to the test case, and the anchor tag's text is text describing the test case.

Test suites are executed via Selenium's Test Runner page. The Test Runner is a web page from which tests are executed and test results displayed. By default, Selenium looks for test suites in a default directory, although this can be overridden.

### Example Tests

Selenium is easy to use once you've seen it in action, but installing it and writing the first tests can be a bit daunting. In this section we'll go through installing Selenium into a Java EE web app and writing a couple of simple tests.

Start by downloading the latest release of Selenium. The Selenium download is a ZIP file that includes the Selenium runtime engine and documentation. To install Selenium into your Java EE application, copy the selenium folder from the Selenium distribution to the root of your application's WAR file. That's all—Selenium is now installed. Next, you need to write some tests.

Before tackling an Ajax test we'll first investigate testing a "normal" HTTP request. This example simulates the login process for a web application. The user enters a login ID and clicks the Login button. The next page echoes the login ID. Figure 2-19 shows the example login page and the next page that echoes the login ID.

**Figure 2-19.** *The login page (left) and the next page echoing the login ID*

Listing 2-6 shows the source code for the login page, and Listing 2-7 lists the source code for the following page.

**Listing 2-6.** *login.jsp*

```
<!DOCTYPE HTML PUBLIC "-//W3C//DTD HTML 4.01 Transitional//EN"
    "http://www.w3.org/TR/html4/loose.dtd">
<html>
    <head>
        <meta http-equiv="Content-Type" content="text/html; charset=UTF-8">
        <title>Example Login</title>
    </head>
    <body>
        <h1>Please Login Here</h1>
        <form id="loginForm" action="loggedIn.jsp" method="get">
            Login ID:
            <input type="text" id="loginId" name="loginId" value=""/>
            <input type="submit" value="Login"
                                    id="loginButton" name="loginButton"/>
        </form>
    </body>
</html>
```

**Listing 2-7.** *loggedIn.jsp*

```
<%@page contentType="text/html"%>
<%@page pageEncoding="UTF-8"%>
<html>
    <head>
        <meta http-equiv="Content-Type" content="text/html; charset=UTF-8">
        <title>JSP Page</title>
    </head>
    <body>
    <h1>Successful Login</h1>
    <%= request.getParameter("loginId")%> is successfully logged in.
    </body>
</html>
```

This is a very simple example, but it illustrates how to write a simple Selenium test. The test should simulate the user entering a user ID into the input field and then clicking the Login button. The next screen should echo the user ID with text saying that the login was successful.

Listing 2-8 lists the HTML page that executes this test scenario. As explained earlier, the test is written as a three-column table within an HTML page. This test consists of four tasks: opening the login page, entering text into the input box, clicking the Login button, and verifying that the next page contains the entered login ID. Each task gets its own row on the table, but note that the table has five rows because Selenium ignores the first row so it can be used for the test case's name.

**Listing 2-8.** *testLogin.html*

```
<!DOCTYPE HTML PUBLIC "-//W3C//DTD HTML 4.01 Transitional//EN">
<html>
    <head>
        <title></title>
    </head>
    <body>
        <table border="1">
            <tr>
            <td colspan="3">Test Echoing Login ID</td>
            <tr>
                <td>open</td>
                <td>/chapter02/login.jsp</td>
                <td> </td>
            </tr>
            <tr>
                <td>type</td>
                <td>loginId</td>
                <td>tsryana</td>
            </tr>
            <tr>
                <td>clickAndWait</td>
                <td>loginButton</td>
                <td> </td>
            </tr>
            <tr>
                <td>verifyTextPresent</td>
                <td>tsryana</td>
                <td> </td>
            </tr>
        </table>
    </body>
</html>
```

The commands are rather self-explanatory. The open command tells Selenium to point the browser to the login page. The type command tells Selenium to enter the text "tsryana" into the DOM element whose id attribute value is loginButton. The following command, clickAndWait, clicks the DOM element whose id attribute value is loginButton and waits for the next page to appear. Finally, the verifyTextPresent assertion verifies that the application correctly echoes the user ID entered into the text box on the login page.

That's all! By writing a simple HTML file we've written a repeatable test case that will run in multiple browsers on multiple platforms. Before we actually execute the test in Selenium's Test Runner we'll write a second test, this time testing a simple Ajax function.

The Ajax example retrieves a single line of text from the server and displays the text on the page. Selenium will verify that the text retrieved from the server appears on the page, verifying that the Ajax request finished successfully. Figure 2-20 illustrates the page before and after the Ajax request.

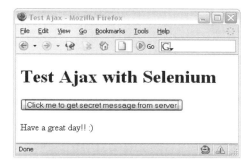

**Figure 2-20.** *Retrieving simple text via Ajax*

Listing 2-9 lists the JSP page source code, including the JavaScript that takes care of the Ajax request, which by now should be quite familiar to you. Listing 2-10 is the JSP that responds to the Ajax request.

**Listing 2-9.** *testAjax.jsp*

```
<%@page contentType="text/html"%>
<!DOCTYPE HTML PUBLIC "-//W3C//DTD HTML 4.01 Transitional//EN"
    "http://www.w3.org/TR/html4/loose.dtd">
<html>
    <head>
        <meta http-equiv="Content-Type" content="text/html; charset=UTF-8">
        <title>Test Ajax</title>
```

```
<script type="text/javascript">
    var xmlHttp;
    function createXMLHttpRequest() {
        if (window.ActiveXObject) {
            xmlHttp = new ActiveXObject("Microsoft.XMLHTTP");
        }
        else if (window.XMLHttpRequest) {
            xmlHttp = new XMLHttpRequest();
        }
    }
    function getSecretMessage() {
        createXMLHttpRequest();
        xmlHttp.onreadystatechange = handleStateChange;
        xmlHttp.open("GET", "ajaxResponse.jsp", true);
        xmlHttp.send(null);
    }
    function handleStateChange() {
        if(xmlHttp.readyState == 4) {
            if(xmlHttp.status == 200) {
                document.getElementById("secretMessage").innerHTML =
                                    xmlHttp.responseText;
            }
        }
    }
</script>
</head>
<body>
    <h1>Test Ajax with Selenium</h1>
    <input type="button" id="button" name="button"
    value="Click me to get secret message from server"
    onclick="getSecretMessage();"/>
    <br/><br/>
    <div id="secretMessage">
    </div>
</body>
</html>
```

**Listing 2-10.** *ajaxResponse.jsp*

```
<%@page contentType="text/plain"%>
Have a great day!! :)
```

As in the first example, the test case is written as an HTML page containing a three-column table, which is shown in Listing 2-11. This test case consists of four tasks. The first task is the open task, which points the browser to the desired page. The next task, click, clicks the DOM element whose id attribute is button. Note that this differs from the clickAndWait task used in the previous example; in this case, the click task does not wait for a new page to load.

Unlike a normal HTTP request, the asynchronous nature of the Ajax request means that a new page is not loaded. Instead, the JavaScript that launched the Ajax request continues on without waiting for the Ajax request to finish. So Selenium can't use the clickAndWait task because a new page is not being loaded. After initiating the click task, which clicks the web page's button, you can use Selenium's pause task to wait a specified amount of time, giving the Ajax request time to complete. In this case the pause time is set to 2,000 milliseconds.

Finally, the verifyTextPresent assertion checks that the text returned by the server in response to the Ajax request appears on the page. Listing 2-11 is the complete HTML source for this test case.

**Listing 2-11.** *testAjax.html*

```
<!DOCTYPE HTML PUBLIC "-//W3C//DTD HTML 4.01 Transitional//EN">
<html>
    <head>
        <title></title>
    </head>
    <body>
        <table border="1">
            <tr>
            <td colspan="3">Test Echoing Login ID</td>
            <tr>
                <td>open</td>
                <td>/chapter02/testAjax.jsp</td>
                <td> </td>
            </tr>
            <tr>
                <td>click</td>
                <td>button</td>
                <td> </td>
            </tr>
```

```
        <tr>
            <td>pause</td>
            <td>2000</td>
            <td> </td>
        </tr>
        <tr>
            <td>verifyTextPresent</td>
            <td>Have a great day!! :)</td>
            <td> </td>
        </tr>
      </table>
   </body>
</html>
```

With both test cases written we can now turn our focus to actually running the tests. The first small task we must do is create a test suite that contains these two test cases. As mentioned earlier, a test suite is an HMTL file containing a table that lists the individual test cases. Listing 2-12 lists the source code for the test suite.

**Listing 2-12.** *TestSuite.html*

```
<!DOCTYPE HTML PUBLIC "-//W3C//DTD HTML 4.01 Transitional//EN">
<html>
    <head>
        <title></title>
    </head>
    <body>
        <table>
            <tbody>
                <tr><td><b>Example Test Suite</b></td></tr>
                <tr><td><a href="testLogin.html">Echo Login ID</a></td></tr>
                <tr><td><a href="testAjax.html">Test Ajax</a></td></tr>
            </tbody>
        </table>
    </body>
</html>
```

You are now ready to run the tests. Remember that the Selenium runtime files should reside at the root of your application's WAR file. Deploy the application and point your browser to $application-root/selenium/TestRunner.html. By default, Selenium looks for test suites in the selenium/tests directory. You can point Selenium to your test suite by appending the query parameter ?test=path-to-test-suite to the URL. The path to your test suite is listed relative to the selenium directory.

The Test Runner page will open and list all of the individual tests that exist in the test suite. You can choose to run all of the tests collectively or singularly. Selenium indicates the results of the test using familiar JUnit colors: green is success and red is a failure. Figure 2-21 shows the results of executing the two tests.

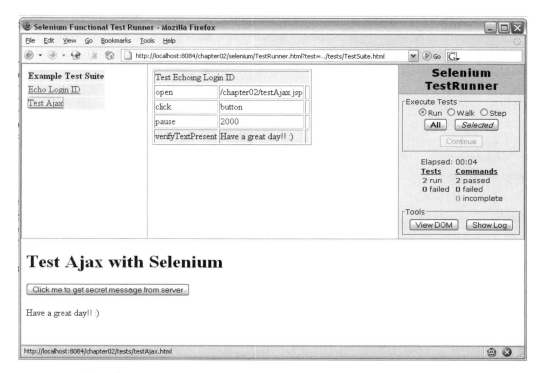

**Figure 2-21.** *The Selenium Test Runner after running two successful tests*

Figure 2-21 indicates that both test cases passed, including the Ajax test case. If you write a test case for an Ajax request that fails, be sure to check that the amount of wait time set by the pause command is sufficient. Sometimes Ajax requests can be slow the first few times they are executed, especially if there are JSPs that need to be compiled. Also note the browser's address bar in Figure 2-21. A query string is used to point the browser to the specific test suite shown in Listing 2-12. The test suite resides in the tests directory which is at the application root, and since Selenium searches relative to the selenium directory, the query string used is ?test=../tests/TestSuite.html.

## Selenium IDE

You've now seen how powerful Selenium is yet also how easy it is to use. Fortunately there's an even easier way to write Selenium tests than by writing simple HTML files: the Selenium IDE.

The Selenium IDE, as described on its home page at `www.openqa.org/selenium-ide`, is an integrated development environment for authoring and executing Selenium tests. Selenium IDE is implemented as a Firefox extension and includes the complete Selenium Core, so you can record and play back scripts directly from the IDE. Selenium IDE not only automatically records scripts but also allows you to create and edit scripts by hand. It even supports autocomplete for the common Selenium commands.

Installing Selenium IDE is as simple as pointing your browser to the installation page at `www.openqa.org/selenium-ide/download.action` and clicking on the link to initiate the installation process. Firefox might first warn you that the page is attempting to install an extension, and if so, you'll need to grant installation rights to the website. Click the download link again and Firefox will open a window confirming your intent to install the extension. Click Install to start the downloading the extension. You must restart Firefox in order to complete the installation of Selenium IDE.

After restarting Firefox you can open Selenium IDE by selecting the Selenium IDE item under the Tools menu. Figure 2-22 shows the main Selenium IDE window.

**Figure 2-22.** *Selenium IDE main window*

The main part of the Selenium IDE window is the Editor tab. The Editor lists all of the commands that appear in the currently opened Selenium test. Here you can add and edit commands by filling in the Command, Target, and Value fields. If you prefer, you can edit the HTML source directly by selecting the Source tab.

You can open an existing test by selecting the Open command from the File menu and navigating to the HTML file representing the Selenium test. Selenium IDE loads the test and lists all of the test's commands in the Editor pane. All of the commands can be edited, moved, copied, or deleted, and new commands can be inserted at any point in the test. Right-click on a command in the Editor pane to see the list of available tasks.

Selenium IDE automatically begins recording browser activity as soon as the Selenium IDE window is opened. You can toggle the recording behavior by clicking on the red circle at the right-hand side of the toolbar just above the Editor pane.

Enough with the basics—let's get busy! We'll do a short example to demonstrate how easy it is to write tests with Selenium IDE. This example will replicate the Ajax test shown earlier and whose Selenium test file is testAjax.html, shown in Listing 2-11. The only difference is that instead of writing the HTML file by hand, we'll use the Selenium IDE to help us write the test.

First, be sure that the web server is running so that the pages will be served correctly. Open Firefox and point it to the testAjax.jsp page. Then, open Selenium IDE.

With the blank Selenium IDE window open, go back to the browser window and click the button. Selenium IDE will automatically detect the button click and fill in some commands, as shown in Figure 2-23.

**Figure 2-23.** *Selenium IDE automatically detects the button click and adds commands to the test.*

You can see that Selenium has automatically added the open command and pointed it to the testAjax.jsp file. Also note that at the top of the window Selenium lists the base URL, which is kept separate from the application context. This is useful in case you ever want to test the application in different domains, such as in a development and prepro-duction domain.

Since Selenium IDE already created the open and click commands for us, all we need to do to make the test identical to the test shown in Listing 2-11 is add the verifyTextPresent command to verify that the Ajax call was successful and the response text was added to the page. To do so, click in the area immediately under the "click" command. The row should become highlighted, and you can now enter the verifyTextPresent command and the text value into their respective input boxes, being sure to enter the text value into the Value input box. Note that as you begin typing verifyTextPresent into the input box, a list of matching commands will appear in the drop-down list, allowing you to select the command while minimizing typing and reducing the chances of errors.

You can click on the Source tab to verify that the command was added correctly to the underlying HTML file. At this point the contents of the Source tab should be nearly identical to Listing 2-11.

With the test complete, all you need to do is run the test. Selenium IDE provides two ways to run the test. The first is to run the test from the browser window as you saw earlier in this chapter. You can do this by clicking the green arrow on the right side of the window next to the red Record button. This will open a browser window in Firefox pointed to the Selenium Test Runner, and you can start the test from here.

The other option is to run the test directly from within Selenium IDE. To do this, click the leftmost green arrow. The test will execute and commands will be highlighted in green if they pass or red if they don't. The successful test is shown in Figure 2-24.

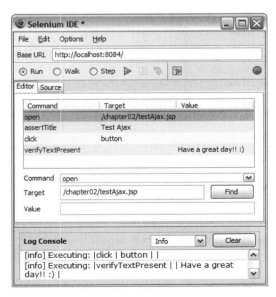

**Figure 2-24.** *A successful test executed from within Selenium IDE*

Using Selenium IDE, we were able create and execute a Selenium test without writing any HTML. In fact, the only typing required was to add the `verifyTextPresent` command, and even then autocomplete helped with that task. The best part of Selenium IDE is that it's easy enough to be used by nontechnical staff, such as by project managers or business owners.

You should consider using Selenium IDE if you're using Selenium, because it offers so many benefits over writing the tests manually. More information on using Selenium IDE can be found on its home page. A video demonstrating how to record a test can be found at `http://wiki.openqa.org/display/SIDE/Recording+a+Test`.

### Which Testing Tool Is Right for Me?

JsUnit and Selenium are powerful tools in their own right. JsUnit is probably the most natural choice for those who are very familiar with JUnit. Selenium sets itself apart from JsUnit by the fact that Selenium tests the functional aspects of an application (instead of testing discrete JavaScript functions) and the way in which test cases are written. Instead of writing JavaScript, Selenium test cases are written as HTML tables, and even then, the Selenium IDE can be used to automatically record and edit tests.

The real answer is that the tools are more complementary to each other than anything else. Selenium is more of a user acceptance or integration testing tool, and the way in which its test cases are written means that nontechnical personnel can potentially write test cases. Selenium could be paired with a more "traditional" unit testing tool like JsUnit to provide a very powerful testing architecture.

# Summary

In this chapter you've been exposed to several tools that can make Ajax development easier. JavaScript editors like JSEclipse are making it easier to write nontrivial amounts of JavaScript with features like syntax highlighting and code completion, and formatting tools help ease working with poorly formatted legacy JavaScript files.

The Dojo JavaScript compressor compresses your JavaScript files, reducing the amount of network bandwidth they consume and providing some obfuscation features in the process, and it can even be integrated into your Ant build process. The Mouseover DOM Inspector is a fast, easy-to-use tool that helps you understand the structure of an HTML document, which can aid in learning and debugging.

NetBean's HTTP Monitor can help track down bugs by showing you exactly how a request was made by the browser and what (if any) parameters were included in the request. Venkman is a powerful JavaScript debugging environment that gives you the ability to step through JavaScript code one line at a time. JavaScript logging frameworks like Log4JS and Lumberjack bring log4j-like logging capabilities to your JavaScript code.

Finally, all of your test-first and unit testing development techniques can be brought to JavaScript development using tools like JsUnit and Selenium. Both are great tools that bring the concepts of repeatable test cases to JavaScript and web applications in general.

These tools and the tools that are sure to continue popping up will help you develop higher-quality Ajax applications in less time and with less effort from you, the developer. Try them out and see how you can integrate them into your development process.

# PART 2

■ ■ ■

# Libraries and Toolkits

Despite what some pundits claim, Ajax isn't rocket science—but that doesn't mean everyone should reinvent the wheel. In fact, with the number of quality libraries and toolkits available, developers can quickly and easily add sophisticated Ajax effects to their applications. Although you certainly can do an awful lot on your own, once you see what others have already done in various libraries and toolkits, why would you? We should point out that Ajax is a very dynamic space, so by the time you read this there will likely be new options, some projects might be dormant, and others may have changed radically. That said, before you start crafting your own solution, you owe it to yourself to explore what's already available.

# CHAPTER 3

■■■

# Java-Agnostic Toolkits

**Y**ou may think it odd that we'd spend time talking about toolkits and libraries that aren't directly related to a Java server-side solution. However, to fully appreciate the current Ajax space, we really need to discuss these options. These solutions work just fine with your Java application! In this chapter, we'll take a look at the popular Prototype framework along with s⬚⬚⬚⬚⬚⬚⬚⬚⬚⬚⬚⬚⬚⬚⬚⬚⬚⬚⬚⬚⬚⬚⬚⬚⬚⬚⬚Ve'll also examine Dojo and Taconit⬚

Obviously, we ⬚⬚⬚⬚⬚⬚⬚⬚⬚⬚⬚⬚⬚⬚⬚⬚⬚⬚⬚⬚⬚⬚⬚⬚⬚⬚ reading this section you'll know enou⬚⬚⬚⬚⬚⬚⬚⬚⬚⬚⬚⬚⬚⬚⬚⬚⬚⬚⬚⬚⬚⬚ own applications. These toolkits are ⬚⬚⬚⬚⬚⬚⬚⬚⬚⬚⬚⬚⬚⬚⬚⬚⬚⬚⬚⬚⬚ a bit by the time you read this.

## Prototype

Prototype (http:/⬚⬚⬚⬚⬚⬚⬚⬚⬚⬚⬚⬚⬚⬚⬚⬚⬚⬚⬚ library written by Sam Stephenson ⬚⬚⬚⬚⬚⬚⬚⬚⬚⬚⬚⬚⬚⬚⬚⬚⬚⬚⬚plications." Although it's not the best-d⬚⬚⬚⬚⬚⬚⬚⬚⬚⬚⬚⬚⬚⬚⬚⬚⬚⬚Behavior, and the ubiquitous script.⬚⬚⬚⬚⬚⬚⬚⬚⬚⬚⬚⬚⬚⬚⬚⬚⬚⬚ritten and pretty easy to read, plus there⬚⬚⬚⬚⬚⬚⬚⬚⬚⬚⬚⬚⬚⬚⬚⬚⬚⬚riptions of how Prototype works.

Of course, much of the interest in Prototype comes from Ruby on Rails (www.rubyonrails.com), which features integrated Prototype support. Despite weighing in at just over 1,000 lines of code (as of release 1.4), Prototype packs quite a punch. Although it might be known for simplifying Ajax development, it also contains a large number of useful utility methods that can be leveraged even if you aren't adding Ajax to your application.

Getting started with Prototype couldn't be easier. Simply download the latest version from http://prototype.conio.net and put the prototype.js file into your application's preferred location for JavaScript files. Let's start by looking at some of the utility methods that you might use regardless of how much Ajax you put into your application.

## $()

As soon as you start working with the DOM, you become very familiar with code like this:

```
var myElement = document.getElementById('foo');
```

Now, this isn't the hardest code to write, but frankly it gets a little monotonous and it's also a bit wordy, which can be an issue in some user interfaces. Prototype recognized these shortcomings and gives us this wonderful shortcut:

```
var myElement = $('foo');
```

Although some may find this approach a bit terse, having written the long form more times than we can count, it really is helpful. We'd also like to point out that using this shorter form shrinks the size of your pages slightly. Although that may not be the biggest issue you'll deal with, smaller pages load faster, which generally improves the perception users have of your application.[1]

Less typing and smaller pages aren't the only plus of using $() though. Unlike getDocumentById(), $() can retrieve multiple elements and return them as an array. So, you can do something like this:

```
var myElements = $('foo', 'bar', 'fooBar');
for (var i = 0; i < myElements.length; i++) {
  myElements[i].value = "new value";
}
```

That can be pretty handy when you're looking to update multiple fields, though there is one issue you need to be aware of. Prototype doesn't bother to check whether the fields you are asking for exist, so if you ask for three elements, you will get an array of length 3 even if two of the elements aren't in the DOM (the array will contain nulls).

With dynamic languages like JavaScript, classes aren't closed, so we're free to extend them and add our own methods. Prototype takes advantage of this (seriously, you should read the code!) by extending the standard document object with a new method called getElementsByClassName(). This method allows you to retrieve DOM elements based on their CSS class name (think getElementsByTagName() except on the className attribute). If a given element has multiple class names, fear not; Prototype will find it!

Why is that interesting you might ask? Imagine you have required fields on your form and you want to run a simple JavaScript check on each one. While you certainly could hard-code the names of the elements into your validation routine, it's much simpler to add a "required" class name to the required elements and then leverage getElementsByClassName() to get the collection of required elements. Your validation check can then iterate over the collection and make sure a value is present!

---

1. www.useit.com/alertbox/9703a.html

---

**TIP** Keep in mind that Prototype (like many Ajax frameworks) isn't namespaced. If you use it in conjunction with other libraries, it's possible that you might have some collisions.

---

## Working with Forms

Web applications revolve around forms. In the Ajax space, we often grab an element, get its value, make a request to a server passing along that value, and then take the response and update some other value on the page. If getting an element is the most frequent thing we do, getting the value of an element has to be a close second. Just as Prototype helps us with the former, it also has a convenience function for the latter. Instead of writing this:

```
var myValue = document.getElementById('foo').value;
```

we can write this:

```
var myValue = $F('foo');
```

That's pretty handy. This works on any input field, but unlike $(), it won't take multiple IDs.

Prototype has some other helpful form methods; in fact it has a Form class. Form has a number of interesting methods:

getElements(form): Returns all the elements of the form as an array

getInputs(form, typeName, name): Returns all the input elements from a form, allowing you to (optionally) filter out results by element type or element name

disable(form): Gets every element of the form, fires the blur event, and sets the disabled attribute to true for every element

enable(form): Gets every element of the form, fires the blur event, and sets the disabled attribute to false for every element

focusFirstElement(form): Places the focus on the first nonhidden, nondisabled form field

reset(form): Calls reset on the form element

serialize(form): Formats a string for posting the form to the server via Ajax, in other words something like "foo=value1&bar=value2"

## Manipulating the DOM

A major part of Ajax is manipulating the DOM—adding, showing, hiding, and removing elements, and so on. Although none of this code is terribly hard to write, it can get repetitious. To simplify this, Prototype adds static methods to the Element class (or in the case of browsers that do not properly support Element, it adds the class) that we can use to manipulate parts of the DOM. Let's start with simplifying hiding or showing elements. How often have you seen code like Listing 3-1?

**Listing 3-1.** *Hide/Show (The Old Way)*

```html
<html>
  <head>
    <title>HideShow</title>
    <script type="text/javascript">
        function toggle(name) {
            var element = document.getElementById(name);
            if(element.style.display == 'none') {
                element.style.display = '';
            }
            else {
                element.style.display = 'none';
            }
        }
    </script>
  </head>
  <body>
    <h1>Hide/Show</h1>
    <div id="hideShow">
        Now you see me...
    </div>
    <br>
    <input type="button" value="Toggle" onclick="toggle('hideShow');"/>
  </body>
</html>
```

This code produces a simple page (see Figure 3-1), and clicking on the button causes the text in the div to disappear (see Figure 3-2).

**Figure 3-1.** *Hide/Show—now you see me...*

**Figure 3-2.** *Hide/Show—now you don't!*

Let's compare that to using Prototype's toggle() method (see Listing 3-2).

**Listing 3-2.** *Hide/Show Using Prototype*

```
<html>
  <head>
    <title>Prototype Hide Show</title>
    <script src="scripts/prototype.js" type="text/javascript"></script>
  </head>
  <body>
    <h1>Hide/Show with Prototype</h1>
    <div id="hideShow">
        Now you see me...
    </div>
    <br>
    <input type="button" value="Toggle" onclick="Element.toggle('hideShow');"/>
  </body>
</html>
```

That's a tad easier, no? But toggle() isn't the only function that Element gives us. Along the same lines as toggle(), we have hide() and show(). As you would expect, hide() takes any number of elements and sets each element's display style to none, thus rendering the element invisible. Obviously, show() does the opposite.

Sometimes simply hiding a part of the DOM isn't enough. After all, if a hidden element contained a form, that data would still get submitted along with the page. We can take hiding a step further by actually removing the element from the DOM. For us to write this ourselves, we would have to do something like the following:

```
function remove(name) {
  var element = document.getElementById(name);
  element.parentNode.removeChild(element);
}
```

We can just leverage Prototype to do the same thing: Element.remove(name). Element also provides methods to add or remove CSS classes to an element—addClassName(element, className) and removeClassName(element, className), respectively. Another method will tell you if a given element has a class already defined on it, hasClassName(element, className). There is a method to get the offset height of an element (getHeight(element)), and you can remove child nodes that only have white space via the cleanWhitespace(element) function.

OK, so we've shown how Prototype can help us hide, show, and remove things from the DOM, but what about adding elements? How would we do something like the dynamic lists found in Backpack (see Figure 3-3)?

Well, leveraging Prototype, we can start to mimic that. To handle the adding of elements, Prototype introduces a class called Insertion that allows us interject content at various points such as the top or bottom of an element (like a list). We aren't limited to just the top or bottom though; we can also insert before or after the element. Let's take a look at some simple code that will let us add items to the bottom of a list (see Listing 3-3).

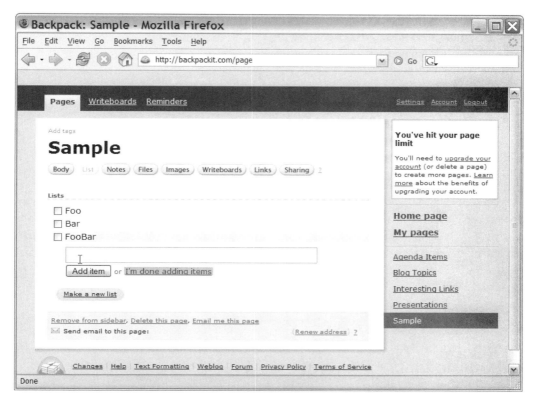

**Figure 3-3.** *Backpack's dynamic list functionality*

**Listing 3-3.** *Insertion in Action*

```html
<html>
  <head>
    <title>Dynamic Lists</title>
    <script src="scripts/prototype.js" type="text/javascript"></script>
    <script type="text/javascript">
      function addItem() {
        var val = $F('newItem');
        new Insertion.Bottom('groceries', '<li>' + val + '</li>');
        new Field.clear('newItem');
      }
    </script>
  </head>
```

```
<body>
  <h1>Dynamic Lists</h1>
  <ul id="groceries">
    <li>Bread</li>
  </ul>
  <input type="text" id="newItem"/>
  <input type="button" value="Add Item"
    onclick="addItem();"/>
</body>
</html>
```

You'll notice that we're taking advantage of a couple of features besides just the Insertion class. We're using $F() to get the value we want to add to the list, and then we use the Field class to clear out the input field. Obviously we've hard-coded some of this for simplicity, but it wouldn't be hard to spiff this up. In the end, this gives us a page like Figure 3-4.

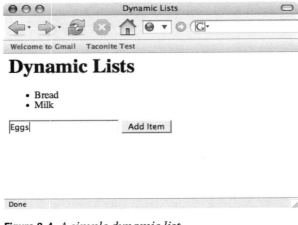

**Figure 3-4.** *A simple dynamic list*

The first thing you should notice about working with the Insertion class is that we have to provide the appropriate HTML around the thing we want to insert. Since this example shows a list, we have to wrap our text with the <li> tags. Despite this minor drawback, the Insertion class is a very powerful addition to our toolkit. Of course at this point you might be asking, what is the difference between Insertion.Top() and Insertion.Before()? Well, let's take our dynamic list example and tweak it a bit so it looks like Listing 3-3 (see Listing 3-4).

**Listing 3-4.** *Insertion Explained*

```html
<html>
  <head>
    <title>Insertion Explained</title>
    <script src="scripts/prototype.js" type="text/javascript"></script>
    <script type="text/javascript">
      function addItemBefore() {
        var val = $F('newItem');
        new Insertion.Before('groceries', '<h2>' + val + '</h2>');
        new Field.clear('newItem');
      }
      function addItemTop() {
        var val = $F('newItem');
        new Insertion.Top('groceries', '<li>' + val + '</li>');
        new Field.clear('newItem');
      }
      function addItemBottom() {
        var val = $F('newItem');
        new Insertion.Bottom('groceries', '<li>' + val + '</li>');
        new Field.clear('newItem');
      }
      function addItemAfter() {
        var val = $F('newItem');
        new Insertion.After('groceries', '<h2>' + val + '</h2>');
        new Field.clear('newItem');
      }
    </script>
  </head>
  <body>
    <h1>Insertion Explained</h1>
    <ul id="groceries">
      <li>Bread</li>
    </ul>
    <input type="text" id="newItem"/>
    <input type="button" value="Add Item Before"
      onclick="addItemBefore();"/>
    <input type="button" value="Add Item Top"
      onclick="addItemTop();"/>
    <input type="button" value="Add Item Bottom"
      onclick="addItemBottom();"/>
```

```
    <input type="button" value="Add Item After"
      onclick="addItemAfter();"/>
  </body>
</html>
```

Basically, we've just added functions to use the other three insertion points so you could see how they differ in practice. This code will result in something that looks like Figure 3-5 (depending on which buttons you click).

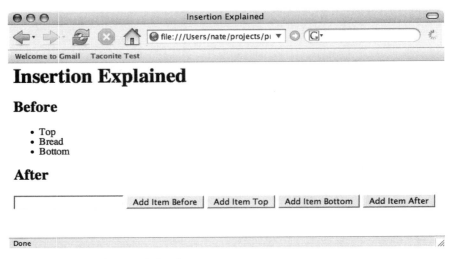

**Figure 3-5.** *Insertion explained*

## Try: Simplified Browser Detection

Compared to the early days, JavaScript support across browsers has improved greatly; however, there are still some things that just don't work everywhere. Although we can always do browser checks on our own, sometimes things change. For instance, in Internet Explorer 7, XHR will be implemented as a JavaScript object instead of an ActiveX object, meaning all of the Ajax apps that try to create an ActiveX object first might need to change their implementation. Often, we will write a set of functions, one for each browser peculiarity. Rather than do our own error or browser detection, we can use the Try class, which will run each function in sequence, returning the result of the successful call. Listing 3-5 shows a contrived example of how to use Try.

**Listing 3-5.** *Using the Try Class*

```html
<html>
  <head>
    <title>Prototype's Try</title>
    <script src="scripts/prototype.js" type="text/javascript"></script>
    <script type="text/javascript">
      function giveItATry() {
        var value = Try.these (
          function () {
            asdf; //deliberate error
            return 1;
          },
          function () {
            return 2;
          }
        );
        alert("path: " + value);
      }
    </script>
  </head>
  <body>
    <h1>Prototype's Try</h1>
    <input type="button" value="Try Me"
      onclick="giveItATry();"/>
  </body>
</html>
```

As you would expect, running this example results in the second path executing (see Figure 3-6).

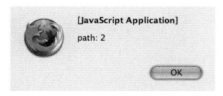

**Figure 3-6.** *Result of Try.these*

## Ajax Support

We've seen how Prototype has some very handy methods that can help with common behavior related to forms and the DOM, but what about its support for Ajax? As you would expect, Prototype provides an easy-to-use wrapper around XHR as well as basic user interface support. The Prototype's Ajax object handles the cross-browser issues related to getting an instance of XHR. On top of this, Prototype builds the Ajax.Request class that makes calling the server a breeze. A simple use is shown in Listing 3-6.

**Listing 3-6.** *A Simple Use of Ajax.Request*

```html
<html>
  <head>
    <title>Prototype's Ajax Request</title>
    <script src="scripts/prototype.js" type="text/javascript"></script>
    <script type="text/javascript">
      function doFoo() {
        var url = "simpleResponse.xml";
        new Ajax.Request(url, {
            asynchronous: true,
            method: "get",
            parameters: "foo=bar",
            onComplete: function(request) {
                showResults(request.responseText);
            }
        });
      }
      function showResults(responseText) {
        alert("The server returned: " + responseText);
      }
    </script>
  </head>
  <body>
    <h1>Prototype's Ajax Request</h1>
    <input type="button" value="Do Foo"
      onclick="doFoo();"/>
  </body>
</html>
```

We're actually mocking the server here by using a simple XML file that simply contains the text "Hello from the server!" (We're showing how to pass a parameter, though we aren't actually using them here.) Mocking the server by using a basic XML, HTML, or text file to represent the response from the server can be a great way to test your client-side code. Ajax applications add an additional layer of complexity, and being able to hold at least one variable constant can greatly simplify development. As you would expect, running this code results in the pop-up shown in Figure 3-7.

**JavaScript**
The server returned: Hello from the server!

OK

**Figure 3-7.** *Showing the results from the server*

So what did we do here? First, we created a new instance of `Ajax.Request` and established that the first argument of the constructor is a URL of the server-side resource (here just a simple XML file). Next, we indicate whether the request is asynchronous or not. Most of the time we'll leave this true. (Omitting this has the same effect.) After that, we indicate which HTTP method we want to use: GET, POST, etc. Now we pass in any parameters we might need. (Obviously these aren't actually used; they are just for demonstration purposes.) Next we indicate the callback function. Here we use the `onComplete` attribute, meaning that `showResults` will be called when the XHR's `readyState` attribute is 4. We also could have defined a callback function for a successful completion (`onSuccess`) or failure (`onFailure`).

Of course we don't always want to send back just plain text from the server. Sometimes we want to return JavaScript that is then evaluated on the client. This can be done quite easily with `Ajax.Request` as shown in Listing 3-7. Here we're taking advantage of the `eval()` function to execute JavaScript.

**Listing 3-7.** *Returning JavaScript*

```
<html>
  <head>
    <title>Prototype's Ajax Request - Using Eval</title>
    <script src="scripts/prototype.js" type="text/javascript"></script>
    <script type="text/javascript">
      function evalFoo() {
        var url = "evalResponse.xml";
        new Ajax.Request(url, {
            asynchronous: true,
            method: "get",
```

```
            onSuccess: function(request) {
                eval(request.responseText);
            }
        });
    }
  </script>
</head>
<body>
  <h1>Prototype's Ajax Request - Using Eval</h1>
  <input type="button" value="Eval Foo"
    onclick="evalFoo();"/>
</body>
</html>
```

We could just as easily return pure HTML from our server as well. In some cases this is the easiest thing to do if you are adding Ajax to an existing web application that is expecting to create a complete chunk of HTML. Of course we'll take that generated HTML and update some element's innerHTML property. Instead of using Ajax.Request, we'll use Ajax.Updater, which is quite similar except that it takes the id attribute of the element to update. A simple example is shown in Listing 3-8.

**Listing 3-8.** *Using Ajax.Updater*

```
<html>
  <head>
    <title>Prototype's Ajax Updater</title>
    <script src="scripts/prototype.js" type="text/javascript"></script>
    <script type="text/javascript">
      function update() {
        var url = "inner.html";
        new Ajax.Updater("replaceMe", url, {
            asynchronous: true,
            method: "get"
        });
      }
    </script>
  </head>
  <body>
    <h1>Prototype's Ajax Updater</h1>
    <div id="replaceMe">
      <h2>Before</h2>
    </div>
```

```
    <input type="button" value="Update"
      onclick="update();"/>
  </body>
</html>
```

The results are shown in Figures 3-8 and 3-9.

**Figure 3-8.** *Using Ajax.Updater—before*

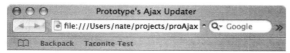

**Figure 3-9.** *Using Ajax.Updater—after*

Believe it or not, this doesn't quite cover everything Prototype has to offer. In addition to what we've shown you, Prototype also includes helpful ways to determine the current position of rendered elements (useful in a variety of UI manipulations), an `Enumerable` component to simplify working with collections of data, some helpful additions to the `String` object, numerous extensions to the `Event` object, and a simple way to call the server repeatedly at intervals (for the prototypical auto update feature). As an important aspect of the Ruby on Rails framework, expect to see other useful additions to Prototype by the time you read this.

**ISSUES WITH INNERHTML**

Many of the current Ajax frameworks rely heavily on the use of innerHTML, but this approach is not without its limitations. Like the XMLHttpRequest object, innerHTML is not a W3C standard, though it is widely supported in a number of modern browsers. Believe it or not, there are even browser quirks.

For instance, the innerHTML property is read-only for the following elements: COL, COLGROUP, FRAMESET, HTML, STYLE, TABLE, TBODY, TFOOT, THEAD, TITLE, and TR. In practice, this means there are a number of things we cannot do with the innerHTML property in IE. Say you want to append a row to a table or insert a row between two others. If you want to use innerHTML, you'd have to reproduce the entire table.

Of course if you're writing your web pages in XHTML, you're out of luck; innerHTML doesn't apply to XHTML documents.

# script.aculo.us

Prototype is a fantastic framework, but Thomas Fuchs has taken it further with the script.aculo.us (http://script.aculo.us) library. Script.aculo.us supplies a number of rich interface effects that are compatible across a number of modern browsers, coming prepackaged with visual effects, drag-and-drop, and the Ajax stalwart autocomplete text fields. Getting started with script.aculo.us couldn't be easier. Go to the download page (http://script.aculo.us/downloads), grab the latest version in your preferred archive, and drop prototype.js, scriptaculous.js, builder.js, effects.js, dragdrop.js, slider.js, and controls.js into the your favorite folder for script files in your application. Keep in mind that script.aculo.us builds upon Prototype, so make sure that you have the proper version of that installed as well. (Expect to see it bundled, but if it's not, the readme file should tell you what version you need.)

## Effect

The lack of interesting visual effects has traditionally separated thin applications from their thick cousins. Script.aculo.us recognizes this limitation and contains five core effects along with a number of combination effects that build upon the core effects. The general syntax for using Effect is

```
new Effect.EffectName(element, required-params, [options]);
```

Let's break this down a bit. First, the core effects are: Opacity, Scale, MoveBy, Highlight, and Parallel. Taking a look at the basic call, the element attribute can either be a DOM element or the ID of the element. As expected, the required-params may or may not be needed depending on the effect. If the effect has any additional customization points, they will be specified in the options arguments. The standard options that you might pass to an effect are summarized in Table 3-1.

**Table 3-1.** *Common Effect Options[a]*

| Option | Description |
|---|---|
| duration | A float (defaults to 1.0) that defines how long the effect will last in seconds. |
| fps | Frames per second to target (defaults to 25, can't exceed 100). |
| transition | The algorithm to use to modify the current point of the effect. The supplied transitions are: Effect.Transitions.sinodial (which is the default), Effect.Transitions.linear, Effect.Transitions.reverse, Effect.Transitions.wobble, Effect.Transitions.pulse, and Effect.Transitions.flicker. |
| from | The starting point of the transition expressed as a float between 0.0 and 1.0 (defaults to 0.0). |
| to | The end point of the transition expressed as a float between 0.0 and 1.0 (defaults to 1.0). |
| synch | Determines whether the effect should automatically render new frames (defaults to true). |

a. http://wiki.script.aculo.us/scriptaculous/show/CoreEffects

You can also insert your own JavaScript called at various points in the execution of an effect by passing in various callback methods as optional parameters. These callback points are summarized in Table 3-2. The callback methods get a reference to the effect object on which you can access a number of attributes (see Table 3-3).

**Table 3-2.** *Callback Functions*

| Callback | Description |
|---|---|
| beforeStart | Called before the main rendering loop has started |
| beforeUpdate | Called on each iteration of the rendering loop before the redraw |
| afterUpdate | Called on each iteration of the rendering loop after the redraw |
| afterFinish | Called after the last redraw |

**Table 3-3.** *Effect Variables*

| Variable | Description |
|---|---|
| element | The HTML element the effect is applied to |
| options | The list of options you passed to the effect |
| currentFrame | Number of the last frame rendered |
| startOn | The time the effect was started (in milliseconds) |
| finishOn | The time the effect will finish (in milliseconds) |
| effects[] | The array of individual effects that make up a parallel effect (Effect.Parallel only) |

Now that we know the basics, let's look at some actual effects.

### Effect.Opacity

As you would expect, this changes the opacity of the element. (Opacity defines the transparency of the element; the lesser the opacity, the more transparent it is.) To use this, we will use the from and to options to set an element's opacity between 100 percent (represented as a 1.0) and 0 percent (represented as 0.0). Keep in mind, you've only hidden (or obscured) the element; this isn't the same as Prototype's hide() and show(). To really appreciate how Opacity works, let's look at some code (see Listing 3-9).

**Listing 3-9.** *Using Effect.Opacity*

```html
<html>
  <head>
    <title>Script.aculo.us: Effect.Opacity</title>
    <script src="scripts/prototype.js" type="text/javascript"></script>
    <script src="scripts/effects.js" type="text/javascript"></script>
    <script type="text/javascript">
      function fade() {
        new Effect.Opacity('default',
          { duration: 3.0, from: 1.0, to: 0.0 });
      }
      function wobble() {
        new Effect.Opacity('wobble',
          { duration: 3.0, from: 1.0, to: 0.0,
            transition: Effect.Transitions.wobble });
      }
    </script>
  </head>
```

```
<body>
  <h1>Script.aculo.us: Effect.Opacity</h1>
  <div id="default">
    <h2>Watch me slowly fade away...</h2>
  </div>
  <input type="button" value="Disappear"
    onclick="fade();"/>
  <div id="wobble">
    <h2>Watch me wobble!</h2>
  </div>
  <input type="button" value="Wobble"
    onclick="wobble();"/>
</body>
</html>
```

So what are we doing here? First, you'll note that we've included both the prototype.js and effects.js files. Here, we've created two different effects. In the first function (fade()), the element we passed in will gradually fade away over the course of 3 seconds while in the second (wobble()), the element will "bounce" in and out over 3 seconds until it completely disappears from the page. As you can see from the screen shot (see Figure 3-10), both effects can occur together. Although this adds quite a bit of flair to your sites, don't go too overboard with them.

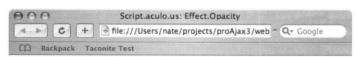

**Figure 3-10.** *Effect.Opacity in action*

## Effect.Scale

Sometimes you just want to resize something on the page. Effect.Scale lets us do this easily. As you would expect, there are a number of parameters that are specific to scale (see Table 3-4). This effect will take care of the relative scaling of contained elements, though there are some issues with contained text. Unless you've specified the font size in em units, the text won't be resized along with its container.

**Table 3-4.** *Effect.Scale Specific Parameters*

| Option | Description |
| --- | --- |
| scaleX | Determines whether the element should scale horizontally (defaults to true) |
| scaleY | Determines whether the element should scale vertically (defaults to true) |
| scaleContent | Determines whether the content scaling should be enabled (defaults to true) |
| scaleFromCenter | If set to true, the center of the element stays in its current position (defaults to false) |
| scaleMode | Scale on the portion of the element that is visible (box, the default) or scale everything (content) |
| scaleFrom | The starting percentage of the scaling (defaults to 100.0) |

## Effect.Highlight

As we've described, Ajax allows us to call the server asynchronously and then modify part of the page. Although this is a great step forward for our users, we've trained them to expect a full page refresh when something has changed, so they might miss a minor change to the page. The most common solution to this is one we discussed in Chapter 1: the Fade Anything Technique where we modify the background color of the thing that changed and then slowly fade it back to the original color. Script.aculo.us makes this really simple to implement with Effect.Highlight.

Effect.Highlight takes three effect specific parameters, as seen in Table 3-5. If you omit the restorecolor, Effect.Highlight will try to determine the current background color of the element you are applying the effect to. However, if the color wasn't declared as a CSS RGB triplet, the results are less than reliable.

**Table 3-5.** *Effect.Highlight Specific Parameters*

| Option | Description |
| --- | --- |
| startcolor | The color the background of the element starts as (defaults to light yellow) |
| endcolor | The color the background of the element ends at (defaults to white) |
| restorecolor | The color the background of the element is set to after the effect finishes |

The code in Listing 3-10 will fade the element from maroon to gold and then reset the background color to white.

**Listing 3-10.** *Using Effect.Highlight*

```html
<html>
  <head>
    <title>Script.aculo.us: Effect.Highlight</title>
    <script src="scripts/prototype.js" type="text/javascript"></script>
    <script src="scripts/effects.js" type="text/javascript"></script>
    <script type="text/javascript">
      function fadeAnything() {
        new Effect.Highlight('fadeMe',
          { startcolor: '660000',
            endcolor: 'FFFF00',
            restorecolor: '#ffffff'});
      }
    </script>
  </head>
  <body>
    <h1>Script.aculo.us: Effect.Highlight</h1>
    <div id="fadeMe">
      <h2>The Fade Anything Technique!</h2>
    </div>
    <input type="button" value="Fade Me!"
      onclick="fadeAnything();"/>
  </body>
</html>
```

## Effect.Parallel

While the core effects alone give us some powerful tools, combining several effects together
can allow us to do even more interesting things. To accommodate this, `Effect.Parallel`
takes an array of subeffects as its first parameter (as opposed to the standard element).
Keep in mind that you don't have to apply the effects to the same element. This just allows
you to simultaneously (remember, effects are asynchronous) call a number of effects. The
code in Listing 3-11 not only fades the element as before, but also moves it (see Figures 3-11,
3-12, and 3-13).

**Listing 3-11.** *Using Effect.Parallel*

```html
<html>
  <head>
    <title>Script.aculo.us: Effect.Parallel</title>
    <script src="scripts/prototype.js" type="text/javascript"></script>
    <script src="scripts/effects.js" type="text/javascript"></script>
    <script type="text/javascript">
```

```
      function parallel() {
        new Effect.Parallel(
          [ new Effect.MoveBy('affected', 100, 50,
               { sync: true }),
            new Effect.Highlight('affected',
              { sync: true,
                startcolor: '660000',
                endcolor: 'FFFF00',
                restorecolor: '#ffffff'}),
          ],
          { duration: 2.0});
      }
    </script>
  </head>
  <body>
    <h1>Script.aculo.us: Effect.Parallel</h1>
    <div id="affected">
      <h2>Showing Multiple Effects at Once!</h2>
    </div>
    <input type="button" value="Parallel"
      onclick="parallel();"/>
  </body>
</html>
```

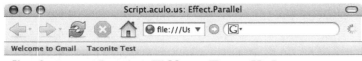

**Figure 3-11.** *Effect.Parallel—before*

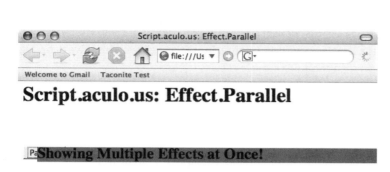

**Figure 3-12.** *Effect.Parallel—during*

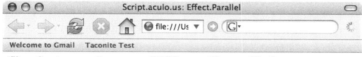

**Figure 3-13.** *Effect.Parallel—after*

## Combination Effects

As you can probably imagine, the possible combinations afforded with Effect.Parallel are limitless. Although you certainly could create your own effects (truthfully, once you get going, it's a bit addictive) script.aculo.us comes prepackaged with a number of useful combinations that are built upon the core effects. Besides serving as example effects, they're simple to use.

As we stated before, just because you can do something doesn't mean you should. Don't make your users search for a "Skip animation" link. Although judicial use of these effects can significantly improve the user experience of your application, if you go too far, all you'll do is help your competitors. To see these effects in action, take a look at the Combination Effects

Demo at `http://wiki.script.aculo.us/scriptaculous/show/CombinationEffectsDemo`. You'll also want to consult the most recent documentation. Some effects don't work on all elements in all browsers, and some require simple HTML tricks.

- `Effect.Appear`: Causes a hidden element to appear via `Effect.Opacity`

- `Effect.Fade`: Causes an element to disappear via `Effect.Opacity`

- `Effect.Puff`: Causes an element to grow and fade, disappearing like a "puff of smoke"

- `Effect.DropOut`: Causes an element to drop and fade away

- `Effect.Shake`: Causes an element to shift left and right again and again

- `Effect.SwitchOff`: Mimics an old TV turning off; the element is scaled down while also combining `Effect.Opacity` and the flicker transition

- `Effect.BlindDown`: Mimics a window blind; element is visible at the end

- `Effect.BlindUp`: Mimics a window blind; element is not visible at the end

- `Effect.SlideDown`: Similar to `Effect.BlindDown`; requires a wrapper `div` to work properly

- `Effect.SlideUp`: Similar to `Effect.BlindUp`; requires a wrapper `div` to work properly

- `Effect.Pulsate`: Causes the element to blink on and off

- `Effect.Squish`: Causes the element to scale down to nothing (towards the upper left)

- `Effect.Fold`: Similar to `Effect.Squish` but scales from the bottom up and then right to left

- `Effect.Grow`: Causes an element to disappear, then scale up to its original size from the center

- `Effect.Shrink`: Similar to `Effect.Squish` but with movement toward the center

## Autocomplete

In our experience designing web applications, one of the most asked-for widgets is an autocompleting text entry field. Until Ajax, it's always been frustrating to explain why it just couldn't be done. Although the code isn't terribly complex, to truly mimic Google

Suggest requires quite a bit of code. Luckily for us, script.aculo.us contains a number of helpful controls, including an autocomplete widget.

The script.aculo.us `Ajax.Autocompleter` couldn't be easier to use. The basic syntax looks like this:

```
new Ajax.Autocompleter(textField, div, url, options)
```

The `textField` is the text field that we want to autocomplete, and the `div` represents where we want the drop-down effect to go. Obviously `url` is the server resource we are calling, and the `options` include things like the minimum number of characters required to actually trigger the server call (defaults to 1) and the frequency to look for changes and call the server (defaults to 0.4 seconds).

First things first—we need a server resource to call. Since this is a Java-based book, we'll code up a really simple servlet (see Listing 3-12). Our servlet will return a list of names that start with what is passed to the servlet. To work with the `Ajax.Autocompleter`, our code must return an unordered list to the client. Keep in mind that this is just example code, so the list is hard-coded. In a real-world situation you'd run off to the database.

**Listing 3-12.** *A Simple Servlet*

```java
package proajax.chap3;
import java.io.*;
import java.util.ArrayList;
import java.util.Iterator;
import java.util.List;
import javax.servlet.*;
import javax.servlet.http.*;
public class AutoCompleteServlet extends HttpServlet {
    private List names = new ArrayList();
    public void init(ServletConfig config) throws ServletException {
        names.add("Abe");
        names.add("Abel");
        names.add("Abigail");
        names.add("Abner");
        names.add("Abraham");
        names.add("Marcus");
        names.add("Marcy");
        names.add("Marge");
        names.add("Marie");
    }
    protected void doGet(HttpServletRequest request, HttpServletResponse response)
    throws ServletException, IOException {
        String prefix = request.getParameter("name");
```

```java
NameService service = NameService.getInstance(names);
List matching = service.findNames(prefix);
if (matching.size() > 0) {
    PrintWriter out = response.getWriter();
    response.setContentType("text/html");
    StringBuffer results = new StringBuffer("<ul>");
    Iterator iter = matching.iterator();
    while(iter.hasNext()) {
        String name = (String) iter.next();
        results.append("<li>" + name + "</li>");
    }
    results.append("</ul>");
    matching = null;
    service = null;
    out.println(results);
    out.close();
} else {
    response.setStatus(HttpServletResponse.SC_NO_CONTENT);
}
}
```

Now that we have something to call, let's set up our client code. On the client side, we need to have a text field, a div to hold the results, and an instance of the Ajax.Autocompleter (see Listing 3-13). Out of the box, our results look something like Figure 3-14.

**Listing 3-13.** *The Client-Side Code*

```html
<html>
  <head>
    <title>Script.aculo.us: Ajax.Autocompleter</title>
    <script src="scripts/prototype.js" type="text/javascript"></script>
    <script src="scripts/effects.js" type="text/javascript"></script>
    <script src="scripts/controls.js" type="text/javascript"></script>
  </head>
  <body>
    <h1>Script.aculo.us: Ajax.Autocompleter</h1>
    <input autocomplete="off" type="text" id="name" name="name"/>
    <div class="auto_complete" id="results"></div>
    <script type="text/javascript">
      new Ajax.Autocompleter('name', 'results', 'AutoCompleteServlet', {})
    </script>
  </body>
</html>
```

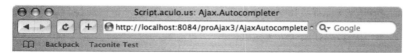

**Figure 3-14.** *The basic Ajax.Autocompleter*

Although this is OK, it isn't quite as pretty as we'd like. Our results are just displayed as a bulleted list, and the only way we can select an option is to use the mouse. Lucky for us, script.aculo.us provides us some styles that will sharpen this up a bit (see Listing 3-14). These styles allow us to use the arrow keys to navigate the list and press Enter to select a name. In addition, it puts the line around the div so it looks more like a drop-down list. Also, the bullets are gone, and the selected item is highlighted in light yellow (see Figure 3-15).

**Listing 3-14.** *Cleaning Up the Results*

```
<style>
    div.auto_complete {
      width: 350px;
      background: #fff;
    }
    div.auto_complete ul {
      border:1px solid #888;
      margin:0;
      padding:0;
      width:100%;
      list-style-type:none;
    }
    div.auto_complete ul li {
      margin:0;
      padding:3px;
    }
    div.auto_complete ul li.selected {
      background-color: #ffb;
    }
```

```
div.auto_complete ul strong.highlight {
  color: #800;
  margin:0;
  padding:0;
}
```

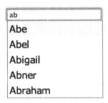

**Figure 3-15.** *The* Autocompleter *styled up*

# Dojo Toolkit

Dojo Toolkit[2] is an open source JavaScript toolkit that simplifies Ajax development. Like Prototype and script.aculo.us, it provides effects and widgets that are built on top of a number of packages. Unlike the previous two libraries, Dojo isn't quite as lightweight or focused (which we don't mean as a negative!). It includes a logging module, widget-authoring utilities, a math module, even a collections library. Essentially, Dojo is a set of JavaScript utilities and functions that are independent of one another but that can be bound together via the packaging system. Dojo really gives developers a tremendous amount of power and flexibility.

Although you could grab the source code for Dojo and build it yourself, you have the option of downloading an edition which is just a custom build that combines various pieces of Dojo into a single file. At the time of this writing, you have the choice of five editions: Ajax, I/O, Event + I/O, Widgets, and the Kitchen Sink. For the sake of simplicity, we're going to work with the Kitchen Sink, but you may want to try other editions or even build your own. We want to stress that Dojo has a lot to offer and that we will only just scratch the surface of what it can do here. To install Dojo, pick an edition (or build your

---

2. http://dojotoolkit.org

own) and move the included JavaScript files to the directory your web applications use for scripts.

## Animations

An animation simply describes the transition of an object between two states. These states can be anything, such as an element's color, opacity, or position; to the animation it just doesn't matter. Creating an animation involves four attributes (see Table 3-6).

**Table 3-6.** *Animation Attributes*

| Attribute | Description |
| --- | --- |
| curve | Any object that defines a getValue(n) method that takes a value between 0 and 1 and returns an array of numbers. Dojo's math module contains some prebuilt curves. |
| duration | How long the animation will last (in milliseconds). |
| accel | Determines whether the animation is accelerating or decelerating (not implemented at the time of this writing). |
| repeatCount | The number of times to repeat the animation (setting to –1 will cause an infinite loop). |

Creating curves is not as hard as you think. They're just objects with an algorithm to determine an array of numbers that map to a current state. Listing 3-15 shows the Line example from the Dojo wiki.

**Listing 3-15.** *Dojo's Line Curve*

```
function Line(start, end) {
  this.start = start;
  this.end = end;
  this.dimensions = start.length;
  //simple function to find point on an n-dimensional, straight line
  this.getValue = function(n) {
    var retVal = new Array(this.dimensions);
    for(var i=0;i<this.dimensions;i++)
      retVal[i] = ((this.end[i] - this.start[i]) * n) + this.start[i];
      return retVal;
    }
  return this;
}
```

To actually use an animation, we need to tie into Dojo's event library. As you've seen in most of the examples thus far, Ajax applications become quite interested in the "on" events that are generated in a browser (such as onclick, onblur, and onchange). We have to hard-wire the functionality into the markup.[3] With Dojo, we "connect" a node, an event, and a function together, in effect registering listeners to events. A basic example looks like this:

```
var element = document.getElementById("foo");
dojo.event.connect(element, "onclick", object, "bar");
```

Besides engendering cleaner markup, this allows us to easily associate multiple functions with an event. For example, say we have an element and we want two functions to be called on the onkeydown event. We simply add a second dojo.event.connect(…). Keep in mind that the listener functions will be called in the order they are registered.

The Dojo event framework gives us another advantage in that its definition of an event is quite a bit broader than those defined by the DOM standard. In fact, with Dojo, you can listen for an arbitrary method call. So, if you want to fire a second() method anytime first() is called, Dojo lets you do that using the same syntax shown earlier. Now that we understand the event model a bit better, let's take a look at a simple animation (see Listing 3-16).

**Listing 3-16.** *A Simple Dojo Fade-in Animation*

```
<html>
  <head>
    <title>Dojo Animation</title>
    <script src="scripts/dojo.js" type="text/javascript"></script>
    <script type="text/javascript">
      function fadeIn() {
        var element = document.getElementById("fadeMe");
        var animation = new dojo.animation.Animation (
          new dojo.math.curves.Line([0],[100]),
          3000,
          0 //the yet to be implemented accel attribute
        );
        dojo.event.connect(animation, "onAnimate", function(e) {
          element.style.opacity = e.x;
        });
        animation.play();
      }
    </script>
  </head>
```

---

3. For an interesting solution to this problem, see David Goodlad's write-up "Beautiful JavaScript-Powered Pages" at http://david.goodlad.ca/articles/2005/11/10/beautiful-javascript-powered-pages.

```
<body>
  <h1>Dojo Animation</h1>
  <div id="fadeMe" style="opacity: 0">
      Hello There!
  </div>
  <input type="button" value="Fade In" onclick="fadeIn();"/>
</body>
</html>
```

So what exactly is the fadeIn() code doing? First, we have to grab the element we want to animate. Here it's just a div. Next, we create an animation that will cycle from 0 to 100 in a linear fashion over 3,000 milliseconds. Next, we need to glue that animation to an event listener. Here it's the onAnimate function, which is called for every frame of the animation. In this case, we've used an anonymous function that will modify the opacity of the element through the course of the animation. Once we have the wiring in place, we ask the animation to play, which causes the element to fade in.

## Effects

While you could certainly build some pretty nifty effects with the animations framework, most of the time, you'll simply use Dojo's built-in effects. The Dojo effects return references to the Animation object created, so you're free to do anything with it that you would had you created your own. All of the effects methods are found in the dojo.graphics. htmlEffects module. Tweaking our previous example produces the simplified code found in Listing 3-17.

**Listing 3-17.** *Using Dojo Effects*

```
<html>
  <head>
    <title>Dojo Effects</title>
    <script src="scripts/dojo.js" type="text/javascript"></script>
    <script type="text/javascript">
      function fadeIn() {
        var element = document.getElementById("fadeMe");
        dojo.graphics.htmlEffects.fadeIn(element, 2000);
      }
    </script>
  </head>
```

```
<body>
  <h1>Dojo Effects</h1>
  <div id="fadeMe" style="opacity: 0">
      Hello There!
  </div>
  <input type="button" value="Fade In" onclick="fadeIn();"/>
</body>
</html>
```

That's a bit easier now, isn't it? This particular method also takes an optional `callback` argument that allows us to call an additional function when the animation is finished. Of course we aren't just limited to `fadeIn`. Dojo comes with quite a hefty collection of effects. Some of these aren't documented as of this writing, and chances are by the time you read this there will be others. However, the following list gives you a taste of what Dojo can do for you. (Note, all of these define an optional callback function that we've left out for simplicity.)

`fadeOut(element, duration)`: Fades the element from its current opacity to 0 over a given duration in milliseconds

`fadeIn(element, duration)`: Fades an element's opacity to 100 over a given duration in milliseconds

`fadeHide(element, duration)`: Like `fadeOut` except the element's display is set to none when the effect is finished

`fadeShow(element, duration)`: Like `fadeIn` but guarantees that the element will be displayed

`fade(element, duration, startOpacity, endOpacity, callBackObject)`: Fades a node from `startOpacity` to `endOpacity` over a given duration in milliseconds

`slideTo(element, endCoords, duration)`: Moves an element from its current position to the end coordinates (expressed as an array with two elements, the X and Y coordinates [X, Y]) over a given duration in milliseconds

`slideBy(element, coords, duration)`: Moves an element from its current position by a given set of coordinates (expressed as an array with two elements, the X and Y coordinates [X, Y]) over a given duration in milliseconds

`slide(element, startCoords, endCoords, duration)`: Moves an element from a set of coordinates to a given set of coordinates (expressed as an array with two elements, the X and Y coordinates [X, Y]) over a given duration in milliseconds

`colorFadeIn(element, startColor, duration)`: Fades an element's background color from a starting color (expressed as an array with three elements, the RGB value of the color) to its background color over a given duration in milliseconds

colorFadeOut(element, endColor, duration): Fades an element's background color from its background color to an ending color (expressed as an array with three elements, the RGB value of the color) over a given duration in milliseconds

wipeIn(element, duration): Sets the height of an element to 0 then grows it back to its original size over a given duration in milliseconds

wipeOut(element, duration): Shrinks an element from its height to 0 over a given duration in milliseconds

## dojo.io.bind

Like Prototype and script.aculo.us, Dojo gives us a simplified way of making asynchronous requests of the server. We don't have to deal directly with the XHR object or worry about browser compatibility; Dojo takes care of that for us with dojo.io.bind. Dojo provides a significant advantage over using raw XHR: graceful degradation. Obviously, Dojo handles the monotonous browser check, but if your user has a browser that doesn't support XHR, it can fall back on using an iFrame. Of course you can always override this and specify that you only want Dojo to use XHR.

Setting up a call with dojo.io.bind is fairly similar to what we've seen with Prototype (see Listing 3-18). The results of this simple code are shown in Figures 3-16 and 3-17.

**Listing 3-18.** *Using dojo.io.bind*

```
<html>
  <head>
    <title>dojo.io.bind</title>
    <script src="scripts/dojo.js" type="text/javascript"></script>
    <script type="text/javascript">
      function doFoo() {
        var url = "dojoResponse.html";
        dojo.io.bind({
        url: url,
        load: function(type, data, evt){ show(data) },
        mimetype: "text/plain"
        });
      }
      function show(data) {
        document.getElementById("show").innerHTML = data;
      }
</script>
  </head>
```

```
<body>
  <h1>dojo.io.bind</h1>
  <input type="button" value="Do Foo"
    onclick="doFoo();"/>
  <div id="show"></div>
</body>
</html>
```

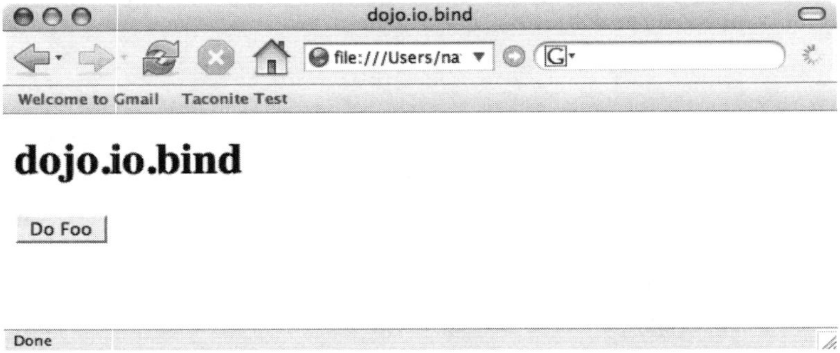

**Figure 3-16.** *Before calling the "server"*

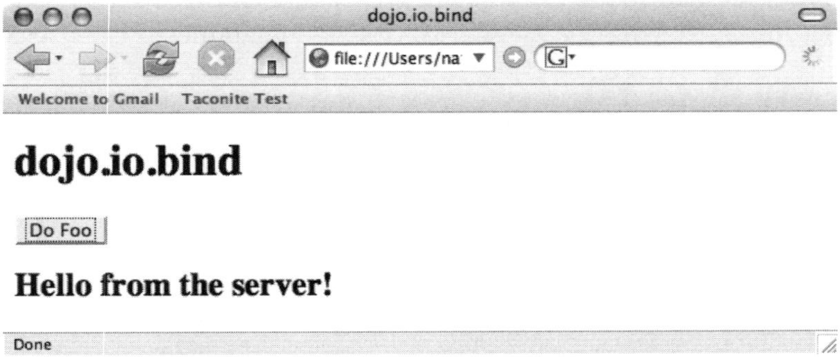

**Figure 3-17.** *After calling the "server"*

As you can see, this is pretty straightforward. We pass in the URL of the server resource to call, provide a callback function, and specify what the return type will be. The load key is equivalent to the onreadystatechange on the XHR object, but Dojo takes care of checking the actual readyState (in other words, the function specified only gets called when the status is 4). The callback method has access to three objects:

- type: Provides more information about the response, such as whether it was successful (load) or whether there was a problem (error)

- data: The response from the server (from the responseText)

- evt: A DOM event

We also could have used the error key to define a function to call if the request wasn't successful or we could have used a single handler that would interpret the type returned by Dojo and react accordingly. We also use Dojo to return JavaScript from the browser by simply changing the mimetype to text/javascript. This will cause the JavaScript returned from the server to be evaluated on the client.

Of course one of the common things people do with Ajax is use it to submit an entire form, something that can be a bit tedious with raw XHR. Fortunately for us, Dojo makes this pretty straightforward:

```
dojo.io.bind({
  url: url,
  load: function(type, evalObj){ /* do foo */ },
  formNode: document.getElementById("myForm")
});
```

That is quite a helpful feature. There are some other options on dojo.io.bind. You can specify the HTTP method using the method key, pass specific request parameters as a hash using content (content: { key1: 'value1', key2: 'value2' }) and postContent (used only if the method is POST), perform the request synchronously with synch: true, and use a local cache useCache: true.

## Handling the Back and Forward Buttons

As we discussed in Chapter 1, Ajax applications don't handle the Back button in a manner that most users expect. Although an iFrame will modify the browser's history cache, XHR will not. Luckily for us, Dojo has support for intercepting the Back and Forward buttons. Unfortunately, as of this writing this solution will not work on Safari. According to the Dojo documentation, its Back and Forward buttons aren't interceptable.

Dojo allows us to call a function on the Back and Forward buttons so that we can perform whatever cleanup activities we need to do. All we have to do is add a couple more keys to our dojo.io.bind call (see Listing 3-19).

**Listing 3-19.** *Dojo Intercepts Clicks of the Back and Forward Buttons*

```
dojo.io.bind({
  url: url,
  load: function(type, evalObj){ /* do foo */ },
  backButton: function() { doBack(); }
  forwardButton: function() { doForward(); }
  formNode: document.getElementById("myForm")
});
```

One thing to note: these particular Back and Forward intercepts are only bound to this particular action. If they perform some other `bind()` request, this instance wouldn't be fired. So, let's say you have an "add" function that dynamically inserts a row into your page. If your user clicks the Back and Forward buttons, the functions defined in `bind()` that added the row would be invoked. However, if they engaged another dynamic feature, say selecting a new feature that changes the price of their widget, you would need to define a new set of back and forward functions that are associated with that particular invocation of `bind()`.

### Bookmarking

Bookmarking is another gotcha we mentioned in Chapter 1. After all, it's why Google Maps has a "Link to this page" link. Although you could certainly do something similar and create some unique hash that tells your server exactly how to reconstruct the page, you could always just let Dojo do the heavy lifting for you.

There is yet another parameter to `dojo.io.bind`, `changeURL`. Passing in a value of "true" means your URL will have a timestamp attached to it. If you want to attach your own values, you can do that as well by passing `changeURL: your values here`. For example, say you pass a value of "fooBar" to the `changeURL` parameter. The resulting URL would look something like this: `http://yoursite.com/ajaxRules#fooBar`.

# Taconite

Taconite is a lightweight Ajax library found at `http://taconite.sourceforge.net`. Unlike many server-side technology-agnostic libraries, Taconite provides both a client-side JavaScript library and a formula for composing the server-side response, which can be implemented in any server-side language.

Taconite's client-side library is modeled after the W3C's DOM Level 3 Load and Save specification, which outlines a standard for Ajax-like interactions. Taconite closely mirrors the API specified by this recommendation. Instead of reinventing the Ajax wheel, Taconite leverages the work already done by the W3C.

Unlike many JavaScript libraries which make liberal use of JavaScript's dynamic nature, Taconite's client-side library is modeled in the style of JavaBeans. The client-side library uses get and set methods for accessing an object's properties, which will feel comfortably familiar to longtime Java developers.

Another aspect that sets Taconite apart from the crowd is that it completely avoids the use of the `innerHTML` property to update the DOM. Instead, Taconite uses the standard DOM manipulation methods like `createElement` or `appendChild` to create and modify content on the page. The advantage to this is that Taconite can insert or modify content anywhere on the page. The `innerHTML` property is much more limited. By sticking to W3C standards, Taconite should work in all standards-compliant browsers. Taconite also automatically handles some browser incompatibilities so you don't have to worry about it.

So, how exactly does Taconite work? On the browser side, Taconite provides an `AjaxRequest` object that encapsulates all the data necessary for sending an Ajax request to the server. The `AjaxRequest` object exposes a series of set and get style methods that provide easy access to specifying the object's properties. The `AjaxRequest` object also provides functionality for automatically building a query string based on the values of input elements.

On the server side, all you need to do is specify your new or updated view as you normally would, as XHTML, probably in a JSP page. You embed the XHTML in a few simple Taconite-specific XML tags, make sure that the response's content type is set to `text/xml`, and Taconite takes care of the rest.

## Taconite on the Client Side

As mentioned earlier, the heart of Taconite's client-side library is the `AjaxRequest` object, which encapsulates the properties and behavior of sending an Ajax request to the server.

Listing 3-20 illustrates a simple example of using the `AjaxRequest` object. An instance of `AjaxRequest` is first created by passing the destination URL to the constructor. The next line adds the value of a form element to the query string using the `addFormElementsById` method; the query string will be sent to the server as part of the Ajax request. Finally, the Ajax request is initiated by calling the `sendRequest` method. You can see that an Ajax request can be sent by writing only a few lines of JavaScript and that working with the `AjaxRequest` object is quite easy thanks to its JavaBeans-style accessors.

**Listing 3-20.** *Sending an Ajax Request with the `AjaxRequest` Object*

```
function sendAjaxRequest() {
  var ajaxRequest = new AjaxRequest("URL");
  ajaxRequest.addFormElementsById("name");
  ajaxRequest.sendRequest();
}
```

Table 3-7 lists some of the methods you're most likely to use on the AjaxRequest object.

**Table 3-7.** *Common Methods of the AjaxRequest Object*

| Method | Description |
|---|---|
| addFormElements(formId) | Adds all of the form elements in the specified form to the query string. |
| addFormElementsById(id1, [id2], …) | Adds all the specified input elements to the query string. |
| addNamedFormElements(name1, [name2], …) | Adds all of the specified form elements to the query string. |
| getXMLHttpRequestObject() | Returns the XMLHttpRequest object wrapped by this object. |
| sendRequest() | Sends the Ajax request. |
| setEchoDebugInfo() | Enables client-side debugging. Debug information is written to the page. |
| setPostRequest(function) | Sets the function that is called after the server response is received. |

## Taconite on the Server

You may have noticed that the AjaxRequest request doesn't appear to do anything to handle the server's response and update the DOM. Instead, the instructions for updating the DOM are specified by the server response.

As explained earlier, a valid Taconite response consists of valid XHTML embedded within some Taconite-specific XML tags that define *actions* that tell Taconite what to do with the embedded XHTML. The actions are always specified relative to an existing element in the DOM known as the *context node*. For example, the taconite-append-as-children tag instructs Taconite to append the embedded XHTML as children of the context node, which is specified using its id attribute. Table 3-8 describes the available Taconite commands.

**Table 3-8.** *Taconite Tags for Updating the DOM*

| Tag | Description |
|---|---|
| taconite-append-as-children | Appends the specified content as children of the context node |
| taconite-append-as-first-child | Adds the specified content as the first child of the context node |
| taconite-delete | Deletes the context node and all its children |
| taconite-insert-after | Inserts the content as the immediately following sibling of the context node |

**Table 3-8.** *Taconite Tags for Updating the DOM*

| Tag | Description |
| --- | --- |
| taconite-insert-before | Inserts the content as the immediately preceding sibling of the context node |
| taconite-replace-children | Replaces the children of the context node with the contents of this tag |
| taconite-replace | Replaces the context node with the contents of this tag |
| taconite-set-attributes | Sets the attributes on the context node with the specified values |

Since a valid Taconite response is a valid XML document, any server-side technology that can produce structured XML and set the Content-Type response header to text/xml can send Taconite responses. Java EE can certainly do that, of course, and you can choose from JSPs, Velocity templates, JDOM, Java API for XML Processing (JAXP), or even straight servlets to generate the XML.

## Getting Started with Taconite

Taconite is very easy to use and install, requiring only two small JavaScript files named taconite-client.js and taconite-parser.js (detailed instructions are covered later in this section). This example is as easy as it gets: a simple Ajax request with no parameters and a simple server response. It doesn't do anything exciting, but it demonstrates how easy it is to use Taconite to Ajax-enable your web applications.

Listing 3-21 shows the client HTML page. The page is pretty spartan, with only one link on the page that initiates the Ajax request. You can see that there are two JavaScript files defined: taconite-client.js and taconite-parser.js. The taconite-client.js file is the heart of Taconite's client-side functionality, as it defines the AjaxRequest object. The taconite-parser.js file handles the actual parsing of the server response by updating the DOM according to the actions defined by the response.

**Listing 3-21.** *taconiteHelloWorld.html*

```
<!DOCTYPE html PUBLIC "-//W3C//DTD XHTML 1.0 Strict//EN"
"http://www.w3.org/TR/xhtml1/DTD/xhtml1-strict.dtd">
<html xmlns="http://www.w3.org/1999/xhtml" lang="en" xml:lang="en">
    <head>
        <title>Taconite Example</title>
        <script type="text/javascript" src="js/taconite-client.js"></script>
        <script type="text/javascript" src="js/taconite-parser.js"></script>
```

```
        <script type="text/javascript">
            function doHelloWorld() {
                var ajaxRequest = new AjaxRequest("taconiteHelloWorld.jsp");
                ajaxRequest.sendRequest();
            }
        </script>
    </head>
    <body>
        <a href="javascript:doHelloWorld();">
            Show Taconite's Hello World Message
        </a>
        <br/><br/>
        <div id="helloWorldContainer">
        </div>
    </body>
</html>
```

The lone link on the page simply calls the doHelloWorld JavaScript function. Thanks to Taconite, it's only two lines long. The first line creates an instance of the AjaxRequest object. The AjaxRequest object, as described earlier, encapsulates an Ajax request. Each instance of an AjaxRequest object creates its own instance of the XMLHttpRequest object, so you can create as many as you'd like (or that your browser will support) and not have to worry about instances of XMLHttpRequest overwriting one another.

The AjaxRequest object is created by passing a single argument to the object constructor. The argument is the URL to which the Ajax request will be sent. In this example, the URL points to the JSP that formulates the server response. The second (and last!) line of the doHelloWorld function sends the request to the server. The AjaxRequest object defines a sendRequest method, which is called here to send the request.

At the bottom of the page lies an empty div element with an id attribute value of helloWorldContainer. This is very important. This div is the location to where the server's response will be appended. We'll discuss this more when we look at the server-side components.

And that's all that needs to be done on the client side. Next we'll take a look at the server side.

We want Taconite to print a "Hello World" to the page when the link is clicked. As mentioned earlier, a valid Taconite response consists of XHTML embedded within Taconite-specific tags. In this example we'll use a JSP page to render the response, which is shown in Listing 3-22.

**Listing 3-22.** *taconiteHelloWorld.jsp*

```
<%@page contentType="text/xml"%>
<taconite-root xml:space="preserve">
    <taconite-append-as-children contextNodeID="helloWorldContainer"
        parseInBrowser="true">
        <div style="font-weight:bold;color:orange;">
            Taconite says: Hello World!!!
        </div>
    </taconite-append-as-children>
</taconite-root>
```

We'll start at the top. The first line is a JSP directive indicating that the Content-Type of the page should be returned as text/xml. All Taconite responses must be returned with a Content-Type of text/xml, otherwise the XMLHttpRequest object won't be able to parse it as an XML document.

Next is the taconite-root XML tag, which is the root tag of all Taconite responses. All Taconite responses must have the taconite-root tag as the root tag. The presence of this tag ensures that the response is well-formed XML. Note that the taconite-root tag has a attribute of xml:space="preserve". This is to ensure that Internet Explorer handles white space correctly.

The first child of the taconite-root tag is the taconite-append-as-children tag. This tag says that the child elements of this tag will be appended as children to the *context node*. The context node is specified by the contextNodeID attribute. The value of this attribute must correspond to some element on the XHTML page. Remember the empty div element on the XHTML page, that had an id attribute value of "helloWorldContainer"? This is the *context node* where the message will be appended, because the contextNodeID attribute of the taconite-append-as-children tag has a value of "helloWorldContainer". The second attribute on the taconite-append-as-children tag is parseInBrowser, which has a value of true. This tells the AjaxRequest object that it needs to parse the response as DOM manipulation commands to produce the "Hello World" message.

Finally, the "Hello World" message is defined within the taconite-append-as-children tag. Notice how the message is simply defined as valid XHTML. In fact, the div tag even has an embedded style that makes the message font orange in color! This is the beauty of Taconite: you simply specify the new or updated content as regular ol' XHTML, and Taconite does the rest, without you having to resort to writing a bunch of DOM manipulation code or building XHTML via string concatenation and using the innerHTML property.

Figure 3-18 illustrates the results of clicking the "Hello World" link. Because the response text is always appended to the context node, one message appears each time the link is clicked.

**Figure 3-18.** *The results of clicking the "Hello World" link*

Keep in mind that this is a very simple example that only scratches the surface of Taconite's capabilities. You can use multiple action tags within `taconite-root`, so you could delete an existing DOM node while adding others. You can also send form parameters to the server by using Taconite's built-in support for creating a query string. And since Taconite allows you to specify any sort of XHTML to update the existing page, you can let your imagination run wild with all the potential possibilities. You're not constrained by the tedious task of writing JavaScript code to update the DOM. For more information, check out Taconite's home page at `http://taconite.sourceforge.net`.

# Summary

Although Ajax isn't rocket science, there is a fair amount of tedious code, and creating truly helpful client-side effects can be a challenge. Lucky for us, there are a number of very strong libraries that can aid our effort. We've seen how using the right toolkit can, in just a few lines, give us wizard-like effects, ones that will improve the usability of our application while also being easy to add.

Believe it or not, but we've just scratched the surface of these libraries' capabilities as well as the toolkit space in general. Hopefully, you have enough to go on to perform your own evaluation and decide which of these libraries will improve your application. These libraries are fairly dynamic, so you may want to stop by their home pages from time to time to see what they're up to!

# CHAPTER 4

■ ■ ■

# Java-Specific Frameworks

**O**ne of the strengths of Java is its diversity. From app servers to IDEs, from XML libraries to logging implementations, developers always have a choice. You don't like the logging implementation of the Java Development Kit (JDK)? Use another logging implementation. You just aren't productive in your current IDE? Try one of the many alternatives. The Java ecosystem is a vibrant collection of intermingled tools, utilities, and frameworks that give the developer a wide array of choices.

The tools, utilities, and frameworks both complement and compete with one another. By competing against each other they are forced to offer the features that are most coveted by developers. If not, they will likely fade away as developers choose to use other options. These tools, utilities, and frameworks complement each other by providing somewhat differing features and implementations, allowing developers to choose the one that best fits their particular problem domain.

In Chapter 3 you saw several Ajax frameworks that do not rely on Java. Almost universally these frameworks are implemented completely in JavaScript and designed to execute within the confines of the web browser. These frameworks focus solely on what's happening in the browser and leave the server-side implementation of an Ajax interaction up to developers to build in their preferred server-side language.

In this chapter we'll explore Ajax frameworks that take full advantage of the Java language and platform. Java is such a powerful and flexible platform that it seems almost silly to not use it to its fullest potential. These frameworks all aim to simplify adding Ajax interactions to your web application. They attack the problem a bit differently, too, so you can choose the one (or ones) that most closely align with the specific problem you're trying to solve.

## DWR

Direct Web Remoting, more commonly known as DWR, is an Ajax framework that relies exclusively on Java and JavaScript. DWR is found at `http://getahead.ltd.uk/dwr` and is released under the Apache 2.0 license.

DWR claims to reduce the amount of time it takes to implement Ajax in Java EE–powered applications. It does so by automating common Ajax tasks and reducing the amount of boilerplate code written by the developer. DWR is stable and well documented, with complete documentation on its home page and various tutorials on the web.

In practice DWR is a remote procedure framework. DWR exposes any server-side Java object as a remote object accessible via JavaScript within the browser. DWR does this by dynamically creating JavaScript code based on Java classes, allowing the developer to access server-side Java resources via JavaScript as if the resources were local to the browser. Security is enforced by the developer, as a Java object must be explicitly configured by the developer to be accessible via JavaScript.

DWR automatically translates parameters and return values between JavaScript and Java. For example, DWR automatically converts Java primitive values such as int and boolean (and their class-based cousins) to their JavaScript equivalents and vice versa. Standard Java classes like String and Date are also automatically converted. Better yet, DWR will even convert JavaBeans-style objects into JavaScript associative arrays and vice versa. As you can see, DWR provides great flexibility, as you are not constrained to passing only simple data types between the browser and the server.

That's enough talking for now. Let's take a look at some examples to get a better feel for what DWR can actually do.

## Installation

Despite its vast functionality, DWR is surprisingly easy to install. Start by downloading the server-side library named dwr.jar from DWR's home page. Place dwr.jar in your web application's WEB-INF/lib directory so it's in the application's classpath. Next, you need to add DWR's handler servlet to the web.xml file by specifying the servlet class and a mapping for that servlet. An example servlet definition and mapping are shown in Listing 4-1.

**Listing 4-1.** *DWR Servlet Definition and Mapping*

```
<servlet>
    <description>DWR Servlet</description>
    <servlet-name>dwr-servlet</servlet-name>
    <servlet-class>uk.ltd.getahead.dwr.DWRServlet</servlet-class>
    <init-param>
        <param-name>debug</param-name>
        <param-value>true</param-value>
    </init-param>
</servlet>
<servlet-mapping>
    <servlet-name>dwr-servlet</servlet-name>
    <url-pattern>/dwr/*</url-pattern>
</servlet-mapping>
```

The servlet definition is standard and shouldn't change. The servlet mapping is more flexible, and you're free to configure the mapping as you see fit. In this example, any URLs in which DWR appears after the application context will be forwarded to the DWR servlet.

With the web.xml file correctly configured, you can now set up the dwr.xml file. The dwr.xml file configures the Java bean to be remoted and configures the converters that will be used for converting Java objects to JavaScript and vice versa. Remember that you must explicitly define the Java objects that are available for remoting. The dwr.xml file must be placed in the WEB-INF directory along with the web.xml file.

Listing 4-2 defines an example dwr.xml file that configures one Java object, RemoteBean, as being accessible via JavaScript. The create tag defines classes that can be remoted, and the creator attribute tells DWR to create the remote bean using the new keyword. The javascript attribute defines the name used to access the bean in JavaScript.

**Listing 4-2.** *Example dwr.xml File Defining a Single Java Object That Is Available for Remoting*

```
<!DOCTYPE dwr PUBLIC
    "-//GetAhead Limited//DTD Direct Web Remoting 1.0//EN"
    "http://www.getahead.ltd.uk/dwr/dwr10.dtd">
<dwr>
    <allow>
        <create creator="new" javascript="RemoteBean">
            <param name="class" value="com.proajax.chapt4.RemoteBean"/>
        </create>
    </allow>
</dwr>
```

The param tag tells DWR that a new object of the specified class will be created. The name attribute specifies that an instance of a class will be created, and the value attribute lists the fully qualified name of the class. In this example, the RemoteBean class is made available for remoting.

For now, the RemoteBean class defines only one public method, getServerDate, which returns the server's current date and time. Listing 4-3 lists the Java source code for the RemoteBean class.

**Listing 4-3.** *RemoteBean.java*

```
package com.proajax.chapt4;
import java.util.Date;
public class RemoteBean {
    public String getServerDate() {
        return new Date().toString();
    }
}
```

## Installation Verification

So far you have seen how to update the web.xml file, create the dwr.xml file, and write a class that is available for remoting. You can now deploy the application to your favorite servlet container.

Before writing a single line of JavaScript you should verify the DWR installation and configuration. DWR provides a built-in mechanism for testing the installation and configuration without writing any JavaScript.

Deploy your web application and point your web browser to the DWR servlet as you defined it in the web.xml file. If you configured the DWR servlet as was shown in Listing 4-1, then the correct URL would be http://localhost/your-app-name/dwr. When done correctly, DWR will display a page listing all of the classes known to DWR, as shown in Figure 4-1.

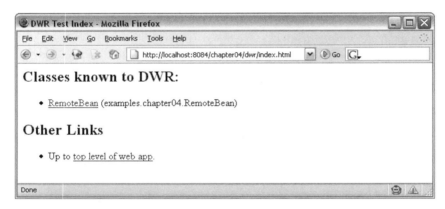

**Figure 4-1.** *DWR lists the classes it's aware of from the* dwr.xml *file.*

Click on the link to view the details for the remoted bean. You'll see a page that looks like Figure 4-2.

A lot of information is provided here, so we'll take a closer look. The top part of the page lists the script tags that should appear within any page that will use this bean. The first script tag defines the JavaScript the represents the remote bean—in this case, the RemoteBean object. Even though the script tag appears to point to a static JavaScript file named RemoteBean.js, it doesn't. In reality, the RemoteBean.js "file" is JavaScript that is dynamically generated by DWR. The second script tag defines DWR's standard JavaScript file named engine.js. Again, this isn't a static JavaScript file but rather dynamic JavaScript generated by the DWR servlet. This is valuable information, as DWR tells you exactly what script tags need to be included in your HTML page.

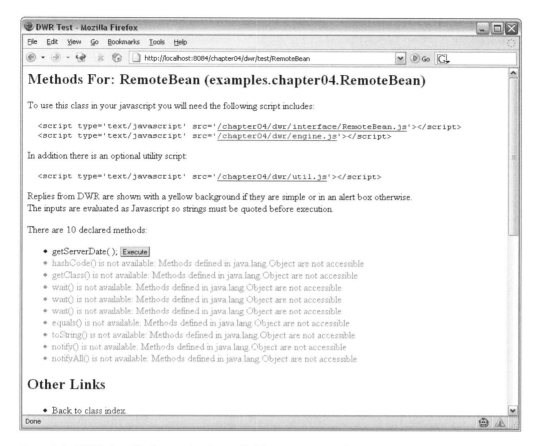

**Figure 4-2.** *DWR details the methods available on a remote bean.*

The next section is especially useful for testing your DWR installation and the remote beans. This section lists all of the methods on the bean that can be accessed via JavaScript and even allows you to execute the methods with the click of a button. In this example, the only publicly and remotely available method on the RemoteBean object is the getServerDate method. You can click the button and see that the method is invoked by DWR, and the return result is displayed after the button, as shown in Figure 4-3.

There are 10 declared methods:

- getServerDate( ); Execute  Sun Jan 22 22:40:37 CST 2006
- hashCode() is not available: Methods defined in java.lang.Objec
- getClass() is not available: Methods defined in java.lang.Object

**Figure 4-3.** *DWR's bean test page provides a way to test accessing a remote bean's methods.*

As you can see, this is a very powerful testing facility that DWR provides. Without writing a single line of JavaScript, you can test your remote beans and at least verify that the DWR installation and configuration are correct and that the remote methods can be accessed successfully. Of course, you won't want your users to be able to access these help pages. To prevent users from seeing these help pages, go to the web.xml file and change the DWR servlet's debug parameter to false. This will prevent you (or anybody else) from accessing these help pages. You don't want potential hackers to be able see every Java object that is exposed by DWR, so be sure to disable the debug facility before moving your application to production.

## Browser Scripting

So far you've seen how to install DWR and create a Java object that will be scriptable via JavaScript in the browser. You then saw how to use DWR's built-in test facility to verify that the remote bean is configured correctly. With that done, you're now ready to start scripting in the browser to leverage DWR's Ajax capabilities.

DWR's strength is that it allows the developer to interact with Java objects located on the remote web server as if the objects were located within the browser. DWR hides the nitty-gritty details of Ajax communication between the browser and server, allowing you to focus on writing business logic instead of messy Ajax plumbing details.

The basic syntax for accessing a remote bean via JavaScript looks like the following pseudo code:

```
BeanName.methodName([parameters, ] callbackFunction);
```

In the previous example, BeanName is the alias assigned to the remote Java object as defined in the dwr.xml file. Recall that the create tag in dwr.xml has a javascript attribute. It's the value of the javascript attribute that must be used when referencing the remote bean via JavaScript. The desired method is referenced using dot notation after the bean name. Here, you reference the method just as you would if you were writing Java code.

You can use pass strings, numbers, Boolean values, and even JavaScript objects as parameters to the method. The big difference is that the last parameter in the parameter list specifies the callback function that should be called after the server responds to the Ajax request.

Remember that the callback function is the function that actually does something with the server response. Since Ajax requests are normally asynchronous, execution of the script continues as soon as the Ajax request is sent; the script doesn't suspend execution and wait for the server to respond. The callback function is the function that is invoked when the request completes, whenever that may be. In JavaScript, functions can be referenced just like variables by using the function name, so to tell DWR which function to call when the request completes successfully, simply name the function as the last parameter in the parameter list.

Enough talk—let's look at some code. The first example presented here is about as easy as it gets. In this example DWR is used to call the getServerDate method on the RemoteBean class, which you saw in Listing 4-3. The getServerDate method takes no parameters and simply returns a string representing the server's system date. Clicking a button on the web page invokes the method, and upon successful completion of the request, the server's date string is added to the web page.

Listing 4-4 lists the fragment of the HTML page that runs this example. There is a single button that executes the getServerDateTime function when the button is clicked. The empty span element is a placeholder for the server response. The server's date string is placed within the span element after the Ajax request completes.

**Listing 4-4.** *HTML Fragment Showing the Button and Empty span Element*

```
Get server date:
<button onclick="getServerDateTime();">
    Get Server Date
</button>
<span id="serverDateTime" class="response"></span>
```

Listing 4-5 shows the two JavaScript functions that service this example. The first JavaScript function, getServerDateTime, is where DWR is used to access the remote bean. Note the syntax of how the call is made. RemoteBean is the alias of the Java object you want to access on the server; the name RemoteBean was specified by the javascript attribute of the create tag in the dwr.xml file. Next, the RemoteBean's getServerDate method is specified using dot notation. Finally, since the getServerDate method takes no parameters, the only parameter we need to specify is the callback function. In this case, the callback function is handleGetServerDateTime, which is also shown in Listing 4-5.

**Listing 4-5.** *The Two JavaScript Functions That Service This Request*

```
function getServerDateTime() {
    RemoteBean.getServerDate(handleGetServerDateTime);
}
function handleGetServerDateTime(dateTime) {
    //dateTime is the string returned by RemoteBean.getServerDate()
    DWRUtil.setValue("serverDateTime", dateTime);
}
```

You may have noticed that the handleGetServerDateTime function takes one parameter named dateTime. DWR automatically feeds the remote method call's return value to the callback function, so you don't have to worry about mining the return data directly from the XMLHttpRequest object.

With the server's response in hand, the only thing left to do is to update the web page by placing the server response inside of the empty span element. To do this we have a couple of options. One option is to directly use the nonstandard innerHTML property of the span element to set the element's text. Another option would be use the standard W3C

DOM methods to create a text node using the `document.createTextNode` method and then append that text node to the `span` element.

Fortunately DWR provides some help with DOM manipulation, too. In general, DWR does not attempt to be a complete JavaScript library for DOM manipulation. Instead, it attempts to provide helper methods for the most common DOM manipulation use cases. DWR's DOM helper functions are accessed from the `util.js` file in the same way that the `engine.js` file is accessed. These helper functions can also be used independently of DWR's Ajax engine.

In this example all we want to do is update the empty `span` element so it contains the text returned by the server. This example uses the `DWRUtil.setValue` function to do just that. The `DWRUtil.setValue` function takes two parameters. The first parameter is a string representing the ID of the element to be updated. The second parameter is a string representing the new value. The `DWRUtil.setValue` function works on HTML elements including selects (where the option with a matching value is selected), input elements, `divs`, and `spans`.

After all that drama, the web page is updated with the server's system date. The example output is shown in Figure 4-4.

**Get Server Date**

Get server date: [ Get Server Date ]  **Tue Jan 24 22:15:34 CST 2006**

**Figure 4-4.** *A button click invokes DWR to get the server's system date.*

## Sending a Single Parameter

So the ability to access the server using Ajax via DWR is a neat trick, right? The previous example is useful, but although it's a good introduction to DWR, it's not a good real-world example. Rarely in the real world will you send an Ajax request without sending at least one parameter to the server. Most use cases will involve sending some sort of entity identifier or edited text to the server.

This example builds on the previous example by sending a parameter as part of the remote bean method call and also introduces a few other wrinkles along the way.

In this example the user enters text into a text field and clicks a button to invoke the method on the remote bean. The text entered by the user is sent as a parameter to the remote bean's method call. The method takes the text entered by the user and sums the character code values for each character in the string and returns the sum back to the browser.

Listing 4-6 shows the HTML fragment for this example. The user enters text into the text box and clicks the button to invoke the method on the remote bean via DWR. The remote method's return value is displayed in the empty `span` element.

**Listing 4-6.** *HTML Fragment Showing the Input Box and the* span *in Which the Server's Response Is Displayed*

```
<h3>Pass a Single Parameter</h3>
<p>
    Calculate the Sum of All Characters in String:
    <input type="text" id="textInput"/>
    <button onclick="getSumOfCharactersInString();">
        Calculate Sum of Characters
    </button>
    <br/>Sum of Characters in String:
    <span id="characterSumResponse" class="response"></span>
</p>
```

A click of the button calls the JavaScript function named getSumOfCharactersInString that uses DWR to call the remote bean. The JavaScript function and the associated callback function, handleGetSumOfCharactersInString, are shown in Listing 4-7. The getSumOfCharactersInString introduces a few new wrinkles. First, note that the first line of the function calls DWRUtil.useLoadingMessage(). This utility function displays a small "Loading…" message in the upper right-hand corner of the page to indicate to the user that a request is in progress. DWR automatically removes the message once the request is complete.

**Listing 4-7.** *The JavaScript Functions That Call the Remote Bean and Handle Its Response*

```
function getSumOfCharactersInString() {
    DWRUtil.useLoadingMessage();
    var textInput = $("textInput").value;
    RemoteBean.calculateCharacterSum(textInput,
handleGetSumOfCharactersInString);
}
function handleGetSumOfCharactersInString(sumOfCharacters) {
    DWRUtil.setValue("characterSumResponse", sumOfCharacters);
}
```

The next line in the getSumOfCharactersInString function retrieves the text entered by the user into the text box. Instead of using the document.getElementById method to access the text box, you'll see that DWR's $() function is used. The $() function was inspired by Prototype's function of the same name that is basically a shortcut for document.getElementById.

Finally, DWR invokes the calculateCharacterSum method on RemoteBean. As before, the method is accessed via dot notation, first by naming the bean and then the method. Since the calculateCharacterSum method takes a string as its lone parameter, the text entered by the user is listed first in the parameter list, followed by a reference to the callback function, handleGetSumOfCharactersInString. Remember that when calling a remote method via DWR, the parameter list should match the remote method's signature except that the callback function is appended as the final parameter.

Figure 4-5 shows the results of calling the remote bean. The remote bean's calculateCharacterSum method sums the character codes for each of the characters in the text entered by the user. The handleGetSumOfCharactersInString function, like the previous example, uses DWRUtil.setValue to set the server response into the appropriate span element.

**Pass a Single Parameter**

Calculate the Sum of All Characters in String : | Um Yah! Yah! |    [ Calculate Sum of Characters ]
Sum of Characters in String: 904

**Figure 4-5.** *The remote bean calculates the sum of the character codes for the characters in the string.*

## Passing Multiple Parameters and JavaScript Closures

By now you should be pretty comfortable with DWR and using it to call Java objects located on a remote server. This final example demonstrates how to send multiple parameters to a remote method invocation, but more important, it shows how to pass parameters other than the remote method's return value to the callback function.

Listing 4-8 shows the HTML fragment that renders this example. There are two input boxes, one for a name and the other for the password. Clicking the button sends the parameters to the remote Java object, which calculates a "lucky number" based on the name and password. A string listing the name, password, and lucky number is displayed upon receiving the server response.

**Listing 4-8.** *A "Lucky Number" Calculated from the Name and Password*

```
<h3>Pass Multiple Parameters</h3>
<p>
    Generate Your Lucky Number for Today:
    <br/>Name: <input type="text" id="nameInput"/>
    <br/>Password: <input type="password" id="passwordInput"/>
    <button onclick="getLuckyNumber();">
        Get Lucky Number
    </button>
    <br/><br/>Your Lucky Number for Today is:
    <span id="luckyNumberResponse" class="response"></span>
</p>
```

Listing 4-9 shows the JavaScript functions that service this example. The getLuckyNumber function is responsible for harvesting the name and password from the input boxes and calling the remote bean's getLuckyNumber method. There is a new concept unveiled in this example in that a JavaScript *closure* is used to pass the name and password values, along with the lucky number returned by the server, to the callback function. The variable named callbackFunction is really just a proxy function that accepts the remote method's return value as its lone parameter. However, since callbackFunction is defined within the getLuckyNumber function, it can also "see" the user name and password values. So, callbackFunction simply calls the "real" callback function, handleGetLuckyNumber, passing to it the remote method's return value along with the name and password values. By default, DWR uses the GET method to send the values to the server, although this can be changed by executing the DWREngine.setVerb("POST") command. Not all browsers implement the POST method on the XMLHttpRequest object, and in this case DWR will revert to the GET method.

**Listing 4-9.** *A JavaScript Closure Used to Send Multiple Parameters to the Callback Function*

```
function getLuckyNumber() {
    var name = $("nameInput").value;
    var password = $("passwordInput").value;
    var callbackFunction = function(luckyNumber) {
        handleGetLuckyNumber(luckyNumber, name, password);
    };
    RemoteBean.getLuckyNumber(name, password, callbackFunction);
}
function handleGetLuckyNumber(luckyNumber, name, password) {
    var message = "Name \"" + name + "\" and password \""
        + password + "\" produce a lucky number of " + luckyNumber;
    DWRUtil.setValue("luckyNumberResponse", message);
}
```

The handleGetLuckyNumber function generates a string that lists the entered name and password along with the generated lucky number from the remote bean. This would not have been possible had a JavaScript closure not been used to pass the name and password to handleGetLuckyNumber. One could argue that the server could have just as easily generated the string and returned it to the browser, eliminating the need for the JavaScript closure. Although true, this would lead to poor separation of concerns between the browser and the server. The bean should only be responsible for generating the lucky number from the given name and password and leave displaying the lucky number to whomever the bean's client might be—in this case, the browser. Figure 4-6 shows the result.

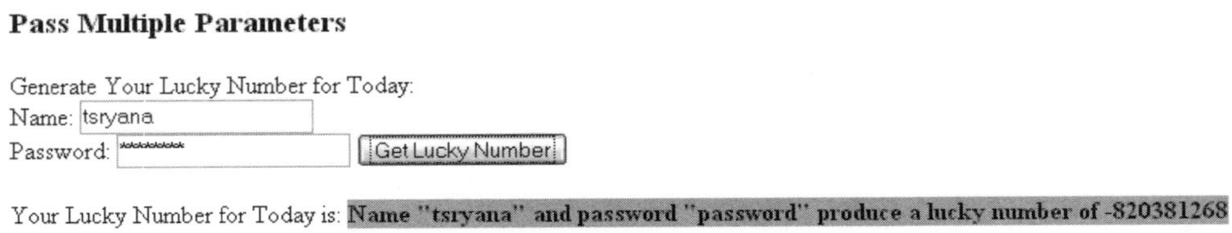

**Pass Multiple Parameters**

Generate Your Lucky Number for Today:
Name: tsryana
Password: ✱✱✱✱✱✱✱✱    [Get Lucky Number]

Your Lucky Number for Today is: Name "tsryana" and password "password" produce a lucky number of -820381268

**Figure 4-6.** *The remote object generates a lucky number from a user name and password.*

## Passing Object Parameters

By now you should be pretty comfortable with using DWR to invoke a method on a remote Java object. All of the previous examples have passed simple parameters like strings and integers to the remote methods.

DWR can also handle JavaBeans-style objects as method parameters with minimal configuration by the developer. This ability greatly increases DWR's usefulness as you can now design your own data transfer objects to ferry information between the browser and the remote server. You don't have to rely on sending only strings, numbers, and Booleans between the browser and the server. Instead, you can customize the browser-to-server interactions by using custom objects to encapsulate the data.

This example involves a Person class that encapsulates properties of a person such as first name, last name, and age. An instance of a Person object also holds a collection of Address objects that encapsulate address information. The source code for the Person and Address classes are shown in Listings 4-10 and 4-11, respectively.

**Listing 4-10.** *Person.java*

```java
package com.proajax.chapt4;
import java.util.ArrayList;
import java.util.Collection;
public class Person {
    private String firstName = "";
    private String lastName = "";
    private int age = 0;
    private Collection addresses = new ArrayList();
    public String getFirstName() {
        return firstName;
    }
    public void setFirstName(String firstName) {
        this.firstName = firstName;
    }
```

```java
    public String getLastName() {
        return lastName;
    }
    public void setLastName(String lastName) {
        this.lastName = lastName;
    }
    public int getAge() {
        return age;
    }
    public void setAge(int age) {
        this.age = age;
    }
    public Collection getAddresses() {
        return addresses;
    }
    public void addAddress(Address addr) {
        addresses.add(addr);
    }
}
```

**Listing 4-11.** *Address.java*

```java
package com.proajax.chapt4;
public class Address {
    private long id = 0;
    private String addressLine1 = "";
    private String addressLine2 = "";
    private String city = "";
    private String state = "";
    private String zip = "";
    public String getAddressLine1() {
        return addressLine1;
    }
    public void setAddressLine1(String addressLine1) {
        this.addressLine1 = addressLine1;
    }
    public String getAddressLine2() {
        return addressLine2;
    }
    public void setAddressLine2(String addressLine2) {
        this.addressLine2 = addressLine2;
    }
```

```java
    public String getCity() {
        return city;
    }
    public void setCity(String city) {
        this.city = city;
    }
    public String getState() {
        return state;
    }
    public void setState(String state) {
        this.state = state;
    }
    public String getZip() {
        return zip;
    }
    public void setZip(String zip) {
        this.zip = zip;
    }
    public long getId() {
        return id;
    }
    public void setId(long id) {
        this.id = id;
    }
}
```

You can see that both the Person and Address classes follow the JavaBean specification: they both have a default no-argument constructor, and the classes' properties are private but accessible via getter and setter methods.

Since these classes follow the JavaBeans specification, we can use DWR's built-in Java-Bean converter to convert object instances of these classes into their equivalent JavaScript objects and vice versa. First we need to configure DWR so it recognizes these classes and applies the appropriate converter.

Remember, earlier we learned that when configuring DWR through the dwr.xml file, DWR expects that remote beans are *created* and parameters are *converted.* You saw in Listing 4-2 how to define the remote bean in the dwr.xml file using the create tag. Since the Person and Address classes are parameters and not remote beans, we need to configure them in the dwr.xml file using the convert tag.

Listing 4-12 shows the additions to the dwr.xml file that configure the Person and Address classes as parameters in DWR. The convert tag tells DWR that these classes can be converted from Java objects to their JavaScript equivalents and vice versa. The converter attribute specifies to DWR the converter that should be used to perform the conversions. DWR includes a number of built-in converters; since this example uses JavaBeans-style objects, it uses the bean converter, which is specified by giving the converter attribute a value of "bean". The match attribute tells DWR to which classes to apply the converter. This attribute accepts wildcard characters, but we recommend that you specify only one class in each convert tag.

**Listing 4-12.** *Additions to the* dwr.xml *File to Configure the* Person *and* Address *Classes as Parameters*

```
<convert converter="bean" match="com.proajax.chapt4.Person">
    <param name="include" value="firstName, lastName, age, addresses"/>
</convert>
<convert converter="bean" match="com.proajax.chapt4.Address">
    <param name="include" value="id, addressLine1, addressLine2, city,
                                                     state, zip"/>
</convert>
```

The nested param tag tells DWR which properties should be included in the conversion process. DWR supports white-listing of properties by using the name="include" attribute, and properties are excluded from the conversion process by using the name="exclude" attribute. This example uses white-listing to specify the class properties that are included in the conversion process. For example, the firstName, lastName, age, and addresses properties of the Person class will be converted to the equivalent JavaScript object. White-listing is a very powerful security concept that is often implemented by network firewalls. Most network firewalls by default deny all access to all ports except for those that are specifically made available, which maximizes protection. The same concept applies to how DWR converts Java objects to their JavaScript equivalents. Only those properties that you explicitly declare as being available for conversion will exist on the JavaScript object.

Astute readers will recognize a bit of a discrepancy right now. The addresses property of the Person class is a Collection, not a simple type like a String or an int. How does DWR handle this situation? Fortunately DWR is smart enough to convert Java collections to JavaScript arrays. DWR looks at the first element in the collection to determine the object type of the collection's contents, so be sure that all objects in the collection are of the same object type. Also note that DWR can only handle converting Java collections to JavaScript arrays. It won't convert from a JavaScript array to a Java collection.

Now that dwr.xml has been properly configured with the new parameter classes, you can look at using them as part of an Ajax request. Listing 4-13 shows a getPerson method that is added to the RemoteBean class. The getPerson method creates an instance of the Person class and then adds a couple of Address objects to the Person. The method finishes by returning the Person object to the calling method, which in this case will be a JavaScript function running in the browser.

**Listing 4-13.** *The* getPerson *Method of the* RemoteBean *Class*

```java
public Person getPerson() {
    Person person = new Person();
    person.setAge(24);
    person.setFirstName("Erik");
    person.setLastName("Tennent");
    Address address = new Address();
    address.setId(12);
    address.setAddressLine1("4288 N. James St.");
    address.setCity("Apple Valley");
    address.setState("MN");
    address.setZip("55341-2160");
    person.addAddress(address);
    address = new Address();
    address.setId(25);
    address.setAddressLine1("3074 E Bush Lake Road");
    address.setCity("Minneapolis");
    address.setState("MN");
    address.setZip("55041");
    person.addAddress(address);
    return person;
}
```

Before we look at the JavaScript that calls this method and handles the response we'll look at the UI code. The HTML is quite simple. Once the Person object is returned by the remote method, the Person's first name, last name, and age will be added to the page. Following that, a table listing all of the Address objects associated to the Person is shown. Listing 4-14 lists the HTML snippet that renders the user interface.

**Listing 4-14.** *The HTML Code That Renders the Details of a* Person *Object and the* Person's Address *Objects*

```html
<h3>Communicating Using Objects</h3>
<p>
    <button onclick="getPerson();">Get Person</button>
    <br/>
    First Name: <span id="firstName"></span>
    <br/>
    Last Name: <span id="lastName"></span>
    <br/>
    Age: <span id="age"></span>
</p>
```

```
<p>Addresses:</p>
<table id="addresses" border="1">
    <thead>
        <tr>
            <th>Address Line 1</th>
            <th>Address Line 2</th>
            <th>City</th>
            <th>State</th>
            <th>Zip</th>
            <th>Action</th>
        </tr>
    </thead>
    <tbody id="addressesTbody">
        <tr><td colspan="6">No Results</td></tr>
    </tbody>
</table>
```

You can see that there is a button that invokes a function named getPerson that calls the remote bean. The getPerson function calls the getPerson method of the RemoteBean object and specifies the handleGetPerson function as the callback function. The handleGetPerson function takes a single parameter, which is the Person object returned by the RemoteBean's getPerson method. DWR automatically converts an instance of the Person object into an equivalent JavaScript object. The getPerson and handleGetPerson functions are shown in Listing 4-15.

**Listing 4-15.** *DWR Automatically Converts a Person Object to the Equivalent JavaScript Object*

```
function getPerson() {
    RemoteBean.getPerson(handleGetPerson);
}
function handleGetPerson(person) {
    DWRUtil.setValue("firstName", person.firstName);
    DWRUtil.setValue("lastName", person.lastName);
    DWRUtil.setValue("age", person.age);
    removeChildren($("addressesTbody"));
    var row = null;
    var address = null;
    var button = null;
    for(var i = 0; i < person.addresses.length; i++) {
        address = person.addresses[i];
        row = document.createElement("tr");
```

```
        row.appendChild(createCellWithText(
            address.addressLine1, "addr1-" + address.id));
        row.appendChild(createCellWithText(
            address.addressLine2, "addr2-" + address.id));
        row.appendChild(createCellWithText(address.city, "city-" + address.id));
        row.appendChild(createCellWithText(address.state, "state-" + address.id));
        row.appendChild(createCellWithText(address.zip, "zip-" + address.id));
        row.appendChild(createSaveButtonCell(address.id));
        $("addressesTbody").appendChild(row);
    }
}
```

Once you have a JavaScript instance of the Person object, you can use the method of your choice to update the DOM with information from the Person object. One method would be to create HTML via string concatenation and set the HTML using the innerHTML property of various elements on the page. This example avoids the use of innerHTML and instead uses the standard W3C DOM methods to update the web page. There are a few helper methods that assist the handleGetPerson with generating content from the Person object and its associated Address objects. In particular, note how the table of addresses is constructed from the array of Address objects that are accessed from the Person object. The JavaScript functions that produce the output on the web page are shown in Listing 4-16.

**Listing 4-16.** *JavaScript Helper Functions That Update the Web Page Based on Person and Address Objects*

```
function createCellWithText(text, id) {
    var cell = document.createElement("td");
    var input = document.createElement("input");
    input.setAttribute("type", "text");
    input.setAttribute("id", id);
    input.value = text;
    cell.appendChild(input);
    return cell;
}
function createSaveButtonCell(id) {
    var button = document.createElement("button");
    button.onclick = function() { saveAddress(id); };
    button.appendChild(document.createTextNode("Save"));
    var cell = document.createElement("td");
    cell.appendChild(button);
    return cell;
}
```

```
function removeChildren(node) {
    while(node.childNodes.length > 0) {
        node.removeChild(node.childNodes[0]);
    }
}
```

The result of clicking the button and the ensuing web page updates are shown in Figure 4-7. You can see that each row of the address table has a Save button, indicating that the values can be edited and saved. We'll get back to that in a minute.

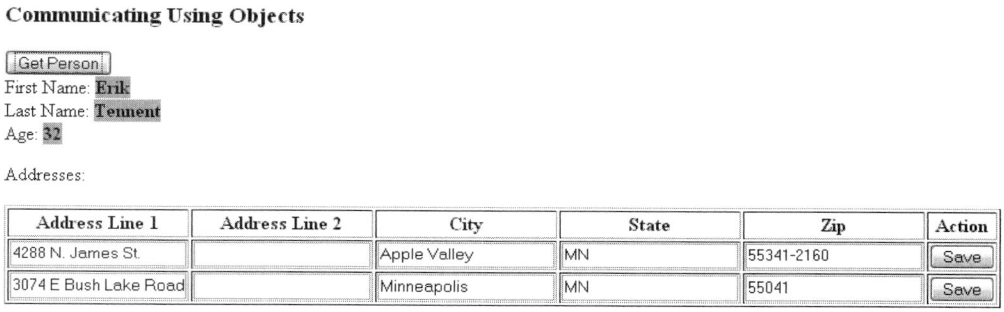

**Communicating Using Objects**

[ Get Person ]
First Name: Erik
Last Name: Tennent
Age: 32

Addresses:

| Address Line 1 | Address Line 2 | City | State | Zip | Action |
|---|---|---|---|---|---|
| 4288 N. James St. | | Apple Valley | MN | 55341-2160 | Save |
| 3074 E Bush Lake Road | | Minneapolis | MN | 55041 | Save |

**Figure 4-7.** *The web page is updated using W3C DOM methods from JavaScript objects built by DWR from their Java equivalents.*

## Sending an Object to the Remote Method

Since you've been eagerly reading this text and studiously dissecting the example code, you've noticed that the entries in the address table are contained in input boxes with a Save button at the end of the row. The previous example showed how DWR could convert a Java object into an equivalent JavaScript object; this example demonstrates how DWR converts a JavaScript object to its Java equivalent.

All of the fields in a row in the address table are editable. Clicking the Save button at the end of a row will trigger a call to a method called saveAddress on the RemoteBean object. The saveAddress method takes a single parameter: the Address object whose data should be saved. DWR will convert a JavaScript object representing an address to an Address object and pass it to the saveAddress method.

There's no need to bore you with the mundane details of actually saving the Address object. Instead, the saveAddress method will simply write out the Address parameter's properties so you can ensure that they match what was entered in the UI. The saveAddress method is shown in Listing 4-17.

**Listing 4-17.** *The saveAddress Method Accepts a Single Address Object That Was Converted by DWR*

```
public void saveAddress(Address addr) {
    StringBuffer buf = new StringBuffer();
    buf.append("**** Saving Address ****");
    buf.append("\nID: " + addr.getId());
    buf.append("\nAddress Line 1: ");
    buf.append(addr.getAddressLine1());
    buf.append("\nAddress Line 2: ");
    buf.append(addr.getAddressLine2());
    buf.append("\nCity: ");
    buf.append(addr.getCity());
    buf.append("\nState: ");
    buf.append(addr.getState());
    buf.append("\nZip: ");
    buf.append(addr.getZip());
    System.out.println(buf.toString());
}
```

If you study Listing 4-16, specifically the createSaveButtonCell function, you'll see that the onclick event handler for each button passes that row's address ID to the saveAddress function. The saveAddress function, shown in Listing 4-18, handles the details of creating a JavaScript Address object, populating the object's properties with the data entered on the screen, and calling the RemoteBean's saveAddress method, using the JavaScript Address object as the method parameter. The JavaScript Address object is first created by creating a generic JavaScript object by using the new operator. Note that each property name must match the property name of the equivalent Java Address object. Then, each property is added to the object by naming the property within quotes within brackets. Each property value is retrieved from the input boxes by using the $() function.

Before calling the remote saveAddress method, the saveAddress function uses DWR's toDescriptiveString function to show the Address object's properties in an alert window. Finally the remote saveAddress method is called, passing the Address object as a parameter and specifying the handleSaveAddress as the callback function.

**Listing 4-18.** *The saveAddress Method Constructs a JavaScript Object Which DWR Converts to a Java Object*

```
function saveAddress(id) {
    var address = new Object();
    address["id"] = id;
    address["addressLine1"] = $("addr1-" + id).value;
    address["addressLine2"] = $("addr2-" + id).value;
```

```
    address["city"] = $("city-" + id).value;
    address["state"] = $("state-" + id).value;
    address["zip"] = $("zip-" + id).value;
    alert(DWRUtil.toDescriptiveString(address, 1));
    RemoteBean.saveAddress(address, handleSaveAddress);
}
function handleSaveAddress(status) {
    alert("Save Status: " + status);
}
```

Figure 4-8 displays an example console that shows a successful save of an Address object.

```
chapter04 (run) ×  Bundled Tomcat (5.5.9) Log  ×  Bundled Tomcat (5.5.9) ×

    **** Saving Address ****
    ID: 12
    Address Line 1: New Address Line 1
    Address Line 2: New Address Line 2
    City: Hanska
    State: MN
    Zip: 56001
```

**Figure 4-8.** *The successful save of an updated Address object*

## JavaScript Templates

As you can see, DWR is a very powerful Ajax tool. Using DWR gives you the ability to pass simple and complex objects between the browser and the server. DWR hides the complexity of converting Java objects to their JavaScript equivalents (and vice versa) and shields the developer from the mundane details of Ajax plumbing.

DWR's weakness is that it doesn't provide much help for updating the DOM with new or updated content. DWR does provide some help for creating tables and select boxes and the like, but the functionality is limited and confined to simple use cases. For the most part, when using DWR, you're on your own when it comes to manipulating the DOM.

JavaScript Templates (http://trimpath.com/project/wiki/JavaScriptTemplates) is a templating engine written entirely in JavaScript that allows for template-based programming within a browser. JST is dual-licensed under the Apache and GPL licenses. As its name suggests, JST allows for a JSP-like template environment that runs entirely in the browser. JST can be used with any server-side technology.

So why is JST being mentioned here? Refer to Listings 4-15 and 4-16. These listings, measuring roughly 50 lines long, are made up predominantly of code that updates the DOM with the information returned by the browser. The code uses the W3C DOM methods to build elements and element attributes and adds them to the DOM to produce the desired output. Although not particularly hard, creating content this way is unnatural for Java EE developers and also somewhat difficult to read. Java EE developers likely use a templating technology like JSP or Apache's Velocity to dynamically create HTML content from a template.

Enter JST, the perfect complement to DWR to dynamically produce HTML content from JavaScript objects returned by DWR. Instead of using tedious DOM methods to update the DOM, you can write a template that will convert a DWR JavaScript object into HTML. To show you how easy JST is to use, we'll repeat the previous example, this time using JST to update the DOM.

### Installing JavaScript Templates

JST consists of a single JavaScript file that can be downloaded from JST's home page. The file is named template.js and is only 400 or so lines long.

You must reference the template.js file in the HTML file that will use JST. For this example, the template.js file is located in a directory named js, so the following line is added to the HTML page's head section to reference the template.js file:

```
<script type="text/javascript" src="js/template.js"></script>
```

### Writing the Template

Like the previous example, you want to create new page content based on the data in the Person object returned by the getPerson remote method. Instead of writing DOM methods to create the content, you will write a template that reads through the Person object's properties and generates the correct output.

Before you write the template, you must decide where to put the template. In the Java EE world, JSPs live and execute on the server, and their results are sent back to the browser. In the case of JST, the template is evaluated in the browser, so we somehow need to keep the template on the browser. The creators of JST recommend hiding JST templates in textarea elements that are themselves hidden from the user's view. They note that textarea elements are the ideal choice because textarea elements won't interfere with the formatting of the markup residing within the text area. This is important because the template is made up of HTML and special JST markers that must not be changed. If you don't want to hide the JST templates in textarea elements, you could also load the templates dynamically via Ajax. This example hides the template within a hidden textarea element.

The heart of JST is focused around a *context object*. The context object is the root object from which JST will search for property values. For those familiar with Struts and Struts JSP tags, the context object is similar to the ActionForm object from which Struts HTML tags read properties. JST supports nested properties that can be referenced using dot notation.

The Person object is the context object for the purposes of this example. The Person object has three primary properties that are written to the page: firstName, lastName, and age. In addition, the Person object has an array of Address objects, with each Address object having five properties in which we're interested: addressLine1, addressLine2, city, state, and zip.

Listing 4-19 shows the JST template embedded within a textarea element. Note how the textarea itself is hidden from the user's view.

**Listing 4-19.** *The JST Template to Produce HTML from a Person Object*

```
<textarea id="personTemplate" style="display:none;">
    <p>
        <br/>
        First Name: <span class="response">${firstName}</span>
        <br/>
        Last Name: <span class="response">${lastName}</span>
        <br/>
        Age: <span class="response">${age}</span>
    </p>
    <table border="1">
        <thead>
            <tr>
                <th>Address Line 1</th>
                <th>Address Line 2</th>
                <th>City</th>
                <th>State</th>
                <th>Zip</th>
                <th>Action</th>
            </tr>
        </thead>
        <tbody>
            {for address in addresses}
                <tr>
                    <td><input type="text" id="addr1-jst-${address.id}"
                    value="${address.addressLine1}"/></td>
                    <td><input type="text" id="addr2-jst-${address.id}"
                    value="${address.addressLine2}"/></td>
                    <td><input type="text" id="city-jst-${address.id}"
                    value="${address.city}"/></td>
                    <td><input type="text" id="state-jst-${address.id}"
                    value="${address.state}"/></td>
                    <td><input type="text" id="zip-jst-${address.id}"
                    value="${address.zip}"/></td>
                    <td>
```

```
                        <button
                        onclick="saveAddressFromJstTable(${address.id});">
                        Save</button></td>
                    </tr>
                {/for}
            </tbody>
        </table>
    </textarea>
```

If you carefully read Listing 4-19 you should be able to discern exactly what is going on. In fact, the template embedded within the textarea element should look strikingly similar to a JSP that would render similar output.

At the top of the template is a p element in which the person's first name, last name, and age are listed. The JST syntax for retrieving object properties is to embed the property name within curly braces which are preceded by a dollar sign. Assuming for a moment that a Person object has been set as the context object (more on how that's done in a minute), you can access the Person object's firstName property by using ${firstName}. This syntax will look familiar to anybody who has used JSTL tags within a JSP.

Following the output of the Person's primary properties you can turn to building the table of addresses. Remembering that the Person object has an array of Address objects, it seems reasonable that you'll want to use some sort of iteration mechanism to loop through all of the Address objects and build a table row for each Address object.

Fortunately JST has built-in iteration support. The {for address in addresses} statement iterates over all of the Address objects in the addresses property of the Person object. The current Address is assigned to the address variable, which can then be used inside the iteration loop. Inside of the for loop is the template for building an individual table row that represents a single Address object. Note how the address variable is referenced inside of the id, value, and onclick attributes and that the individual properties of the address object such as addressLine1 and city are referenced via dot notation. Be sure to close the for loop with the closing {/for} statement.

That's all for the template! As you can see, the template is much easier to write than W3C DOM JavaScript methods, and it's much easier to read, too. The last thing we need to do is wire together the Person object returned by DWR and the JST template.

### Evaluating the Template

Now that the template is written, the rest of the JavaScript to retrieve the Person object from the remote bean using DWR and update the DOM using JST is trivial. Listing 4-20 lists all the necessary JavaScript.

**Listing 4-20.** *Combining JST with DWR Eliminates a Significant Amount of JavaScript*

```
function getPersonUsingJst() {
    RemoteBean.getPerson(handleSaveAddressUsingJst);
}
function handleSaveAddressUsingJst(person) {
    var result = TrimPath.processDOMTemplate("personTemplate", person);
    $("jstOutput").innerHTML = result;
}
```

The getPersonUsingJst function is nearly identical to the getPerson function from the previous example. All this function does is use DWR to call the remote bean's getPerson method and specify the handleSaveAddressUsingJst function as the callback function.

The handleSaveAddressUsingJst function takes as its lone function parameter the Person object returned by the server. The first line of the function is where the template is evaluated against the context object. JST defines a TrimPath object that has a processDOMTemplate method. This method takes two parameters: a string that identifies the element whose innerHTML property holds the JST template, and the context object. In this example, the textarea element in which the JST template is hidden has an id attribute value of personTemplate; this is the first parameter to the processDOMTemplate method. The Person object returned by the server is the context object, so person is provided as the second method parameter to processDOMTemplate.

The processDOMTemplate method returns a string representing the fully evaluated template which is stored in a variable named result. The second line of the handleSaveAddressUsingJst function sets the innerHTML property of a div element whose id is jsOutput to result, thus updating the page with the Person information returned by the server. The result should be identical to the output shown in Figure 4-7.

The amount of JavaScript in this example is nearly nonexistent compared to the previous example. Instead of using JavaScript to update the DOM, this example used a JST template to do so, drastically reducing the amount of JavaScript. The improvements of using JST templates over JavaScript is comparable to the advantages of using JSPs over println statements inside of servlets.

# AjaxTags

AjaxTags is an open source JSP tag library found at ajaxtags.sourceforge.net using the Apache 2.0 license. AjaxTags is designed for Java EE developers who may not be well-versed in browser technologies like JavaScript yet still need to Ajax-enable their web applications. AjaxTags only requires that the developer drop a custom JSP tag onto the page and write the appropriate server-side code to support the Ajax request. No JavaScript coding is required. AjaxTags supports the following use cases: an autocomplete text box, select box population based on input from another field, pop-up balloons, and more.

AjaxTags is implemented as a custom JSP tag library that also ships with some supporting JavaScript and CSS files. All you need to use AjaxTags is JDK 1.4 or greater and a servlet container.

## The Ajax "Killer Application"

One of the first killer applications of Ajax was for autocomplete components. Thanks to Google Suggest, the endless possibilities presented by Ajax spread through the Internet like wildfire. Google Suggest showed that Ajax could be used to deliver highly interactive web applications that approached thick client applications in terms of usability and interactivity. Soon the Internet and developer community was abuzz with all of the potential uses for Ajax.

Developers everywhere moved to implement autocomplete components in their web applications. The collective thud you heard was all of those developers banging their heads against the wall in unison thinking, "This is *hard*." The actual Ajax request and response that powers the typical autocomplete component is straightforward, but updating the DOM to display the drop-down list with the list of available selections, and making the drop-down list respond to key press events like arrow up or enter, is complex and error-prone. What we need is a drop-in component that hides the complexities of the autocomplete widget.

## AjaxTags Autocomplete Component

AjaxTags provides a drop-in autocomplete component. Without writing a single line of JavaScript you can add an autocomplete text field to your web page. Instead of writing all of the code necessary to produce the autocomplete drop-down you can focus on the server-side code that actually services and populates the drop-down list.

This example demonstrates an autocomplete text box that searches for names starting with an "A" or an "M." Instead of using an external database to perform an actual search, this example will use a hard-coded list of names to search. Listing 4-21 lists the NameService class that is responsible for searching through a list of names and returning the ones that match the given input. The NameService class' constructor takes a List of names as the names that can be used in the search.

**Listing 4-21.** *NameService.java*

```java
package com.proajax.chapt4;
import java.util.ArrayList;
import java.util.Iterator;
import java.util.List;
```

```
public class NameService {
    private List names;
    private NameService(List listOfNames) {
        this.names = listOfNames;
    }
    public static NameService getInstance(List listOfNames) {
        return new NameService(listOfNames);
    }
    public List findNames(String prefix) {
        String prefixUpperCase = prefix.toUpperCase();
        List matches = new ArrayList();
        Iterator iter = names.iterator();
        while(iter.hasNext()) {
            String name = (String) iter.next();
            String nameUpperCase = name.toUpperCase();
            if(nameUpperCase.startsWith(prefixUpperCase)) {
                boolean result = matches.add(name);
            }
        }
        return matches;
    }
}
```

Now that the search implementation is complete, let's turn our attention towards the JSP page itself. AjaxTags does a wonderful job handling the messy details of creating the drop-down list and populating it from the server response. All you need to do is drop the JSP tag on the page. Listing 4-22 shows the example JSP page.

**Listing 4-22.** *ajaxTagsAutocomplete.jsp*

```
<%@ taglib uri="http://ajaxtags.org/tags/ajax" prefix="ajax" %>
<%@page contentType="text/html"%>
<!DOCTYPE html PUBLIC "-//W3C//DTD XHTML 1.0 Strict//EN"
                "http://www.w3.org/TR/xhtml1/DTD/xhtml1-strict.dtd">
<html xmlns="http://www.w3.org/1999/xhtml">
    <head>
        <title>AjaxTags Examples</title>
        <script type="text/javascript"
            src="js/ajaxtags/prototype-1.3.1.js"></script>
        <script type="text/javascript"
            src="js/ajaxtags/ajaxtags-1.1.5.js"></script>
        <link rel="stylesheet" type="text/css" href="css/ajaxtags.css" />
    </head>
```

```
<body>
    <h1>AjaxTags Autocomplete</h1>
    <form action="#">
        <p>
            <label for="firstName">Search for a Name: </label>
            <input id="firstName" name="firstName" type="text" size="30" />
        </p>
    </form>
    <ajax:autocomplete
    baseUrl="AutoCompleteServlet"
    source="firstName"
    target="firstName"
    parameters="search={firstName}"
    className="autocomplete"
    minimumCharacters="1" />
    <script type="text/javascript">
        var popup = document.getElementById("ajaxAutocompletePopup");
        popup.style.display = "none";
    </script>
</body>
</html>
```

The JSP page starts with a JSP directive that defines the AjaxTags custom tag library. All of the AjaxTags tags that appear on the page will use the ajax prefix. Within the head section there are two JavaScript files defined: prototype-1.3.1.js and ajaxtags-1.1.5.js. AjaxTags is dependent on the Prototype JavaScript library (see Chapter 3), although AjaxTags supplies its own JavaScript library. Following the JavaScript source file declarations is a CSS file named ajaxtags.css that provides the style information for the drop-down list. The contents of this CSS file were condensed from an example CSS file provided by the AjaxTags distribution. You are free to customize it as you see fit.

The body of the JSP is very simple. Here you can see the input box into which the user can enter text. The text entered by the user into this text field is used by the NameService class to find a list of matching names. You can see that there's nothing special about this input field; it's simply a regular old text box. The autocomplete drop-down magic is all handled by AjaxTags.

Following the input box is the autocomplete JSP tag. There's likely nothing you haven't seen here before if you've ever used a custom JSP tag. All you need to do is fill in the required parameters, and the rest should just work. Table 4-1 lists the parameters required for the autocomplete tag and their intended use.

**Table 4-1.** *The Attributes Required by the* autocomplete *Tag*

| Attribute Name | Meaning/Use |
| --- | --- |
| baseUrl | The URL to which the Ajax requests will be sent. |
| source | The ID of the input box that is providing the text on which to search. The drop-down list will appear under this input box. |
| target | The ID of the input box into which the selected autocomplete value will be placed. Often this will be the same as the source input box. |
| parameters | A comma-separated list of parameters that will be sent to the server as part of the Ajax request. |
| className | The CSS class to apply to the drop-down list. |
| minimumCharacters | The minimum number of characters that must appear in the source input box before an Ajax request is made. |

In this example, a servlet mapped to the AutoCompleteServlet URL will handle the Ajax request, so this value is placed in the baseUrl attribute. The input box that the user types into has an id attribute value of firstName, so this value is used for the source attribute. Since we want the user's selection to appear in the firstName input box, this value is also used for the target attribute.

The parameters attribute is quite useful. This attribute allows you to specify a comma-separated list of name/value pairs that will be sent to the server as part of the Ajax request. You can see that in this example, the parameters attribute is set to search={firstName}. Note how the firstName text appears within curly braces. The curly braces tell AjaxTags to use the value of the input box that has an id of firstName as the value for this name/value pair. In short, this is how the value entered into the text box by the user is sent to the server for further processing.

The last two attributes are className and minimumCharacters. The className attribute names the CSS class that applies to the drop-down list. In this example, the autocomplete CSS class is defined in the ajaxtags.css file. Finally, the minimumCharacters attribute lists the minimum number of characters that must be present in the input box before the Ajax request will be sent. For this example the value is set to 1, but in real-world applications you may wish to use a higher value to help limit the number of results that will appear in the drop-down list.

Now that we have the JSP and the search service complete, we need to tie them together. This example uses a servlet to accept the Ajax request and return the results to the server. The servlet is responsible for accepting the Ajax request, using the NameService object to find a list of names that match the given input, and returning the matching names to the client in a format which can be used by AjaxTags to build the drop-down list.

Before we look at the servlet, let's quickly look at the format required by AjaxTags to render the drop-down list. AjaxTags expects an XML document to be returned by the server. The XML document is rather basic and most easily described using an example, which is shown in Listing 4-23.

**Listing 4-23.** *An Example AjaxTags Server Response*

```
<?xml version="1.0" encoding="UTF-8"?>
<ajax-response>
  <response>
    <item>
      <name>Abe</name>
      <value>Abe</value>
    </item>
    <item>
      <name>Abel</name>
      <value>Abel</value>
    </item>
    <item>
      <name>Abigail</name>
      <value>Abigail</value>
    </item>
  </response>
</ajax-response>
```

The root of the XML document is always the ajax-response tag. The immediate child of this tag is the response tag. The response tag contains any number of item tags, each with its own name and value child tags. In this example, since we're simply displaying names in the drop-down list, the name and value tags will each have the same text.

Listing 4-24 lists the servlet that processes the response for the autocomplete Ajax request. The doGet method is where all of the work happens. The first thing this method does is retrieve the text that was entered by the user into the text box. This value is sent as the value of the search parameter. (Remember that this was set as an attribute to the autocomplete custom tag; see Listing 4-22.) Next, the value is sent to NameService which returns the List of names that match the given string. Finally, an XML string that matches the structure of the example in Listing 4-23 is constructed and sent back to the browser. Remember to set the response's content type to text/xml and to disable caching before returning the response.

**Listing 4-24.** *AutoCompleteServlet.java*

```java
package com.proajax.chapt4;
import java.io.*;
import java.util.ArrayList;
import java.util.Iterator;
import java.util.List;
import javax.servlet.*;
import javax.servlet.http.*;
public class AutoCompleteServlet extends HttpServlet {
    private List names = new ArrayList();
    public void init(ServletConfig config) throws ServletException {
        names.add("Abe");
        names.add("Abel");
        names.add("Abigail");
        names.add("Abner");
        names.add("Abraham");
        names.add("Marcus");
        names.add("Marcy");
        names.add("Marge");
        names.add("Marie");
    }
    protected void doGet(HttpServletRequest request
                                        , HttpServletResponse response)
    throws ServletException, IOException {
        String prefix = request.getParameter("search");
        NameService service = NameService.getInstance(names);
        List matching = service.findNames(prefix);
        if (matching.size() > 0) {
            PrintWriter out = response.getWriter();
            response.setContentType("text/xml");
            response.setHeader("Cache-Control", "no-cache");
            out.println("<?xml version=\"1.0\" encoding=\"UTF-8\"?>");
            out.println("<ajax-response><response>");
            Iterator iter = matching.iterator();
            while(iter.hasNext()) {
                String name = (String) iter.next();
                out.println("<item>");
                out.println("<name>" + name + "</name>");
                out.println("<value>" + name + "</value>");
                out.println("</item>");
            }
```

```
                out.println("</response></ajax-response>");
                matching = null;
                service = null;
                out.close();
            }
            else {
                response.setStatus(HttpServletResponse.SC_NO_CONTENT);
            }
        }
        protected void doPost(HttpServletRequest request
                                            , HttpServletResponse response)
        throws ServletException, IOException {
            doGet(request, response);
        }
}
```

The final result is an autocomplete text box that drops down a list of matching items when the user types into the text box. The items in the drop-down list can be navigated using the up and down arrows. The Escape key closes the drop-down list, and the Enter or Return key selects the current item. All of this functionality comes without writing a single line of JavaScript. The example autocomplete widget is shown in Figure 4-9.

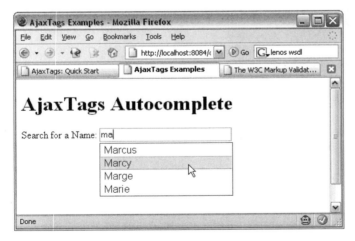

**Figure 4-9.** *An Ajax-enabled autocomplete text box can be implemented without writing a single line of JavaScript, thanks to AjaxTags.*

# Other Options

DWR and AjaxTags aren't the only Ajax-Java frameworks out there. JSON-RPC-Java (`http://oss.metaparadigm.com/jsonrpc`) is a framework similar to DWR. It uses JavaScript Object Notation (JSON) as the data interchange format and can be used in any servlet container. Like DWR, JSON-RPC-Java focuses on the data exchange between the browser and server and does little to help with manipulating the DOM.

AjaxAnywhere (`http://ajaxanywhere.sourceforge.net`), as described on its website, is designed to turn any set of existing JSP or JSF components into Ajax-aware components without a lot of custom JavaScript. AjaxAnywhere is implemented as a servlet filter and a set of JSP tags that allow you to specify certain "zones" of a page that can be refreshed via Ajax. If Ajax is available, then the zones will be updated via Ajax; if Ajax is not available, then the zones are reloaded using a traditional full-page refresh. AjaxAnywhere can be easily integrated with existing solutions as it does not require changing the existing application code.

For a list of other available Java Ajax frameworks you can visit `http://ajaxpatterns.org/Java_Ajax_Frameworks`.

# Summary

Between Chapter 3 and this chapter you've been exposed to several libraries and frameworks designed to simplify the process of Ajax-enabling your web applications. Now, the big question is: which one is right for you?

Not surprisingly, the correct answer is, "it depends." You need to choose the library or framework that best fits your skills and the problem you're trying to solve. Some libraries are geared towards visual effects. Others focus on encapsulating the communication between the browser and the server. Some frameworks require that you write a bit of JavaScript; others eliminate the need to write any JavaScript.

When choosing an Ajax library or framework you'll want to consider a few different criteria. Do you want to write a lot of JavaScript? Some frameworks require that you write lots of JavaScript. If you're not comfortable with this you may wish to look elsewhere.

Does the framework solve the problem you're trying to solve? For example, DWR is great for passing objects between the browser and server but doesn't help much with manipulating the DOM, although it can be paired with JST. In contrast, Taconite does a great job in updating the DOM but isn't as sophisticated in its ability to pass data to and from the server. Most likely, if you start to use Ajax frequently in your applications you'll use multiple Ajax frameworks and libraries. For example, you may wish to use AjaxTag's autocomplete component for its simplicity but use another library for a different task.

Is the framework or library flexible enough for your needs? For example, AjaxTags is very powerful, but it can only do what its specific components are designed to do. DWR is very flexible but requires more custom coding on your part. The ability to tweak the framework's behavior may be important to you.

Not all frameworks use JavaScript namespacing, which could lead to problems if two frameworks used together both define a JavaScript object with the same name. Be sure to investigate whether multiple libraries can be used together in the same environment without causing errors.

The last thing you may want to consider is community involvement and available support. Ajax is currently a hot topic in the industry, and lots of frameworks and libraries have sprung up. At some point there will be some consolidation within this market as developers gravitate towards the most useful frameworks. A framework or library that's here today may not be here tomorrow, so choose one that appears to have strong community support or one that you're comfortable supporting on your own if the original author ends support.

The bottom line is this: there are plenty of libraries and frameworks available to help you with Ajax-related development. You shouldn't have to worry about the mundane details of creating the `XMLHttpRequest` object or how to correctly position a drop-down list under an input box. Instead, you can focus on implementing business functionality for your users, and the user experience is enhanced by the use of Ajax. The libraries and frameworks listed here will help you do just that.

# PART 3

■■■

# Web Frameworks

**A**jax is primarily a technique that lives in the web tier of a multitiered web application. The typical Ajax request will likely require the use of the service and database tiers, but for the most part the Ajax request itself will be handled by the web tier and then passed along as needed to the other tiers.

Most of the examples you've seen so far use a Java servlet on the server to handle the incoming Ajax request. Servlets are a vital part of the Java EE standard that provide the ability to handle incoming HTTP requests. Without servlets we would have to write our own sockets to accept HTTP requests and handle writing the response out to a stream all by ourselves. Servlets do all of this heavy lifting for us, relieving of us the duty to work with the low-level HTTP specification.

Now, a quick survey: how many of you actually write servlets on a daily basis? Even though you may spend a majority of your time working on Java-based web applications, it's a good bet that you probably don't work directly with servlets. Servlets shield us from the low-level details of the HTTP specification, but today servlets themselves are even considered too low-level to work with on a daily basis.

Most likely you use some type of web framework in your Java EE web applications. Whether it's Struts or Spring MVC, Tapestry or JSF, these frameworks insulate you from working directly with servlets and instead provide a higher-level abstraction over the standard servlet API. Make no doubt about it: all of these frameworks use servlets under the covers in some shape or form.

Since you're likely using a web framework already there's no need to start writing servlets again to simply service your Ajax requests. Remember, an Ajax request is just like any other HTTP request. The only difference is that the browser sends the Ajax request asynchronously so that the browser remains responsive to user input. So, why not use your favorite web framework to service the requests instead of writing servlets? By using a web framework, you'll also be able to leverage the features and services offered by that framework.

We'll spend the next few chapters reviewing the most popular Java web frameworks and how they integrate with Ajax. We'll also show how each framework's special features can be used to make the most of Ajax.

# CHAPTER 5

■■■

# Struts and Ajax

**S**truts is the granddaddy of all the Java web frameworks. Craig R. McClanahan launched Struts in May 2000, with the 1.0 release following in July 2001. Since that time Struts has arguably become the most popular Java web framework and due to its relatively old age is sometimes considered to be "legacy." Struts pioneered the Model 2 model-view-controller (MVC) pattern that has become the standard among Java web frameworks. The Model 2 MVC pattern uses a servlet to control application flow, making it the controller. The controller typically delegates to a handler object that acts as the adapter between the request and the model. The model, of course, represents the application's business objects or domain layer. After processing the request the controller forwards the request to the appropriate view, which is usually implemented using JSPs.

In addition to providing a Model 2 MVC implementation for Java web applications, Struts provides a number of services that can help ease the burden of developing modern, interactive web applications. Foremost among these services is the validation framework. Before the availability of the Struts validator, we had to write all of our own validation routines, such as verifying that the user filled out all of the information on the page or that a particular input field was in the correct format. The Struts validator will automatically perform validations on input fields based on definitions stored in an XML file, so instead of writing the tedious code to perform validations, you can simply specify validations in an XML file and the Struts validator will take care of the rest.

## Struts Design

The following is not meant to be a complete Struts tutorial but rather a refresher on Struts' design and implementation. You've likely worked with Struts at some point in your career as a Java web application developer, but even if you haven't, you'll likely be familiar with its concepts as other Java web application frameworks (even homebuilt ones) often mirror Struts' implementation.

The core of Struts is a servlet that acts as the controller within the MVC implementation. The Struts controller servlet is responsible for acting as a bridge between the application model and the web view. The controller passes requests to a request handler which is an instance of an `Action` class. The typical web application will use many different `Action` objects, and the controller servlet knows which `Action` to pass the request based on mappings in the `struts-config.xml` file.

The `Action` accesses the model to query or update the application's state, or both. The `Action` itself should have no business logic and should simply delegate all of the grunt work to the model or a façade that accesses the model. By keeping business logic out of the `Action` objects, you can minimize the amount of coupling between your service/business tier and the web tier and from Struts in general.

Data from the HTTP request is passed to the `Action` object via an `ActionForm` object. The `ActionForm` is a simple JavaBeans-style object that helps transfer data between the model and the view. Struts automatically populates the `ActionForm` object with the parameters sent as part of an HTTP GET or POST operation. Thanks to the autopopulating of the `ActionForm` you don't need to get the request parameters using the request object's `getParameter` method.

The previous few paragraphs are all well and good, but like the old saying goes, a picture is worth a thousand words. Figure 5-1 is a UML sequence diagram that shows the key Struts classes and how they interact when servicing a web request.

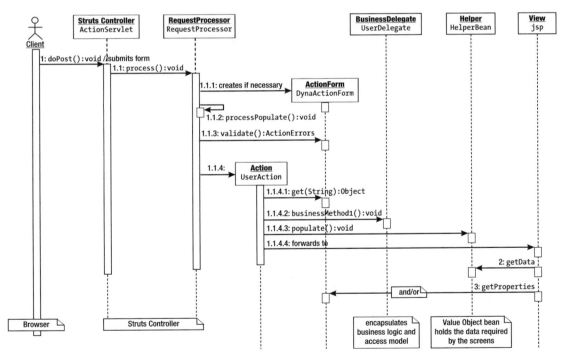

**Figure 5-1.** *UML sequence diagram describing the interactions of Struts classes while servicing an HTTP request[1]*

---

1. Submitted diagrams by Jean-Michel Garnier on October 2. Based on an article by Jean-Michel Garnier on the `http://rollerjm.free.fr` website. Copyright © 1999–2002 by The Apache Software Foundation. All rights reserved.

The diagram in Figure 5-1 shows the interaction of the main Struts classes. As described previously, the Struts controller servlet handles all requests and delegates to the `RequestProcessor` the task of passing the requests to their appropriate handlers.

The `RequestProcessor` populates an instance of an `ActionForm` class from the request's parameters, saving you from having to access the request object directly to retrieve the parameters.

Once populated, the `ActionForm` is subjected to two different methods for validating the request parameters. First, Struts uses the Jakarta Commons Validator library to validate the `ActionForm`'s properties based on the validation rules defined in the `validation.xml` file, if any exist. Following that, if no validation errors occurred, the `ActionForm`'s `validate` method is called. Developers may override the base `ActionForm`'s `validate` method to validate the object's properties.

Once all the validation routines complete, and assuming that there were no validation errors, the `Action` is called. The `Action` is responsible for accessing the model and service layers where the real work is performed. The `Action` interacts with the `ActionForm` to access the request parameters and provide them to the service and model layers.

After accessing the service and model layers, the `Action` is responsible for preparing the response that is sent back to the browser. The `Action` populates the `ActionForm` or, as the diagram depicts, a helper object that contains the data will eventually appear in the view.

Finally the `Action` forwards the request to the view, which in most Java web applications is a JSP. Struts can work with a number of different views, including Velocity templates and XML/XSLT, in addition to JSP. The view populates itself using the data from the `ActionForm` and any helper objects.

In the end, the view renders itself as HTML that is sent back to the client browser. The result is a dynamically built web page that is built based on input by the user, in contrast to traditional static HTML pages that never change.

# Ajax Validation

A key component of any web framework is the ability to validate information entered by the user. Traditional thick-client applications often rely on custom input widgets that only allow valid input. Many thick-client applications provide a date widget in which the user can only enter numbers, and the widget also ensures that the input constitutes a valid date; for example, it does not allow the user to enter a date greater than the number of days in the specified month.

The web world has no concept of these types of complex input widgets. Many of the same effects can be handled with JavaScript, but writing the JavaScript to perform these duties can be tedious, error-prone, and time-consuming, not to mention unreliable—validation will not occur if the user has disabled JavaScript. As a result, in the web world, input validation has traditionally occurred on the server when the form data is posted to the server. The advantage of performing input validation on the server is that it's guaranteed to always be executed (it runs regardless of whether JavaScript is enabled on the browser) and the validation routines can be as complex as needed, from simply verifying the correct format of a date string to accessing a database to ensure that a unique key is still unique.

The downside to performing validation on the server, of course, is that the validation is being performed *on the server* after the user has submitted the form. We would much rather perform the validation as soon as possible so any feedback can be presented to the user as quickly as possible. Doing so provides a much richer and more interactive user experience. But, alas, how can we seamlessly invoke server-side validation routines without posting the form and waiting for the whole page to refresh?

Ajax, of course! (Not that you didn't already know.) One of the most common applications of Ajax is to invoke server-side validation routines to provide immediate feedback to the user. The following example demonstrates how the built-in Struts validators are easily leveraged using Ajax techniques.

# Struts Validation

Struts allows developers to validate user input three ways. The first way is by using the XML-based Commons Validator. Commons Validator allows form input validation to be configured via rules defined in an XML file named validation.xml. Commons Validator covers many of the simple yet repetitive validation routines such as ensuring that a particular element has received some input, that an input string consists of all numeric digits, or that an input string matches a predefined pattern. These cases and more are provided by Commons Validator, and all the developer needs to do is specify the rule (or rules) that must be applied to a particular input field. Much if not all of a form's input validation can be performed by specifying rules in an XML file writing nary a line of Java code. Commons Validator is best used for simple validations such as a form element being required or an input string that must consist entirely of numeric digits.

The second way in which Struts allows for input validation is through the validate method of any instance of the ActionForm class. All subclasses of the ActionForm may override the default implementation of the validate method, which does nothing. Struts always calls the ActionForm's validate method after performing any validation specified in validation.xml but before passing the request to an Action class. The validate method is a great place to perform validation that is too complex to be covered by Commons Validator. If/else conditions that are nearly impossible to specify in validation.xml but relatively easy to do in Java code are a good example of validations that can be performed within an ActionForm's validate method.

The final place in which validation can be performed is within a Struts Action class. Like an ActionForm, validation that occurs within an Action must be written in Java. The key difference is that the Action class has access to the application's domain and service tiers, so validations that involve querying the database or accessing business rules in the domain tier are best placed within an Action. All Action classes can access the ActionMessages object to which error messages can be added.

# Struts and Ajax Integration

Struts is an ideal framework on which to add Ajax interactions. Struts does a good job of encapsulating all of the redundant details of MVC Model 2 development while still providing enough access to the "nuts and bolts" of the application so it can be customized as desired by the developer. One area in which Struts particularly shines is its flexibility when it comes to validating user input, and thanks to Struts' various validation extension points, it can be easily integrated with Ajax.

This example demonstrates how well Struts validation can be integrated using Ajax. The example is a fictional hotel room reservation system. The web page collects the necessary information like the desired dates, whether a smoking or nonsmoking room is desired, any special requests, and the customer's name and telephone number. The example web page is shown in Figure 5-2.

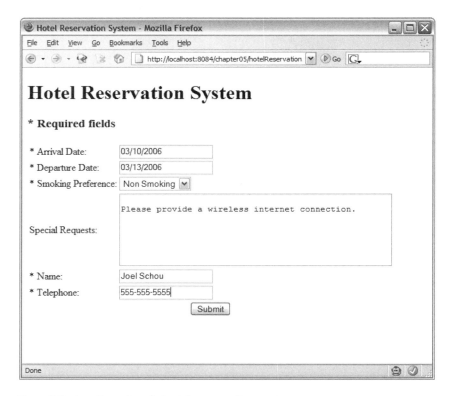

**Figure 5-2.** *A rather simple hotel reservation system*

Listing 5-1 lists the JSP page that renders this screen. As you can see, there is no rocket science occurring within this JSP. Struts HTML custom tags like `text` and `textarea` are used to render the input elements, while the `errors` tag is used to display any error messages.

**Listing 5-1.** *hotelReservation.jsp*

```
<%@taglib uri="http://struts.apache.org/tags-html" prefix="html" %>
<html:xhtml/>

<!DOCTYPE html PUBLIC "-//W3C//DTD XHTML 1.0 Strict//EN"
                          "http://www.w3.org/TR/xhtml1/DTD/xhtml1-strict.dtd">

<html xmlns="http://www.w3.org/1999/xhtml">
    <head>
        <title>Hotel Reservation System</title>
        <script type="text/javascript" src="js/hotelReservation.js"></script>
        <script type="text/javascript" src="js/prototype-1.4.0.js"></script>
    </head>
    <body>

    <h1>Hotel Reservation System</h1>
    <h3>* Required fields</h3>

    <div id="errors">
        <html:errors/>
    </div>

    <html:form action="saveReservation.do" method="post"
        styleId="reservationForm">

        <table border="0">
            <tbody>
                <tr>
                    <td>
                        <label>* Arrival Date:</label>
                    </td>
                    <td>
                        <html:text property="arrivalDate"
                            styleId="arrivalDate" onblur="validateForm();"/>
                    </td>
                </tr>
                <tr>
                    <td>
                        <label>* Departure Date:</label>
                    </td>
```

```
        <td>
            <html:text property="departDate"
                styleId="departDate" onblur="validateForm();"/>
        </td>
    </tr>
    <tr>
        <td>
            <label>* Smoking Preference:</label>
        </td>
        <td>
            <html:select property="smokingPref"
                                          styleId="smokingPref">

                <html:option value="">Select One</html:option>
                <html:option value="smoking">Smoking</html:option>
                <html:option value="Non Smoking">
                    Non Smoking
                </html:option>
            </html:select>
        </td>
    </tr>
    <tr>
        <td>
            <label>Special Requests:</label>
        </td>
        <td>
            <html:textarea property="requests"
                styleId="requests" rows="6" cols="50" />
        </td>
    </tr>
    <tr>
        <td>
            <label>* Name:</label>
        </td>
        <td>
            <html:text property="name"
                                            styleId="name" />
        </td>
    </tr>
    <tr>
```

```
                    <td>
                        <label>* Telephone:</label>
                    </td>
                    <td>
                        <html:text property="telephone"
                                                   styleId="telephone" />
                    </td>
                </tr>
                <tr>
                    <td colspan="2" align="center">
                        <input type="submit" value="Submit"/>
                    </td>
                </tr>
            </tbody>
        </table>
    </html:form>

    </body>
</html>
```

As you might expect, there is some input validation that needs to occur on this page. All of the fields are required except for the Special Requests text area. In addition, the arrival and departure dates must be valid date formats, and the telephone number must be a valid telephone format. The input elements are validated when the form is submitted, and if any of the validations fail then the page is redisplayed with the error messages shown at the top of the page. So far so good.

Are there any other validations that could occur other than the ones that were just mentioned? In this particular example, the answer is (as we say in Minnesota), "You betcha." The user will want to know as soon as possible whether the desired room is available. For example, the user may request a smoking room for a certain date range. If the hotel has rooms available for that date range, but only nonsmoking rooms, then the user should be told that the selected date range and smoking combination is not available. At that point the user could either choose different dates or try the other smoking selection. Wouldn't it be nice if the user could be told as soon as possible whether the selected date range and smoking selection yielded any available rooms?

Thanks to Ajax, we can indeed provide this functionality to the user. The simple input validations such as required fields being present or dates having the correct format could conceivably be done in the browser using some JavaScript, providing feedback before the user actually submits the form. In the case of checking room availability, we presumably need to access a server-side resource to determine whether the requested room is available. Ajax allows us to do just that without submitting the form.

The ordering of the input fields was specifically chosen to support this feature. By including the arrival and departure dates and the smoking preference as the first items on the page, the user will quickly see if the desired room is available. If it isn't, then the user can either change the selections or quit completely without having to fill in the other input fields.

## Ajax-Powered Validation

This example employs Ajax to determine whether the selected combination of rooms, dates, and smoking preference yield any available rooms. If there are no available rooms for the specified combination, then an error message should be shown to the user.

Since this example uses Ajax, there is bound to be some dreaded JavaScript required to make it work. This example uses the Prototype library that you learned about in Chapter 3 to take care of some of the more mundane JavaScript details like accessing input element values and creating and using XMLHttpRequest objects. You might be surprised to know that the JavaScript that makes all of this Ajax validation work is less than 50 lines long! Listing 5-2 shows the entire JavaScript source code used in this example.

**Listing 5-2.** *hotelReservation.js*

```javascript
function hasEntry(id) {
    return $F(id).length > 0;
}

function isFormReadyForValidation() {
    var ready = false;

    if(hasEntry("arrivalDate")
    && hasEntry("departDate")
    && $F("smokingPref").length > 0) {

        ready = true;
    }

    return ready;
}

function validateForm() {
    var isReady = isFormReadyForValidation();

    if(isReady) {
        sendFormForValidation();
    }
}
```

```
function sendFormForValidation() {
    var queryString = Form.serialize("reservationForm");
    queryString = queryString + "&ts=" + new Date().getTime();
    var url = "validateReservation.do";

    new Ajax.Request(url, {
        asynchronous: true,
        method: "get",
        parameters: queryString,
        onComplete: function(request) {
            handleResponse(request.responseText);
        }
    });
}


function handleResponse(text) {
    $("errors").innerHTML = text;
}
```

As you can see in Figure 5-2, there is only one button on the web page, and that is to submit the form to the server. So how is the Ajax validation actually invoked? If you refer back to Listing 5-1, you'll see that the arrival and departure dates and the smoking preference input fields all implement the onblur event handler. The onblur event handler invokes the specified JavaScript function whenever the input field loses focus. The idea is that the user will fill in the input fields in sequential order, and as soon as the arrival and departure dates and the smoking preference are filled in an Ajax request will be sent to the server to verify whether a room is available for the specified combination. The onblur event handlers for the arrival and departure dates and the smoking preference call the validateForm function shown in Listing 5-2.

The validateForm method first determines whether the arrival and departure dates and the smoking preference have been filled in by calling the isForReadyForValidation function. The isReadyForValidation function returns true if the arrival date, departure date, and smoking preference all have nonempty selections; it delegates to the hasEntry function for the arrival and departure dates.

Assuming that the isReadyForValidation function returns true, the validateForm function calls sendFormForValidation. The sendFormForValidation function handles the actual sending of the Ajax request. The function starts by using Prototype's Form.serialize method to build a query string of the form values to be sent to the server. Following that, the current time stamp is appended to the query string to ensure that the URL is unique to prevent the browser from caching the request.

With the query string ready to go, the sendFormForValidation function uses Prototype's Ajax.Request object to build and send the Ajax request. The Ajax request is sent to the validate.do URL using the GET method. It also specifies that the request be sent asynchronously and that the handleResponse function should be used to process the server's response. The handleResponse method simply updates the innerHTML property of a div at the top of the page to show the error messages (if any) returned by the server.

That's all the JavaScript that's required! Thanks to the Prototype library it takes less than 50 lines of code to implement this functionality, which is a small price to pay for the order of magnitude increase in richness and usability we are adding to the application.

The browser side is now done. You've seen the HTML that makes up the home page and the JavaScript that powers the Ajax request. Now you'll turn your attention to the server side where Struts will help us handle the request and perform the necessary validations.

## Implementing Struts

The client-side work with the JavaScript was the hardest part of this whole exercise. If you've ever worked with Struts or another action-based Web MVC framework the rest of this example will come very easily to you.

The heart of Struts is found in the struts-config.xml file. The struts-config.xml file is the glue that binds the various actions, action forms, requests, and validations together to make a usable web application. We'll be referring to this example's struts-config.xml file a lot over the next several pages, so it's best that you see it right away. Listing 5-3 shows the struts-config.xml file used in this example.

**Listing 5-3.** *struts-config.xml*

```xml
<?xml version="1.0" encoding="ISO-8859-1" ?>

<!DOCTYPE struts-config PUBLIC
        "-//Apache Software Foundation//DTD Struts Configuration 1.2//EN"
        "http://jakarta.apache.org/struts/dtds/struts-config_1_2.dtd">

<struts-config>

    <form-beans>
        <form-bean name="reservationForm"
        type="com.proajax.chapt5.validation.ui.ReservationForm"/>
    </form-beans>

    <action-mappings>
        <action path="/reservation"
            type="org.apache.struts.actions.ForwardAction"
            name="reservationForm"
            scope="request"
            parameter="/hotelReservation.jsp" />
```

```xml
    <action path="/validateReservation"
        type="com.proajax.chapt5.validation.ui.ValidateReservationAction"
        name="reservationForm" validate="true"
        input="/jsp/validation/reservationErrors.jsp" >
        <forward name="valid" path="/jsp/validation/blank.jsp"/>
        <forward name="invalid"
        path="/jsp/validation/reservationErrors.jsp"/>
    </action>

    <action path="/saveReservation"
        type="com.proajax.chapt5.validation.ui.SaveReservationAction"
        name="reservationForm"
        validate="true"
        input="/hotelReservation.jsp">

        <forward name="success"
        path="/jsp/validation/reservationSuccessful.jsp"/>

        <forward name="fail" path="/hotelReservation.jsp"/>
    </action>
</action-mappings>

<controller
processorClass="org.apache.struts.tiles.TilesRequestProcessor"/>

<message-resources parameter="MessageResources" />

<plug-in className="org.apache.struts.tiles.TilesPlugin" >

    <!-- Path to XML definition file -->
    <set-property property="definitions-config"
    value="/WEB-INF/tiles-defs.xml" />

    <!-- Set Module-awareness to true -->
    <set-property property="moduleAware" value="true" />
</plug-in>
```

```
<plug-in className="org.apache.struts.validator.ValidatorPlugIn">
    <set-property
    property="pathnames"
    value="/WEB-INF/validator-rules.xml,/WEB-INF/validation.xml"/>
</plug-in>
```

```
</struts-config>
```

This `struts-config.xml` file was constructed by modifying the file that's bundled with the blank Struts starter application that comes with the Struts download. The most important sections of this file are the `form-beans` and `action-mappings` elements. The `form-beans` element has zero to many `form-bean` child elements that declare the `ActionForm` classes that are used in the application.

For this application there is a single action form: the `ReservationForm` class. The `ReservationForm` class is a simple JavaBeans-style object that extends the `ValidatorActionForm` class and provides public getter and setter methods for each of the form elements. The `ReservationForm` class source code is shown in Listing 5-4.

**Listing 5-4.** *ReservationForm.java*

```java
package com.proajax.chapt5.validation.ui;

import java.text.DateFormat;
import java.text.ParseException;
import java.text.SimpleDateFormat;
import java.util.Date;
import javax.servlet.http.HttpServletRequest;
import org.apache.struts.action.ActionErrors;
import org.apache.struts.action.ActionMapping;
import org.apache.struts.action.ActionMessage;
import org.apache.struts.validator.ValidatorActionForm;

public class ReservationForm extends ValidatorActionForm {
    private String arrivalDate;
    private String departDate;
    private String smokingPref;
    private String requests;
    private String name;
    private String telephone;
    private DateFormat parser = new SimpleDateFormat("MM/dd/yyyy");
```

```java
public String getArrivalDate() {
    return arrivalDate;
}

public Date getArrivalDateAsDate() {
    try {
        return parser.parse(arrivalDate);
    }
    catch(ParseException e) {
        return null;
    }
}

public void setArrivalDate(String arrivalDate) {
    this.arrivalDate = arrivalDate;
}

public Date getDepartDateAsDate() {
    try {
        return parser.parse(departDate);
    }
    catch(ParseException e) {
        return null;
    }
}

public String getDepartDate() {
    return departDate;
}

public void setDepartDate(String departDate) {
    this.departDate = departDate;
}

public String getSmokingPref() {
    return smokingPref;
}

public void setSmokingPref(String smokingPref) {
    this.smokingPref = smokingPref;
}
```

```java
public boolean isSmokingRequest() {
    return smokingPref.equalsIgnoreCase("smoking");
}

public String getRequests() {
    return requests;
}

public void setRequests(String requests) {
    this.requests = requests;
}

public ActionErrors validate(ActionMapping mapping
        , HttpServletRequest request) {
    ActionErrors errors;

    errors = super.validate(mapping, request);

    DateFormat parser = new SimpleDateFormat("MM/dd/yyyy");
    try {
        Date arrival = parser.parse(arrivalDate);
        Date departure = parser.parse(departDate);

        if(departure.before(arrival)) {
            errors.add(ActionErrors.GLOBAL_MESSAGE
                    , new ActionMessage("errors.departure.before.arrival"
                    , true));
        }
    }
    catch (Exception e) {
        // Do nothing -- date format validation is handled in
        // validation.xml.
    }

    return errors;
}

public String getName() {
    return name;
}
```

```
    public void setName(String name) {
        this.name = name;
    }

    public String getTelephone() {
        return telephone;
    }

    public void setTelephone(String telephone) {
        this.telephone = telephone;
    }
}
```

Astute readers will notice that the ReservationForm class extends the Struts ValidatorActionForm class instead of the ValidatorForm class. This choice was quite deliberate. Both ValidatorActionForm and ValidatorForm provide basic field validation based on the validation.xml file. For the ValidatorActionForm, the key passed into the validator is the action element's path attribute, which should match the form-bean's name attribute. For the ValidatorForm, the key passed into the validator is the action element's name attribute, which should match the form-bean's name attribute. Put another way, extending ValidatorActionForm means that the validation rules from validation.xml (Listing 5-6) will be applied to requests based on the request's path; extending ValidatorForm means that validation rules from validation.xml will be applied to requests based on the form bean used by the request.

The real meat of the struts-config.xml file comes in the action-mappings section. Each individual action element is the real glue that binds a request to its form bean and specifies the location to where the request should be directed following the handling of the request by the Action class. The first action listed is the reservation action, which simply displays the empty reservation page.

The next action in Listing 5-4 is the validateReservation action. You probably recall that this action is the destination URL of the Ajax request from Listing 5-2 that handles the validation of the arrival and departure dates and smoking preference combination. There's a lot going on in this action mapping, so we'll try to break it down and explain it piece by piece.

The validateReservation action is configured by the name attribute to use the reservationForm form bean—no surprises there. The validate attribute is set to true so that the form bean's validate method is called before calling the Action object.

The input attribute of the validateReservation action is a key piece of the puzzle. The input attribute tells Struts the response to send if any validation exceptions were recorded. In non-Ajax applications this attribute usually points to the same page that submitted the request to the action. In non-Ajax applications the JSP that submitted the request often uses the Struts custom JSP tags to list the error messages when the page is rendered. However, this example uses Ajax, so the entire page will not be redrawn if any validation errors occur. Instead, only a small section of the page will be updated to list the error messages. Refer back to Listing 5-1. At the top of the page there is a div tag with an id attribute value of errors. This is the area in which any errors that are returned by the server will be placed. You should also recall that the handleResponse JavaScript function in Listing 5-2 updates the errors div with the response from the server.

For the validateReservation action the input attribute points to the reservationErrors.jsp file, which is shown in Listing 5-5. It uses the Struts custom tags to render any error messages that have been logged during the validation routine. Since this is an Ajax request that will only update a small part of the page, that's the only output it needs to render.

**Listing 5-5.** *reservationErrors.jsp*

```
<%@taglib uri="http://struts.apache.org/tags-logic" prefix="logic" %>
<%@taglib uri="http://struts.apache.org/tags-html" prefix="html" %>
<%@taglib uri="http://struts.apache.org/tags-bean" prefix="bean" %>

<logic:messagesPresent>
    <ul>
        <html:messages id="error">
            <li style="color:red;">
                <bean:write name="error"/>
            </li>
        </html:messages>
    </ul>
</logic:messagesPresent>
```

The error messages are built as an unordered list. This example uses the logic:messagesPresent, html:messages, and bean:write tags to build the unordered list of errors. Another option is to simply use the html:errors JSP tag, but the HTML markup for this tag must be specified in the messages properties file.

The validateReservation action has two forward elements: one for the valid case (when no validation messages were recorded) and one for the invalid case. The path for the valid case is a JSP file named blank.jsp. As its name suggests, this file contains almost no content—in fact, its only contents are a nonbreaking space. The nonbreaking space blanks out any messages that may already exist on the page. For example, if the user entered a date in an invalid format and received a validation error saying as much, the error message should be removed from the page as soon as the user fixes the date and tabs off of the input field.

Whew! That brings us to the end of the validateReservation action in the struts-config.xml file. There are a lot of things happening in those eight lines of XML, so if you're still a little foggy on some of the items, you should reread this section until you feel comfortable with what's happening.

Now is a good time to talk about the actual validation implementation. For the past several pages you've been hearing about how user input will be validated using an Ajax request, and you've seen how the struts-config.xml file was set up to wire everything together, but so far you haven't seen the actual validation implementation. Remember the discussion earlier regarding the different ways by which Struts can validate form input, that it could be done through Commons Validator, the form bean's validate method, or even the Action class itself? This example uses a combination of all three. Simple format validation occurs using Commons Validator with the validation rules described in the validation.xml file. Input validation that is too complex for Commons Validator happens in the form bean's validate method. Finally, validation that requires accessing the service and data tiers occurs in the Action class.

You can think of Commons Validator and its integration with Struts as the first line of defense when it comes to input validation. Without writing a line of Java code you cover a large portion of your application's validation needs by editing an XML file. This example uses Commons Validator to perform the simple formatting validations that must occur whenever form input is submitted to the server, whether it be through an Ajax request or a normal form submission.

Listing 5-6 lists the validation.xml file used in this example. This example validates two types of form submissions: the Ajax request that validates the arrival and departure dates format and whether their combination with the smoking preference yields any available rooms, and the "normal" form submission where the entire form is submitted.

**Listing 5-6.** *validation.xml*

```
<?xml version="1.0" encoding="ISO-8859-1" ?>

<!DOCTYPE form-validation PUBLIC
    "-//Apache Software Foundation//DTD Commons Validator Rules
     Configuration 1.1.3//EN"
     "http://jakarta.apache.org/commons/dtds/validator_1_1_3.dtd">

<form-validation>

    <global>
      <constant>
        <constant-name>phoneFormat</constant-name>

        <constant-value>^\(?\d{3}\)?\s|-\d{3}-\d{4}$</constant-value>
      </constant>
```

```xml
  <constant>
    <constant-name>dateFormat</constant-name>

    <constant-value>^\d{1,2}/\d{1,2}/\d{4}$</constant-value>
  </constant>
</global>

<formset>

    <form name="/validateReservation">
        <field property="arrivalDate" depends="required, mask">
            <msg key="errors.date" name="mask"/>
            <arg0 key="label.arrival.date" resource="true"/>
            <arg1 key="format.date"/>
            <var>
                <var-name>mask</var-name>
                <var-value>${dateFormat}</var-value>
            </var>
        </field>

        <field property="departDate" depends="required, date">
            <msg key="errors.date" name="mask"/>
            <arg0 key="label.depart.date" resource="true"/>
            <arg1 key="format.date"/>
            <var>
                <var-name>mask</var-name>
                <var-value>${dateFormat}</var-value>
            </var>
        </field>
    </form>

    <form name="/saveReservation">
        <field property="arrivalDate" depends="required, mask">
            <msg key="errors.date" name="mask"/>
            <arg0 key="label.arrival.date" resource="true"/>
            <arg1 key="format.date"/>
            <var>
                <var-name>mask</var-name>
                <var-value>${dateFormat}</var-value>
            </var>
        </field>
```

```
                <field property="departDate" depends="required, mask">
                    <msg key="errors.date" name="mask"/>
                    <arg0 key="label.depart.date" resource="true"/>
                    <arg1 key="format.date"/>
                    <var>
                        <var-name>mask</var-name>
                        <var-value>${dateFormat}</var-value>
                    </var>
                </field>

                <field property="smokingPref" depends="required">
                    <arg0 key="label.smoking.pref" resource="true"/>
                </field>

                <field property="name" depends="required">
                    <arg0 key="label.name" resource="true"/>
                </field>

                <field property="telephone" depends="required, mask">
                    <msg key="errors.invalid.telephone.format" name="mask"/>
                    <arg0 key="label.telephone" resource="true"/>
                    <var>
                        <var-name>mask</var-name>
                        <var-value>${phoneFormat}</var-value>
                    </var>
                </field>

        </form>
    </formset>

</form-validation>
```

The first form listed is the validateReservation form. This form is identified by the name attribute on the form element. Because the ReservationForm class extends ValidatorActionForm, the name attribute of the form element refers to the URL to which the request is sent—in this case, validateReservation.do. The validation that occurs on this form is the format of the arrival and departure dates and that the arrival and departure dates and smoking preference are required. Figure 5-3 shows the error messages that occur when the user enters invalid arrival and departure dates, selects a smoking preference, and tabs off of the smoking preference select field.

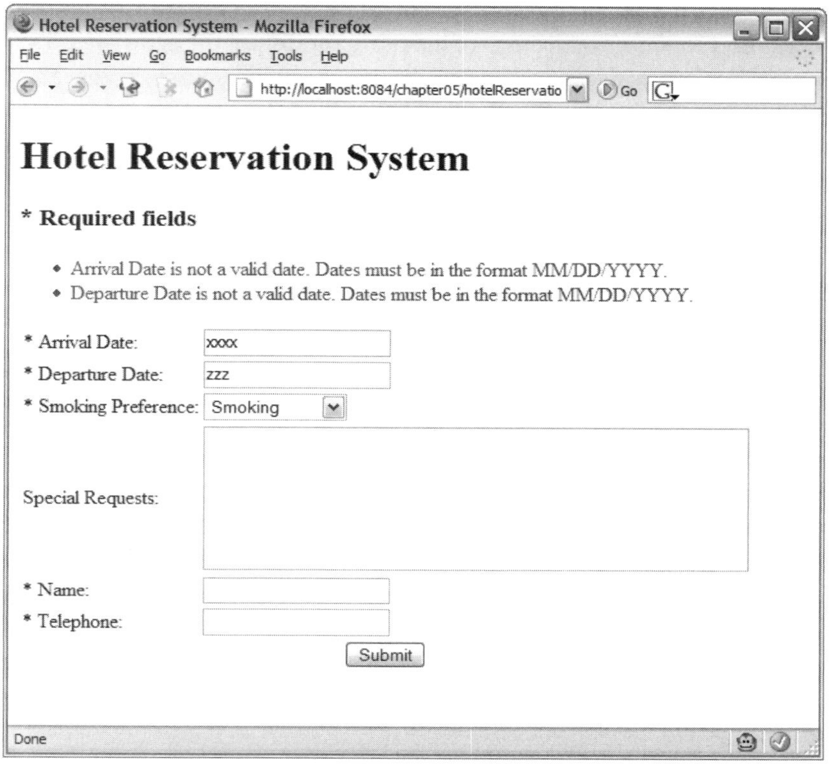

**Figure 5-3.** *The error messages generated by invalid date formats submitted via Ajax*

The second form, which is identified by the saveReservation name attribute, performs the validation for when the complete form is explicitly submitted by the user using the Submit button. It includes the same validation for the arrival and departure dates as the validateReservation form but adds required validations for the name and telephone number in addition to validating the format of the telephone number.

## ALWAYS VALIDATE USER INPUT ON FORM SUBMISSION

Be sure to always validate user input when the form is submitted to the server, even if the form's fields have been validated using Ajax techniques. Why?

The user may be able to disable validation via Ajax but won't be able to disable validation on the server. The user could have JavaScript disabled within the browser, which would render the validation via Ajax useless. Major problems could occur if the form is submitted with invalid data due to the failure of Ajax validation. However, if the form validations are repeated on the server when the form is submitted, then these problems will be avoided.

This example uses regular expressions to validate the date and telephone formats whose formats are listed as constants at the top of the file. In addition, the error messages and labels are externalized to a properties file named `MessageResources.properties`. Note that this file is specified in the `struts-config.xml` file! This file holds the standard error message format used by Commons Validator, and user-defined messages can also be placed here. Listing 5-7 lists the custom labels and error messages added the standard `MessageResources.properties` file.

**Listing 5-7.** *Additions to the* `MessageResources.properties` *File Specific to This Example*

```
label.arrival.date=Arrival Date
label.depart.date=Departure Date
label.smoking.pref=Smoking Preference
label.name=Name
label.telephone=Telephone Number

format.date=MM/DD/YYYY

errors.departure.before.arrival=Arrival date must occur before departure date.
errors.invalid.date.format=Invalid date format.
errors.invalid.telephone.format=Invalid telephone format.
errors.reservation.not.available=The requested reservation is not available.
```

You've now seen the first layer of validation that was performed by Commons Validator. The next layer of validation occurs in the form bean itself. Refer back the source code for the `ReservationForm` class shown in Listing 5-4. Here, the `validate` method ensures that the arrival date entered by the user occurs before the entered departure date. We don't want potential guests to check out before they arrive. This is a great example of a validation that isn't easily handled by Commons Validator but can be easily accomplished with Java code.

If no validation errors were recorded by Commons Validator or the `validate` method of the `ReservationForm`, then the request is passed to the `Action` handler. The Ajax request is handled by the `ValidateReservationAction` class. This class extends the Struts `Action` class and overrides the `execute` method to validate the combination of arrival date, departure date, and smoking preference submitted by the user. More specifically, the `execute` method accesses the service tier and asks it to verify whether any rooms are available for the request arrival and departure dates and smoking preference. The source code for the `ValidateReservationAction` class is shown in Listing 5-8.

**Listing 5-8.** *ValidateReservationAction.java*

```java
package com.proajax.chapt5.validation.ui;

import com.proajax.chapt5.service.ReservationService;
import javax.servlet.http.HttpServletRequest;
import javax.servlet.http.HttpServletResponse;
import org.apache.struts.action.Action;
import org.apache.struts.action.ActionForm;
import org.apache.struts.action.ActionForward;
import org.apache.struts.action.ActionMapping;
import org.apache.struts.action.ActionMessage;
import org.apache.struts.action.ActionMessages;

public class ValidateReservationAction extends  Action {


    public ActionForward execute(ActionMapping mapping, ActionForm actionForm
            , HttpServletRequest request, HttpServletResponse response)
            throws Exception {

        ReservationForm form = (ReservationForm) actionForm;

        ReservationService service = new ReservationService();
        boolean isAvailable =
                service.isReservationAvailable(form.getArrivalDateAsDate()
                    , form.getDepartDateAsDate()
                    , form.isSmokingRequest());

        ActionMessages errors = this.getErrors(request);
        if(!isAvailable) {
            errors.add(ActionMessages.GLOBAL_MESSAGE
                    , new ActionMessage("errors.reservation.not.available"
                    , true));
        }
        saveErrors(request, errors);

        ActionForward forward = null;
        if(errors.size() > 0) {
            forward = mapping.findForward("invalid");
        }
```

```
        else {
            forward = mapping.findForward("valid");
        }
        return forward;
    }
}
```

The Action class is the most logical place to put this type of validation routine. Because it requires Java code, it can't be done by Commons Validator, at least not without writing a custom validator class. It could technically be done in the form bean, but this doesn't make sense because the form bean is intended to be a fairly "dumb" object that doesn't contain too much business logic. The Action, however, is intended from the start to be the bridge between the web tier and the service and data tiers. Since this validation requires accessing a database to see if the requested room is available, it makes the most sense to place the validation here in the Action class.

You've probably noticed that the execute method doesn't actually perform any of the validation itself. Instead, it calls on a ReservationService object that performs the actual lookup to see if there is a room available matching the requested arrival and departure and smoking preference. To keep the example simple, this method uses a random algorithm that will indicate that the desired room is unavailable approximately one-third of the time. The source code for the ReservationService is shown in Listing 5-9.

**Listing 5-9.** *ReservationService.java*

```
package com.proajax.chapt5.service;

import com.proajax.chapt5.exception.ReservationNotAvailableException;
import java.util.Date;
import java.util.Random;

public class ReservationService {
    private static Random random = new Random();

    public boolean isReservationAvailable(Date arrival, Date departure
            , boolean isSmoking) {

        //Of course a real implementation would actually check if the desired
        //reservation was available. Here, just do it randomly so the
        //reservation is unavailable about 1/3 of the time.

        return ! ((random.nextInt(100) % 3) == 0);
    }
```

```
    public void saveReservation(Date arrival, Date departure
            , boolean isSmoking, String requests
            , String name, String telephone)
            throws ReservationNotAvailableException {

        if(!isReservationAvailable(arrival, departure, isSmoking)) {
            throw new ReservationNotAvailableException();
        }

        // Logic to actually save the reservation goes here.
    }
}
```

Over the last several pages we've discussed a lot of concepts and code, so we should step back for a minute and think about what we've been trying to accomplish. The main goal of this example is to provide Ajax-enabled form validation so that the user can receive immediate feedback regarding their input into the form. Not only does the validation perform simple validations like ensuring that input dates are in the correct format, but also that the requested combination of arrival date, departure date, and smoking preference yield an available room. Ajax is used to submit these three items to the server for validation as soon as the user tabs off any of the three fields. If the user enters valid dates for the arrival and departure dates, selects a smoking preference, and tabs off of the smoking preference select field, and the server determines that a room matching that combination is not available, an error message alerting the user to this fact is displayed at the top of the page, as shown in Figure 5-4.

Of course, this mini-application wouldn't be complete if the user couldn't actually try to save a reservation. After entering all of the required information, the user can click the Submit button to save the reservation. Of course, all of the input validation executes to ensure that all of the required input fields have valid selections and that dates and telephone numbers are in the correct format. You've already seen these validations in the validation.xml file and in the form bean's validate method.

The struts-config.xml file is configured to send the save request to the SaveReservationAction class. As in the ValidateReservationAction class you saw before, this class extends the Struts Action class and overrides the execute method. The execute method attempts to save the request reservation to the database by delegating the task to the saveReservation method of the ReservationService class, which you saw previously in Listing 5-9. Notice how the saveReservation method still checks to make sure that the requested reservation is still available. If it's not, a ReservationNotAvailableException is thrown and an error message is displayed.

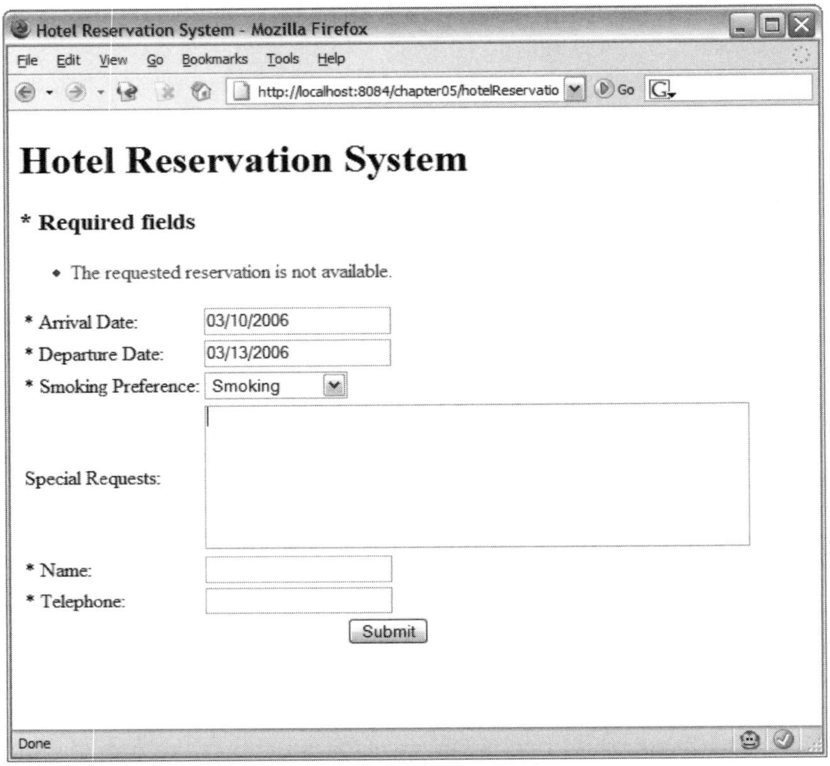

**Figure 5-4.** *The user is immediately alerted if the requested room is not available, thanks to Ajax.*

If all of the input data is in the correct format and a reservation is available, the reservation is saved and the user is shown a confirmation page. The confirmation page, shown in Listing 5-10, simply echoes the data entered by the user. The results of a successful reservation are shown in Figure 5-5.

**Listing 5-10.** *reservationSuccessful.jsp*

```
<!DOCTYPE html PUBLIC "-//W3C//DTD XHTML 1.0 Strict//EN"
                    "http://www.w3.org/TR/xhtml1/DTD/xhtml1-strict.dtd">

<html xmlns="http://www.w3.org/1999/xhtml">
    <head>
        <title>Hotel Reservation Confirmed</title>
    </head>
    <body>
```

```
<h1>
    Congratulations! Your reservation is confirmed.
</h1>
<ul>
    <li>Arrival Date: ${reservationForm.arrivalDate}</li>
    <li>Departure Date: ${reservationForm.departDate}</li>
    <li>Smoking Preference: ${reservationForm.smokingPref}</li>
    <li>Special Requests: ${reservationForm.requests}</li>
    <li>Name: ${reservationForm.name}</li>
    <li>Telephone: ${reservationForm.telephone}</li>
</ul>

</body>
</html>
```

**Figure 5-5.** *A successful reservation*

## Struts and Ajax Design Considerations

The example presented in this chapter represents an in-depth case study of integrating Ajax into Struts-based applications. You've seen how the existing features of Struts can be expanded and given new life with the addition of Ajax techniques.

This example showed building an application from the ground up that leveraged Ajax in specific areas to enhance the user experience. However, this functionality could have been just as easily added to an existing application. Imagine for a moment how this application would have worked without Ajax: there would have been no immediate feedback to the user if the requested room combination (arrival date, departure date, and smoking preference) was not available. The user would have completed the entire form, clicked the

Submit button, and then if the requested room was not available, the page would have been re-rendered with the error message at the top of the page.

In this scenario, the code making up the application would be nearly identical to the Ajax-enabled version. The application would still have the JSPs that render the user interface, an `ActionForm` that contained the user input, an `Action` that handled the Submit request, a service that actually performed the work of making the reservation, and simple form validation using Commons Validator.

The Ajax-enabled version simply adds a new `Action` that specifically handles the Ajax request and a couple of JSPs to render the Ajax response. The `validation.xml` file includes validation for the Ajax request, and even those rules are near-copies of the rules for the complete form submission. It was all topped off with less than 50 lines of JavaScript to make it all work, and that JavaScript is trivial in nature thanks to the use of the Prototype library. The solution demonstrated here also degrades gracefully when JavaScript is disabled in the browser. If JavaScript is disabled, the `onblur` event handlers will never be invoked, preventing the Ajax validation from occurring. However, the form is still validated when it's submitted to the server, which prevents errors caused by invalid input.

The point is that adding Ajax to your existing Struts applications can be a relatively straightforward task that will likely produce a chorus of applause from your users. In the days before Struts became popular, building web applications was rather difficult due to the necessity of working with the low-level servlet API. Struts removed many of the barriers to rapidly building web applications using Java. No longer was it necessary to build a slew of servlet classes and constantly modify the `web.xml` file with each new servlet.

With Struts easing the burden of working with the servlet API, you can exploit it by using Ajax to asynchronously communicate from the browser to the server. Struts makes it easy to write code on the server side that handles the incoming Ajax request. In fact, if you're adding Ajax to an existing Struts application, you'll likely only have to write a new `Action` class and wire it together with existing objects and services.

Because of this, there's no reason not to add some Ajax goodness to your existing Struts applications. Search your applications for areas in which the entire page is refreshed for the sake of updating a small part of the page. Possible examples of this include displaying simple validation messages, sorting a table in response to the user clicking a table header, or adding the results of a search to the page. Your users will love you for updating these scenarios to use Ajax instead of the traditional full-page refresh. Struts makes it easy to build the server-side components, and combined with any of the Ajax frameworks and libraries you've seen from previous chapters, you can add Ajax to your applications in no time with minimal fuss.

# The Future of Struts

A contemporary discussion of Struts would not be complete without discussing the future of Struts development, support, and adoption. At the time of this writing Struts is over five years old, and many within the development community consider Struts to be a legacy framework. The problems they cite with Struts include the inability to use domain objects without duplicate form objects, the difficulty testing Struts modules outside of the container, and the forced inheritance of `ActionForms` and `Actions`, among others.

In addition to the number of modern, direct competitors to Struts, including Spring MVC, Wicket, and Tapestry, there are a few projects whose goal is to build the "next generation" of Struts. We'll briefly take a look at some of these projects so you can get a feel for what's happening it the Struts development world.

## Struts 1.3 and Beyond

Even though the current Struts `Action` framework is considered by some to be legacy code, there are still plans to keep improving it as long as volunteers are willing to do so.

The Struts 1.x Roadmap (`http://struts.apache.org/struts-action/roadmap.html`) lists several possible improvements to Struts. Struts 1.3 aims to implement the "Struts Chain" request processor, meaning that Struts would implement the Chain of Responsibility design pattern for handling requests. This design would be more flexible than the current `Action`-based request handling.

Other potential enhancements to Struts 1.x include support for portlets, combining DTDs, a populate method on the `ActionForm`, support for multiple controllers, and an alternate configuration file.

## Struts Shale

Shale (`http://struts.apache.org/struts-shale`) is a proposal for a modern web application that is fundamentally based on JavaServer Faces. Its goal is to ease the adoption of JavaServer Faces for developers and to provide fine-grained service options that can be combined and extended to meet complex application requirements. The core technologies on which Shale is based are JDK 1.4, servlet API 2.4, JSP 2.0, and JavaServer Faces 1.1.

Shale includes the following features (and more):

- A `ViewController` that backs a Java class with each JavaServer Faces view that provides predefined event handlers for events significant to an application.

- A Dialog Manager that defines a conversation with a user that requires multiple HTTP requests.

- The Application Manager is a traditional application-wide front controller that applies features to every HTTP request.

- Built-in support for Ajax.

- Integration with the Spring framework.

- A built-in test framework consisting of mock objects and a JUnit test case base.

As you can see, Shale is being designed and built from the ground up to be a modern and full-featured MVC framework that utilizes the latest techniques and technologies. Since it's fundamentally based on JavaServer Faces, you'll want to check out Shale if you plan on making use of JavaServer Faces.

## Struts Ti

The goal of Struts Ti (`http://wiki.apache.org/struts/StrutsTi`) is to build a simplified MVC framework that allows the developer better access to the underlying servlet environment. The key goal of Struts Ti is simplicity and it aims to provide the same level of ease of use as Ruby on Rails.

The major announcement of Struts Ti is that it includes a merger between Struts and WebWork (`www.opensymphony.com/webwork`), meaning that Struts Ti will start with the WebWork 2.2 code base. Another goal of Struts Ti is to provide a Struts 1.x compatibility layer to assist in migrating applications to the new framework.

At the time of this writing Struts Ti is in the Struts sandbox for possible eventual acceptance as a Struts subproject. The Struts Ti developers warn that Struts Ti is not yet an official Struts subproject and that it not ready for operational use.

# Summary

As the granddaddy of all Java web MVC frameworks, Struts has built up a loyal following of developers and has innumerable applications built on top of it. Struts frees the developer from having to write directly to the servlet API and constantly edit the `web.xml` file. Struts provides built-in support for validation, internationalization, and a set of JSP custom tags that ease the burden of building rich, web-enabled Java applications.

Ajax integrates very easily with Struts. An Ajax request can call any Struts action by simply sending the request to the correct URL. Once there, the Ajax request is handled the same as any other HTTP request. This, of course, means that the Ajax request has the same access to the Struts validation routines, form beans, and actions, and the benefits provided by each.

Struts and Ajax work very well together, and existing Struts applications can be easily extended by adding Ajax functionality. In many cases Ajax-style interactions can be added to an existing Struts application by adding an `Action` that reuses existing functionality.

# CHAPTER 6

■■■

# Tapestry

Tapestry (http://jakarta.apache.org/tapestry) is an open source framework developed by Howard Lewis Ship. Inspired by Apple's WebObjects framework, the central goal of Tapestry is to make the easiest choice, the right choice. Tapestry puts a stateful, component-based model on top of the stateless, operation-centric model of Java servlets following an approach that is more familiar to traditional desktop-style application programming. The Tapestry framework hides things like HttpSession, HttpServletRequest, and form parameters, allowing developers to focus on components, data, and business logic.

Tapestry applications are simply pages made up of components. With Tapestry, you write HTML pages with little bits of Java code. Tapestry applications are developed in a true object-oriented manner—you create Java objects with methods and properties; you don't concern yourself with URLs and parameters. Tapestry includes a number of components; however, building new ones is a relatively simple task.

Tapestry has four key philosophical principles driven by the overall goal of making the simple choice the correct one:[1]

- Simplicity—Developing web applications shouldn't be impossible; the Java you write is to support your business logic.

- Consistency—Similar problems should have the same solution regardless of the developer.

- Efficiency—Tapestry applications scale and perform well.

- Feedback—When errors do happen, Tapestry provides helpful error messages.

## What Is Tapestry?

Tapestry sits between the servlet container (which thinks of Tapestry as nothing more than another servlet) and your Tapestry-based application. In the classic model-view-controller

---

1. http://jakarta.apache.org/tapestry/#What+is+Tapestry%27s+philosophy%3F

architecture, Tapestry represents the view. While we will focus on HTML, Tapestry is just as happy to serve up XML or WML.

Instead of dealing with the standard servlet API, with Tapestry you write listener methods that are wired to components. These listener methods *do* something on your behalf—such as look up a product in the database, select the next page, and update a row. The typical web application plumbing (session management, dispatching and forwarding, and so on) is handled by Tapestry. Unlike standard operation-centric servlet- or Struts-based web applications, at its core Tapestry is focused on components. Rather than writing a specific servlet to edit an item, with Tapestry you use an existing component that you configure to call a listener method that takes care of your business logic. And unlike other frameworks, with Tapestry, you only need to focus on the listener method. Tapestry figures out when to call your method, what data you need, and how to wire your method to the framework.

Before we go too much further, let's define some common Tapestry terms (please see Table 6-1).

**Table 6-1.** *Common Tapestry Terms*

| Term | Definition |
| --- | --- |
| Page | Tapestry applications are made up of pages, each of which has a template and includes any number of components. |
| Template | A template contains HTML along with special marker tags for Tapestry components. |
| Component | Components are reusable objects that generate HTML when the page is rendered. Components can be made up of other components (to any depth necessary). Some components handle incoming requests, while others facilitate working with forms. |
| Parameter | A component may be bound to a parameter—a value that can be set and retrieved. |
| Bound | The relationship between a component parameter and a value. |
| Engine | The Engine is the central object and is responsible for storing and retrieving the session state of the application. (Essentially, it replaces the HttpSession object in traditional servlet-based applications.) |
| Engine services | Engine services maps Tapestry to the URLs and servlets. They dispatch incoming requests, interpret query results, and encode URLs. |
| Visit object | The Visit object is application-specific and is the way applications access server-side state. The Visit object is a property of the Engine. |
| Global object | Like the Visit object, the Global object is application-specific and is used for storing information that is pertinent to the entire application. |
| OGNL | Object Graph Navigation Language, a Java-based expression language similar to the expression language found in the JavaServer Pages 2.0 specification. |

## WHAT IS OGNL?

Object Graph Navigation Language (www.ognl.org) is an open source expression language that is used to set and retrieve properties of a Java object. OGNL was created as a way to associate UI components and corresponding controllers and though similar to the expression language created with the JSP 2.0 specification, it predates this. Besides Tapestry, OGNL is used by other frameworks such as WebWork and Spring.

OGNL expressions are typically a collection of property names strung together and separated by periods. For example, instead of writing something like getFoo().getBar().getFooBar(), OGNL allows you to say foo.bar.fooBar. However, OGNL is much more powerful than just simple property access. Expressions can be made up of mathematical expressions, and they can invoke methods. Using OGNL, you can create new objects, and you can reference static fields.

# Getting Started

The current release (4.0) of Tapestry requires JDK 1.5 and, to build the examples, Ant 1.6.2 or higher. Navigate to http://jakarta.apache.org/site/downloads/ downloads_tapestry.cgi and download the appropriate archive. Tapestry has a number of dependent libraries (found at http://jakarta.apache.org/tapestry/ dependencies.html), including Commons Logging, HiveMind, and OGNL, that will need to be in the WEB-INF/lib directory of your servlet container. You can either download these yourself or use the Tapestry Ant build script. Once you have all the JARs in place, we can get started on a simple Hello World example.

For better or worse, any time we learn a new language we usually start with the prototypical Hello World example. (Basically, we'll run you through the Quick Start tutorials found at http://jakarta.apache.org/tapestry/QuickStart/helloworld.html). First off, all Tapestry applications have a Home page. It's where the application starts. To begin, we need to create an HTML template called Home.html that is at the root of our web context (see Listing 6-1).

**Listing 6-1.** *Hello World*

```
<html>
  <head>
    <title>Tapestry: Hello World</title>
  </head>
  <body>
    <h1>Tapestry Hello World</h1>
  </body>
</html>
```

Next, we need to configure the Tapestry servlet in the deployment descriptor (see Listing 6-2). The servlet name isn't that important, but for simplicity, the URL pattern has to be /app. (This can be configured if you wish.)

**Listing 6-2.** *Configuring the Tapestry Servlet*

```
<servlet>
    <servlet-name>app</servlet-name>
    <servlet-class>org.apache.tapestry.ApplicationServlet</servlet-class>
    <load-on-startup>0</load-on-startup>
</servlet>
<servlet-mapping>
    <servlet-name>app</servlet-name>
    <url-pattern>/app</url-pattern>
</servlet-mapping>
```

Before we go any further, deploy this code, fire up your server, and point your favorite browser to something similar to this: http://localhost:8084/helloTapestry/app. If everything is configured properly, you'll see something like Figure 6-1.

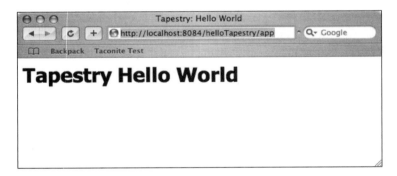

**Figure 6-1.** *Hello World*

Of course this isn't very interesting, and it doesn't really do anything that can't be done with just static HTML. To make this a little more interesting, let's display the current date and time, which in Tapestry means we'll need to add a component. Tapestry components basically look like standard HTML tags except they have additional attributes. For this example, we'll add an instance of the Insert component, which allows us to, well, insert text into the HTML response. We'll provide this component with a value using OGNL. Here, we'll be creating an instance of java.util.Date(). When all is said and done, our HTML page will look something like Listing 6-3.

**Listing 6-3.** *A More Dynamic Example*

```html
<html>
  <head>
    <title>Tapestry: Hello World</title>
  </head>
  <body>
    <h1>Tapestry Hello World</h1>
    <p>
    The current data and time is:
    <strong>
      <span jwcid="@Insert" value="ognl:new java.util.Date()"/>
    </strong>
    </p>
  </body>
</html>
```

Running this code looks something like Figure 6-2. Click the Refresh button and you'll see that the time stamp is updated.

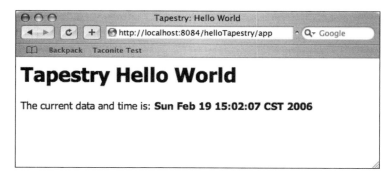

**Figure 6-2.** *Showing today's date and time*

Let's take a closer look at this code. We've already discussed the Insert component. It simply takes the text from the value and puts it into the response. The real magic here is in the OGNL expression `ognl:new java.util.Date()`. So what does this mean? Well, the first part, `ognl`, tells Tapestry that this is an expression and needs to be evaluated. As you would expect, the `new` keyword creates an instance of the class (in this case a `java.util.Date()`), which is then said to be bound to the value parameter of the Insert component. Notice what we didn't have to do here—we didn't have to figure out *how* to render the response or convert the date into a string; the component took care of that for us. Here, the Insert component takes the property of the value parameter (the current date and time), converts it to a string, and renders the appropriate HTML.

Web applications typically are made up of links to other pages, and as you would expect, Tapestry has a set of components to deal with that. For simplicity, let's add a link that refreshes the page. Add the following code into your Home.html template file:

```
<a href="#" jwcid="@PageLink" page="Home">refresh</a>
```

Adding this code will result in something like Figure 6-3, and clicking the link will refresh our page, thus updating the time stamp. If we look at the source code of the page, we'll see that the PageLink component took care of generating the URL, and it will look something like this: /helloTapestry/app?page=Home&amp;service=page. Of course we easily could have hard-coded this value into our page. However, Tapestry is taking care of the session encoding, and it's creating the proper format for the URL.

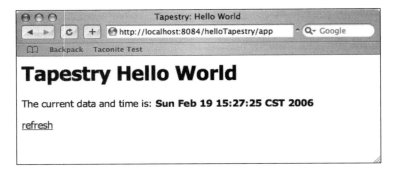

**Figure 6-3.** *Adding the refresh link*

# Calling the Server

While calling standard Java classes has its uses, more often than not, we want to invoke our own server-side logic. To do this, we'll use one of the most commonly used components in Tapestry, DirectLink. This will also expose us to some of the various Tapestry classes. Once again, we'll start with the Home.html (see Listing 6-4) file, which won't look a lot different than the one we created for the Hello World example.[2]

**Listing 6-4.** *Using DirectLink*

```
<html>
  <head>
    <title>Tapestry: Invoking Server Side Logic</title>
  </head>
  <body>
```

---

2. You can choose to either modify the Hello World example or create a brand new project.

```
    <h1>Tapestry Invoking Server Side Logic</h1>
    The current value is:
    <strong>
        <span jwcid="@Insert" value="ognl:counter" />
    </strong>
        <a href="#" jwcid="increment@DirectLink"
            listener="listener:incrementCounter">Increment</a>
  </body>
</html>
```

You should notice a couple of immediate differences. First, while we're using the same Insert component from before, the OGNL looks a little different: here instead of new, we're referencing counter. In the Hello World example, we were creating a new instance of the Java Date class, while here we want to read a property called counter. The next difference is the inclusion of the DirectLink component, which lets us invoke a method specified in the listener attribute. When this link is clicked, the incrementCounter method will be called.

Now that we've got the template created, let's turn our attention to our Java class and convention. The Java class name matches the page name, so we'll create Home.java (see Listing 6-5).

**Listing 6-5.** *The Home.java Class*

```java
package com.proajax.chapt6;

import org.apache.tapestry.annotations.Persist;
import org.apache.tapestry.html.BasePage;

public abstract class Home extends BasePage {
    @Persist
    public abstract int getCounter();
    public abstract void setCounter(int counter);

    public void incrementCounter() {
        int counter = getCounter();
        counter++;
        setCounter(counter);
    }
}
```

A couple of things should jump out at you as you read this code. First, the class is declared abstract. In the Tapestry world, pages are pooled (like database connections) and reused, meaning they need to have any user- and request-specific state stripped from them before entering the pool. While you could always take the time to write the appropriate code to do this yourself, we prefer to let Tapestry take care of the details.

Next, you'll notice we've extended from `BasePage` adding a couple of abstract methods and the `incrementCounter` method we discussed when we created the HTML template. You can clearly see that we're using the `@Persist` annotation on the `getCounter` method. This tells Tapestry that we want the value stored in the session between requests. Adding this simple annotation is a tad easier than hand-rolling the session management in a traditional web application.

### WHAT ARE ANNOTATIONS?

Annotations were added to Java in the 1.5 release of the language. They look a lot like standard Javadoc tags like `@author`, but they provide additional metadata about your code. The general idea of annotations is to replace much of the boilerplate code that is often found in Java programs with easy-to-use tags that are used by a tool or library to generate the necessary code on your behalf.

Tapestry includes a number of annotations (see `http://jakarta.apache.org/tapestry/tapestry-annotations/index.html` for details) that can simplify using pages or components. Keep in mind that using multiple annotations on a given method is not advised and that conflicts between an annotation and the specifications of a component will result in runtime exceptions. Of course to take advantage of annotations you will need to develop with the 1.5 JDK. For more on annotations, please see `http://java.sun.com/j2se/1.5.0/docs/guide/language/annotations.html`.

OK, so now we've got some HTML and some Java. How do we wire them together? To do this, we need to create an application specification. Basically, this is just a bit of XML that sits in our application's `WEB-INF` folder and is named `app.application` where app is the name of the Tapestry servlet. It will look a little something like Listing 6-6. This file tells Tapestry which Java packages to search for page-related classes.

**Listing 6-6.** *The `app.application` File*

```
<?xml version="1.0"?>
<!DOCTYPE application PUBLIC
  "-//Apache Software Foundation//Tapestry Specification 4.0//EN"
  "http://jakarta.apache.org/tapestry/dtd/Tapestry_4_0.dtd">

<application>
  <meta key="org.apache.tapestry.page-class-packages" value="com.proajax.chapt6"/>
</application>
```

At this point, we can run our application. If all went well, we should see something like Figure 6-4. As you would expect, clicking on the Increment link does indeed increase the counter.

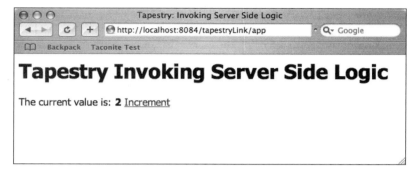

**Figure 6-4.** *Invoking server-side logic*

Of course it sure would be nice if we could reset the counter, so let's add the necessary code to do so. With Tapestry, this is really quite trivial. First, we need to add an additional DirectLink component to our HTML page (see Listing 6-7). This will look very similar to the one we created to increment the counter. However, we'll provide a different ID (reset) for the DirectLink component,[3] and we'll call a different method on our listener class (resetCounter).

**Listing 6-7.** *Adding a Second Link*

```
<p>
    <a href="#" jwcid="reset@DirectLink"
        listener="listener:resetCounter">Reset</a>
</p>
```

Of course we need to add some code to our Java class to actually reset the counter. Add the method from Listing 6-8 to Home.java. Obviously, this is pretty trivial Java code, but notice what we're *not* writing here—we've added what amounts to five lines of code to call a server-side method. Not too shabby!

**Listing 6-8.** *The resetCounter Method*

```
public void resetCounter() {
  setCounter(0);
}
```

---

3. Actually, we can use anonymous components and let Tapestry generate unique component IDs for us; however, the resulting URLs can be harder to read, and $DirectLink_1 isn't terribly descriptive.

If everything worked as expected, you should see something similar to Figure 6-5.

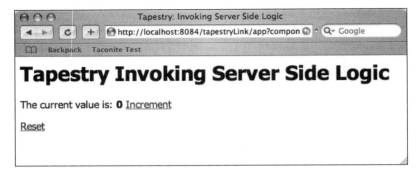

**Figure 6-5.** *The reset method*

At this point, you might be wondering how you would call a method that had a parameter. Let's add another method to the equation. This one will add the parameter to the counter. Add the following code to the Home.java class (see Listing 6-9).

**Listing 6-9.** *The addToCounter Method*

```
public void addToCounter(int value) {
  int counter = getCounter();
  counter += value;
  setCounter(counter);
}
```

Of course we actually have to call this method, so we'll add the following to the Home.html file (see Listing 6-10). This looks pretty much like the other DirectLink components we've worked with so far except that we've added a new attribute: parameters. Once again, we're going to use OGNL to pass a hard-coded "3" to the method. This code results in something like Figure 6-6.

**Listing 6-10.** *Calling the addToCounter Method*

```
<p>
    <a href="#" jwcid="add3@DirectLink" parameters="ognl:3"
        listener="listener:addToCounter">Add 3</a>
</p>
```

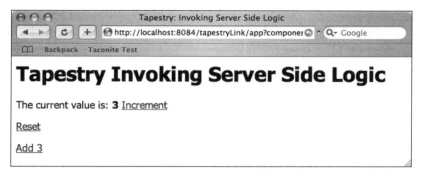

**Figure 6-6.** *Incrementing by three*

It's important to notice what we *didn't* have to do to get our parameter to our server-side logic. We didn't need to worry about grabbing the value out of the request and, more interestingly, we didn't have to convert the value from a string to the int that the method is expecting. That's right, Tapestry handled all the conversion for us. In fact, we could pass any arbitrary object to the listener method provided it was serializable. We don't know about you, but the amount of time we've spent on simply converting values back and forth in web applications makes this particular feature of Tapestry extremely compelling.

# Tapestry Forms

So we've shown how to invoke some server-side logic, but what about data? Obviously we need some type of form, and as you would expect, Tapestry has us covered there. We trust that you know how to talk to a database, so we'll leave that part out of the equation. However, we will demonstrate how you would create a Tapestry page that can take in some data and show the user what they entered. Our example page will help you keep track of your favorite podcasts. We'll collect the names of the podcasts, a short description, a long description, the release date, how long the podcast is, and whether or not you've listened to it.

As before, we'll start with Home.html (see Listing 6-11). While this looks pretty similar to what we've done before, you should notice a couple of differences. First off, we're introducing a new component, Shell. You'll notice that we didn't include some of the normal HTML-related tags like <html>, <head>, and <title>. The Shell component takes care of that for us. The PageLink will be used to take us to the page that has the actual form to fill in, but we'll get to that in a second. Our Home page will look something like Figure 6-7.

**Listing 6-11.** *The* Home.html *for Podcasts*

```
<html jwcid="@Shell" title="My Podcasts">
  <body>
    <h1>My Podcasts</h1>
    <ul>
      <li>
        <a jwcid="@PageLink" page="AddPodcast">Add New Podcast</a>
      </li>
    </ul>
  </body>
</html>
```

**Figure 6-7.** *The My Podcasts page*

Now we have to create the model of our application, the object that will hold our podcast data. One thing you should notice right away—our model class doesn't have to extend any specific class or implement any interfaces. The class is completely abstracted from the Tapestry framework. Our Podcast class will look something like Listing 6-12. This is just a simple class that contains the properties that we talked about earlier along with getter and setter methods.

**Listing 6-12.** *The Podcast Class*

```
package com.proajax.chapt6;

import java.util.Date;

public class Podcast {
```

```java
    private String name;
    private String shortDescription;
    private String longDescription;
    private Date releaseDate;
    private int length;
    private boolean played;

    public Podcast() {
    }

    public String getName() {
        return name;
    }

    public void setName(String name) {
        this.name = name;
    }

    public String getShortDescription() {
        return shortDescription;
    }

    public void setShortDescription(String shortDescription) {
        this.shortDescription = shortDescription;
    }

    public String getLongDescription() {
        return longDescription;
    }

    public void setLongDescription(String longDescription) {
        this.longDescription = longDescription;
    }

    public Date getReleaseDate() {
        return releaseDate;
    }

    public void setReleaseDate(Date releaseDate) {
        this.releaseDate = releaseDate;
    }
```

```
    public int getLength() {
        return length;
    }

    public void setLength(int length) {
        this.length = length;
    }

    public boolean isPlayed() {
        return played;
    }

    public void setListened(boolean played) {
        this.played = played;
    }
}
```

Now it's time to create the HTML page that will be used to actually enter our podcast information. We'll create a new template called AddPodcast. (Remember, that's the name we used in the PageLink component.) Our template will look something like Listing 6-13.

**Listing 6-13.** *The Add New Podcast Page*

```
<html jwcid="@Shell" title="Add New Podcast">
  <body jwcid="@Body">
    <h1>Add New Podcast</h1>
    <form jwcid="form@Form" success="listener:addPodcast">
      <table>
        <tr>
          <th>Podcast Name</th>
          <td>
            <input jwcid="name@TextField" value="ognl:podcast.name" size="40"/>
          </td>
        </tr>
        <tr>
          <th>Short Description</th>
          <td>
            <input jwcid="short@TextField" value="ognl:podcast.shortDescription"
              size="40"/>
          </td>
        </tr>
```

```
      <tr>
        <th>Long Description</th>
        <td>
          <textarea jwcid="long@TextArea" value="ognl:podcast.longDescription"
            rows="5" cols="40"/>
        </td>
      </tr>
      <tr>
        <th>Release Date</th>
        <td>
          <input jwcid="releaseDate@DatePicker"
            value="ognl:podcast.releaseDate"/>
        </td>
      </tr>
      <tr>
        <th>Podcast Length</th>
        <td>
          <input jwcid="length@TextField" value="ognl:podcast.length"/>
        </td>
      </tr>
      <tr>
        <th>Played?</th>
        <td>
          <input jwcid="played@Checkbox" value="ognl:podcast.played"/>
        </td>
      </tr>
    </table>
    <input type="submit" value="Add Podcast"/>
  </form>
  </body>
</html>
```

We've introduced a number of new components in this example. First, you'll see the
Body component, which takes care of the JavaScript for the page. Since you never know
which components might be relying on the JavaScript that is handled by Body, get in the
habit of using it. Next we have Form, which, as you would expect, takes care of the form and
the behavior on submission. You'll notice the success attribute. This tells the form to call
the addPodcast method on the listener class when there are no validation errors.

TextField, TextArea, and Checkbox work just as you would expect. TextField generates
a text input field, TextArea creates a multiline input box, and Checkbox creates a Boolean
input (in other words. . .a checkbox). DatePicker creates a field that is used to select dates,
and it also generates a drop-down list that can be used to select dates. JavaScript must be

enabled for the widget to work. However, even if it's not, the field can still be used to enter a date. Of course these aren't the only components that Tapestry offers!

---

## GRACEFUL DEGRADATION

When developing an Ajax application, developers need to consider graceful degradation. While it is likely that most readers of this book are running on the latest edition of their preferred browser, it is possible that your website has users that are a few generations behind. (That said, check your server log files. You might discover that the few percentage points of usage that indicate browsers from the late '90s might be attributed to spiders and bots). Of course even those users who *do* have the latest and greatest might have ActiveX or JavaScript turned off, meaning the vast majority of your Ajax goodness won't work. It's for this reason (and security) that we run all our validation logic on our server, even if we use a JavaScript function that checks the same thing.

How big of an issue is this? Fundamentally this is a business decision, but it is possible to create an application that degrades well. Some libraries (such as Dojo) handle much of the plumbing for you. Ideally, you would provide a similar user experience to anyone that came to your site, but realistically, you'll probably consider something along the lines of graded browser support as described by Nate Koechely of Yahoo (`http://developer.yahoo.com/yui/articles/gbs/gbs.html`). This approach doesn't say every user sees exactly the same thing as every other user. It focuses on content, saying that the more your browser can support, the richer the experience for the user. That's not to say that we couldn't also tailor our content at the server level with the use of UI components. Of course, depending on your customer base, you *may* be in a position to dictate certain browser levels and settings for your application.

---

Now we need to create the listener class that is tied to this page (see Listing 6-14). Based on Tapestry conventions, this class will be named the same as the page. This looks pretty similar to the one we created before; however, we're implementing the `PageBeginRenderListener` interface. If we had tried to run this example without this interface, we would have had discovered that we didn't have an instance of the `Podcast` class to work with. The solution is to listen for a specific Tapestry lifecycle event—here the `PageBeginRender` event, which is triggered when the page starts to render. In this case, we'll create a new instance of the `Podcast` class that we will discard after the request is over. With Tapestry, this is all we have to do to be informed of this event; it takes care of all the wiring for us.

**Listing 6-14.** *The AddPodcast Class*

```
package com.proajax.chapt6;

import java.util.Date;
import org.apache.tapestry.event.PageBeginRenderListener;
```

```
import org.apache.tapestry.event.PageEvent;
import org.apache.tapestry.html.BasePage;

public abstract class AddPodcast extends BasePage
        implements PageBeginRenderListener {

    public abstract Podcast getPodcast();
    public abstract void setPodcast(Podcast podcast);

    public void pageBeginRender(PageEvent event)
    {
        Podcast podcast = new Podcast();
        podcast.setReleaseDate(new Date());

        setPodcast(podcast);
    }

    public void addPodcast() {
        //do database related code here
    }
}
```

Clicking on the Add New Podcast link from our Home page will take us to the form we just created (see Figure 6-8).

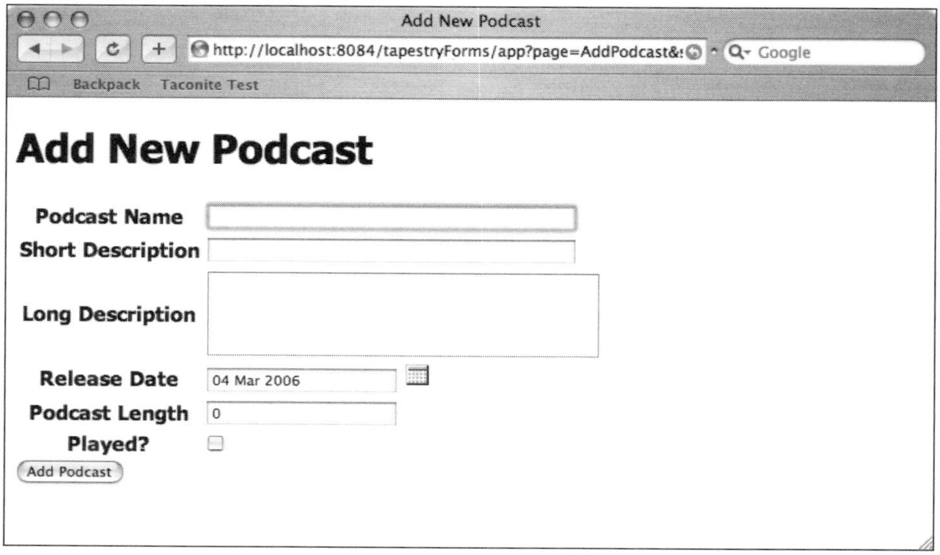

**Figure 6-8.** *The Add New Podcasts page*

So what happens if we actually enter data into this form and click Add Podcast? Well, as of now, nothing much—that we can see. Behind the scenes, Tapestry has actually done quite a bit for us. It pulled the values out of the request and set the properties on the Podcast object, and then the form is just rendered again. Let's modify this code a bit so that when we submit the data, we are taken to a new page that echoes what we entered back to us.

First, we need to create a new HTML page (see Listing 6-15) as well as a matching Java class. The HTML page will look an awful lot like our Add Podcast page except we'll be using the Insert component. As you can probably guess, Insert allows us to put text into the HTML response so it's rendered on the page and formatted if desired. Notice too that we are using OGNL to change what's displayed depending on the value of the played attribute.

**Listing 6-15.** *ShowPage.html*

```
<html jwcid="@Shell" title="Show Podcast">
  <body jwcid="@Body">
    <h1>Show Podcast</h1>
      <table>
        <tr>
          <th align="left">Podcast Name:</th>
          <td>
            <span jwcid="name@Insert" value="ognl:podcast.name"/>
          </td>
        </tr>
        <tr>
          <th align="left">Short Description:</th>
          <td>
            <span jwcid="short@Insert" value="ognl:podcast.shortDescription"/>
          </td>
        </tr>
        <tr>
          <th align="left">Long Description:</th>
          <td>
            <span jwcid="long@Insert" value="ognl:podcast.longDescription"/>
          </td>
        </tr>
        <tr>
          <th align="left">Release Date:</th>
          <td>
            <span jwcid="releaseDate@Insert" value="ognl:podcast.releaseDate"/>
          </td>
        </tr>
```

```
      <tr>
        <th align="left">Podcast Length:</th>
        <td>
          <span jwcid="length@Insert" value="ognl:podcast.length"/>
        </td>
      </tr>
      <tr>
        <th align="left">Played?</th>
        <td>
          <span jwcid="played@Insert"
            value="ognl:podcast.played ? 'Yes' : 'No'"/>
        </td>
      </tr>
    </table>
  </body>
</html>
```

The Java class for this particular page is quite simple, taking just a handful of lines (see Listing 6-16). Essentially, all this class is doing is defining a method that will be called by the addPodcast method from the AddPodcast class.

**Listing 6-16.** *ShowPodcast.*java

```
package com.proajax.chapt6;

import org.apache.tapestry.html.BasePage;

public abstract class ShowPodcast extends BasePage {

    public abstract void setPodcast(Podcast podcast);
}
```

Now that we have the supporting code ready, we need to modify the AddPodcast class a bit to wire them all together. First, we will add the following code to "inject" the ShowPodcast page (this also requires us to import org.apache.tapestry.annotations.InjectPage).

```
@InjectPage("ShowPodcast")
 public abstract ShowPodcast getShowPodcast();
```

Second, we need to change the addPodcast method to call the ShowPodcast code (see Listing 6-17) and return an instance of IPage. By changing the return type from void to IPage, we're telling Tapestry that the returned page is the new active page, the one that will be used to render the response. As we mentioned earlier, it's important to notice what we *didn't* have to do here—no casting or converting of values from the client, no messing around with session or request/response. Tapestry takes care of most of the heavy lifting, allowing developers to focus on developing the business logic.

**Listing 6-17.** *The New addPodcast Method*

```java
public IPage addPodcast() {
    ShowPodcast showPodcast = getShowPodcast();

    showPodcast.setPodcast(getPodcast());

    return showPodcast;
}
```

Submitting the page now results in something like Figure 6-9.

**Figure 6-9.** *The Show Podcasts page*

---

### TAPESTRY CLASSES

Though Tapestry consists of several hundred classes, most developers will have to interact with only a handful of interfaces like IComponent and IPage. In true object-oriented style, most of Tapestry is written against interfaces instead of classes, meaning that you will often see them as arguments and return types. Along with these two key interfaces, you will also work with IRequestCycle (which contains information about the current request), IMarkupWriter (like a Java PrintWriter, used to produce HTML), and IEngine (which manages server-side state and serves as the gateway to Tapestry subsystems).

Obviously, we've only just scratched the surface of Tapestry. As you can see, Tapestry's component model can greatly simplify creation of web applications. The core principles of simplicity, consistency, efficiency, and feedback are visible throughout.

# Tapestry Exceptions

Of course things won't always work out as you expect them to; sometimes errors will happen. One of the guiding principles of Tapestry is that feedback is valuable; and unlike many web frameworks, Tapestry provides a tremendous amount of information to help you figure out what went wrong. For example, let's take a look at the error page that Tapestry displays if we forget to run our servlet container with the 1.5 JDK (see Figure 6-10).

**Figure 6-10.** *The Tapestry error report*

Not only do we get the exception and the stack trace, but if you dig further down the page, you also get a tremendous amount of information about the servlet request, and you'll see the HTTP headers, session data, servlet context, a host of Tapestry-related information, plus a host of JVM settings (where the astute observer would notice that their runtime version was 1.4.2). Compare that to a very contrived error from a regular JSP (see Figure 6-11). Which would you rather have at your side when debugging an error?

**Figure 6-11.** *A standard error report*

# Tapestry and Ajax

The easiest way to inject Ajax into a Tapestry application is to leverage the Tacos component library. Tacos supports several of the libraries we discussed in Chapter 3 including Dojo, Prototype, and script.aculo.us. To get started, point your favorite browser to http://sourceforge.net/projects/tacos and download the latest edition. (Note, this chapter was written using the Tacos 4 beta 1 release).

---

**NOTE** Tapestry's Ajax support is quite fresh, so by the time you read this, we fully expect things to change. Howard Lewis Ship plans to create Ajax components, and Tacos will definitely improve. For those of you blazing the trail though, be prepared to deal with the inevitable issues of beta software. Your results may vary.

---

## Tacos Components

Tacos includes a number of components that you can leverage in your Tapestry applications. Some of these are simple extensions to existing Tapestry components that are needed to enable Ajax, and others are quite unique. As of this writing Tacos contains the following components (see http://tacos.sourceforge.net/components/index.html for the latest information):

- AjaxDirectLink: A version of DirectLink that supports Ajax requests

- AjaxEventSubmit: Generates the necessary JavaScript to submit a form via Ajax

- AjaxForm: A version of the Form component that includes Ajax effects

- AjaxLinkSubmit: Adds Ajax functionality to Tapestry's LinkSubmit component

- AjaxSubmit: Adds Ajax functionality to Tapestry's Submit component

- Autocompleter: Leverages script.aculo.us' Autocompleter to provide client-side autocomplete functionality

- DatePicker: Required to get DatePicker functionality in an AjaxForm component

- Dialog: Allows a modal dialog box by creating a DHTML dialog while disabling the entire form

- DirtyFormWarning: Warns the user if they try to leave a page with unsaved changes

- DropTarget: Provides drag-and-drop functionality

- FisheyeList: Provides a "fisheye lens" zoom component

- InlineEditBox: Allows for dynamically editing a piece of text

- PartialFor: An extension of Tapestry's For component (used for looping over a collection), used for Ajax requests

- ProgressBar: Provides a status bar for server-invoked logic

- Refresh: Similar to AjaxDirectLink except that the generated JavaScript is executed immediately (used by the ProgressBar)

- Tree: Provides an expand/collapse tree structure component used to view hierarchical data

## Setting Up Tacos

Once you've got the latest code, you need to perform some setup tasks. First, we need to edit the application specification to let Tapestry know about Tacos by adding the following lines between the `<application>` tags:

```
<library id="tacos" specification-path="/net/sf/tacos/Tacos.library"/>
<library id="contrib" specification-path="/org/apache/tapestry/contrib/➥
 Contrib.library"/>
```

The second line allows us to take advantage of the Tapestry add-on components. Next, we need to make sure that the Dojo is available to the web application by copying the dojo folder that you'll find in the Tacos download to the preferred location for JavaScript under the application's web directory. Tacos makes extensive use of Dojo, and this folder includes the dojo.js file along with a number of other files including those necessary to create widgets on the fly. Once we have our JavaScript file in place, we need to copy the Tacos JAR file to the WEB-INF/lib directory.

At this point, we need to configure our Tapestry template to use Tacos by setting up a configuration variable and adding the Dojo.js file to the page (see Listing 6-18). Of course you may need to modify the relative path and the source attribute based on your configuration.

**Listing 6-18.** *Configuring Tacos*

```
<script type="text/javascript">
  djConfig = { isDebug: false,
                baseRelativePath: " scripts/dojo/",
                preventBackButtonFix: false };
</script>
<script type="text/javascript" src="scripts/dojo/dojo.js"></script>
```

What is this configuration doing, you might ask? The isDebug flag turns debugging output on or off. If this flag is true, it displays all the Dojo and Tacos debug statements, including the response from the server for Ajax calls. The baseRelativePath is simply the path to the Dojo libraries relative to the context root. At this time, preventBackButtonFix should be set to false. It fixes a bug with the Back and Forward buttons. (Expect this to be fixed by the time you read this.) At this point, you should be good to go with Tacos.

## Using a Component

Now that we've got the basics covered, we can actually leverage a component; in this example, the InlineEditBox. To use a component, there are three things we need to do: add the component to our template, add a page specification, and write a Java class for the component to interact with. So far, we haven't needed to work with page specifications;

the examples we've shown so far didn't require them. However, in order for Tapestry to "understand" the Tacos components it encounters while parsing the templates, we need to provide it some information. Without a page specification, you'll see something like Figure 6-12.

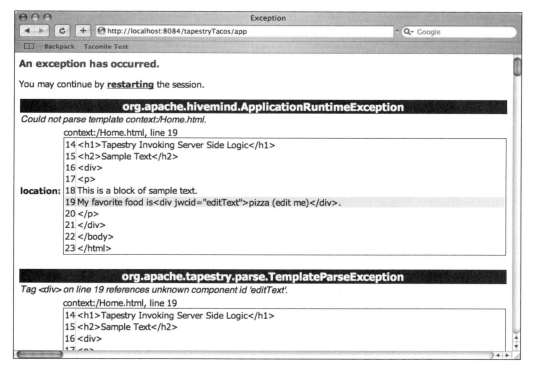

**Figure 6-12.** *A missing page specification*

If you've ever used the JavaServer Pages Standard Tag Library (JSTL) or created your own custom tag library, you've no doubt worked with a tag library descriptor (TLD) file. A TLD describes a tag—what attributes it can accept, whether it can take anything in the body of the tag, its name, and so on. A page specification is similar to a TLD in that it links the component in the template with the class file that it needs to interact with and it wires up the parameters the component takes. To create a page specification, you create a file that has the same name as the template it is tied to with a page extension. (In other words, your Home.html file will have a matching Home.page file.) The specifics for your page specification are defined by the component you are trying to use. For an example, see Listing 6-19. The Tacos documentation provides you with the proper information for each component. Notice that the class attribute of the page specification element will match the name of the class you will create to work with this component.

**Listing 6-19.** *The Page Specification for the InlineEditBox*

```xml
<?xml version="1.0" encoding="UTF-8"?>
<!DOCTYPE page-specification PUBLIC
  "-//Apache Software Foundation//Tapestry Specification 4.0//EN"
  "http://jakarta.apache.org/tapestry/dtd/Tapestry_4_0.dtd">

<page-specification class="com.proajax.chapt6.InlineEditBox">

    <description>In Line Edit Box</description>

    <property name="editedText" persist="session" initial-value="literal:pizza (edit me)"/>

    <component id="editText" type="tacos:InlineEditBox" >
        <binding name="listener" value="listener:processEdit" />
        <binding name="value" value="ognl:editedText" />
        <binding name="direct" value="ognl:false" />
    </component>

</page-specification>
```

Now that we have a page specification, we need to turn our attention to the Java class that will interact with the component. Essentially, these classes aren't any different than the ones we've created so far; they're just wired up to work with a specific component. Once again, the Tacos documentation will provide you with the specifics, but Listing 6-20 shows us the Java necessary for the InlineEditBox.

**Listing 6-20.** *The Java Class for the InlineEditBox*

```java
package com.proajax.chapt6;

import org.apache.commons.logging.Log;
import org.apache.commons.logging.LogFactory;
import org.apache.tapestry.html.BasePage;

public abstract class InlineEditBox extends BasePage {

private static final Log log = LogFactory.getLog(InlineEditBox.class);
```

```
public void processEdit(String newValue) {
    log.debug("processEdit(" + newValue + ")");
    if (newValue != null) {
        setEditedText("--" + newValue + "--");
    }
}

/** Gets the value */
public abstract String getEditedText();
/** Sets the value */
public abstract void setEditedText(String value);
}
```

At this point, we can fully leverage this component in our page. Using a Tacos component is no different than leveraging the standard Tapestry components. The template for this will look something like Listing 6-21. Make sure your template has a Body component; otherwise, you'll see something like Figure 6-13.

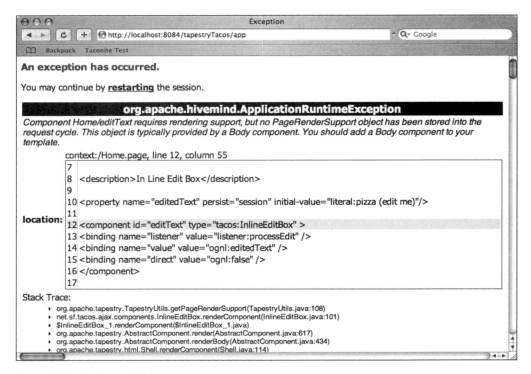

**Figure 6-13.** *A missing Body component*

**Listing 6-21.** *The Template Using the* InlineEditBox

```html
<html jwcid="@Shell" title="Tapestry and Tacos">
  <head>
    <title>Tapestry and Tacos</title>
    <script type="text/javascript">
      djConfig = { isDebug: true,
                   baseRelativePath: "scripts/dojo/",
                   preventBackButtonFix: false };
    </script>
    <script type="text/javascript" src="scripts/dojo/dojo.js"></script>
  </head>
  <body jwcid="@Body">
  <h1>Tapestry And Tacos</h1>
    <h2>The Inline Edit Component</h2>
      <div>
        <p>
         This is a block of sample text.
         My favorite food is <div jwcid="editText">pizza (edit me)</div>.
        </p>
      </div>
  </body>
</html>
```

If everything works according to plan, you'll see something like Figure 6-14 when hovering over the text to edit and, if you click on the text, you'll be given an input box (see Figure 6-15).

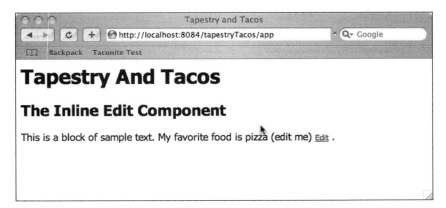

**Figure 6-14.** *The Inline Edit Component in action*

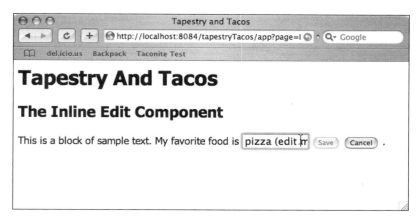

**Figure 6-15.** *The edit box*

## Enabling Debug Information

Provided you followed the preceding steps, everything should work as you would expect. However, Tacos is pretty early in its development, and you might encounter some issues. If you've got everything set up correctly but the component still isn't working, try turning the debug flag to true. This is done in the configuration variable as shown in Listing 6-22. The output will look something like Figure 6-16.

**Listing 6-22.** *Turning on the Debug Flag*

```
<script type="text/javascript">
  djConfig = { isDebug: true,
               baseRelativePath: "scripts/dojo/",
               preventBackButtonFix: false };
</script>
```

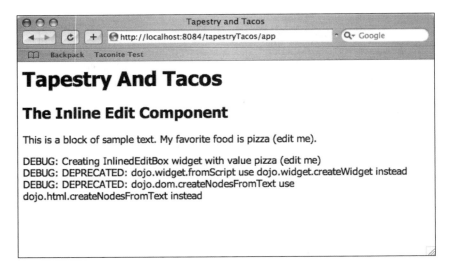

**Figure 6-16.** *Debug information*

## Modifying the Form Example

Now that we've seen the basics of working with Tacos and Tapestry, let's modify the form example from earlier in the chapter so that it submits to the same page. We'll dynamically add information to the page, and we'll take advantage of Dojo's effects to alert our user to the change in the page. For starters, we'll need an HTML template that looks pretty similar to the one we created before (see Listing 6-23).

**Listing 6-23.** *The AddPodcast Template*

```
<html jwcid="@Shell" title="Add Podcast">
<head>
  <script type="text/javascript">
    djConfig = { isDebug: false,
               baseRelativePath: "scripts/dojo/",
               preventBackButtonFix: false };
  </script>
  <script type="text/javascript" src="scripts/dojo/dojo.js"></script>
</head>
<body jwcid="@Body">
  <form jwcid="podcastForm@tacos:AjaxForm">
```

```
<table>
  <tr>
    <th align="left">Podcast Name</th>
    <td>
      <input jwcid="podcastName@TextField" value="ognl:podcast.name"
        displayName="Podcast Name" />
    </td>
  </tr>
  <tr>
    <th align="left">Short Description</th>
    <td>
     <input jwcid="shortDescription@TextField"
       value="ognl:podcast.shortDescription"
       displayName="Short Description" />
    </td>
  </tr>
  <tr>
    <th align="left">Long Description</th>
    <td>
      <input jwcid="long@TextArea" value="ognl:podcast.longDescription"
        displayName="Long Description" rows="5" cols="40"/>
    </td>
  </tr>
  <tr>
    <th align="left">Release Date</th>
    <td>
      <input jwcid="releaseDate@DatePicker"
        value="ognl:podcast.releaseDate"/>
    </td>
  </tr>
  <tr>
    <th align="left">Podcast Length</th>
    <td>
      <input jwcid="length@TextField" value="ognl:podcast.length"/>
    </td>
  </tr>
  <tr>
    <th align="left">Played?</th>
    <td>
      <input jwcid="played@Checkbox" value="ognl:podcast.played"/>
    </td>
  </tr>
</table>
```

```
  <input jwcid="podcast@tacos:AjaxSubmit"
   value="Add Podcast"
   action="listener:addPodcast"
   updateComponents="ognl:{'podcasts'}"
   effects="template:{highlight:{any:'[255,255,184], 500, 500'}}" />
</form>

<div jwcid="@Any" id="podcasts">
  <span jwcid="@If" condition="ognl:podcast.name">
    <table>
      <tbody>
        <tr>
          <th align="left">Podcast Name:</th>
          <th align="left">Short Desc:</th>
          <th align="left">Long Desc:</th>
          <th align="left">Release Date:</th>
          <th align="left">Podcast Length:</th>
          <th align="left">Played?</th>
        </tr>
        <tr>
          <td>
            <span jwcid="@Insert" value="ognl:podcast.name" />
          </td>
          <td>
            <span jwcid="@Insert" value="ognl:podcast.shortDescription" />
          </td>
          <td>
            <span jwcid="@Insert" value="ognl:podcast.longDescription" />
          </td>
          <td>
            <span jwcid="@Insert" value="ognl:podcast.releaseDate" />
          </td>
          <td>
            <span jwcid="@Insert" value="ognl:podcast.length" />
          </td>
          <td>
            <span jwcid="@Insert" value="ognl:podcast.played ? 'Yes' : 'No'" />
          </td>
        </tr>
```

```
      </tbody>
    </table>
  </span>
 </div>
</body>
</html>
```

Most of this code should look pretty familiar. As before, we have our configuration variable. You'll notice that in this example, we're using a Tacos AjaxForm instead of the standard Tapestry Form. The rest of the form is the same as before; however, the submit is taking advantage of Tacos' AjaxSubmit component. There are a couple of interesting things. First, the action="listener:addPodcast" attribute tells Tapestry which Java method to fire on the associated Java class. Second, you'll see updateComponents="ognl:{'podcasts'}" which, as you would expect, indicates what you want to update on the page. The third interesting bit is this line: effects="template:{highlight:{any:'[255,255,184], 500, 500'}}". This attribute allows us to tap into a host of effects from the Dojo library, including

- highlight

- fadeshow

- fadehide

- fade

- wipein

- wipeout

- explode

- implode

- slideto

- slideby

- slide

In this case, we're using the highlight effect to implement the Yellow Fade Technique introduced in Chapter 1. At this point, the rest of the template looks quite a bit like the ShowPodcast.html file from earlier except that it's wrapped by a div (representing the component to update) and we're using the Tapestry If component, which conditionally includes the output in the response if a condition is met (in this case, if the name attribute of the Podcast object has a value).

Instead of having the listener class create the Podcast object, we'll create one via the page specification (see Listing 6-24). This creates a new instance of Podcast and binds it to an attribute called podcast. (Note: you could also use the ognl: prefix to create an instance of the Podcast class as well.)

**Listing 6-24.** *The AddPodcast.page*

```
<?xml version="1.0" encoding="UTF-8"?>
<!DOCTYPE page-specification PUBLIC
  "-//Apache Software Foundation//Tapestry Specification 4.0//EN"
  "http://jakarta.apache.org/tapestry/dtd/Tapestry_4_0.dtd">
<page-specification>

  <property name="podcast" persist="session"
           initial-value="new com.proajax.chapt6.Podcast()" />

</page-specification>
```

At this point, we need to create the listener class mentioned before (see Listing 6-25). This class is really quite basic in this example. In the real world, your addPodcast method would actually do something (like persist the object in the database).

**Listing 6-25.** *The AddPodcast Class*

```
package com.proajax.chapt6;

import org.apache.tapestry.IRequestCycle;
import org.apache.tapestry.html.BasePage;

public abstract class AddPodcast extends BasePage {

  /**
   * Invoked by forms listener:userLogin specification.
   */

  public void addPodcast() {
      //do some persistence logic here
  }
}
```

If everything goes according to plan, you should see something like Figure 6-17 when you submit the form. Obviously this example is just scratching the surface of what you can do with Tapestry and Tacos, but it gives you an idea on where to go from here.

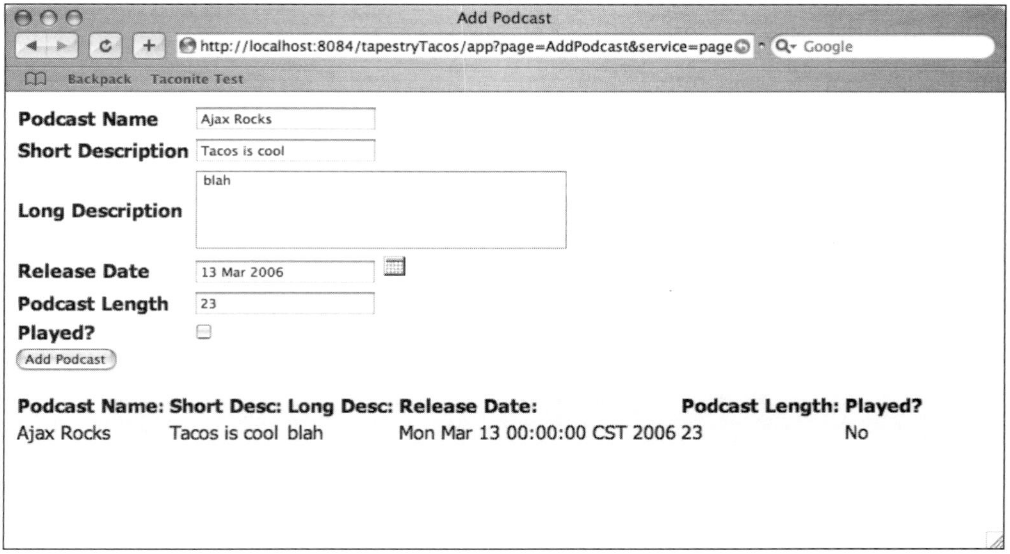

**Figure 6-17.** *Submitting the form to the same page*

# Summary

We've seen how Tapestry adheres to its goal of making the simplest choice the right choice along with its core principles of simplicity, efficiency, consistency, and feedback. Tapestry tackles web applications by breaking them into pages made up of components that are wired into Java classes. In web development with Tapestry the developer focuses on working with components, not dealing with session, URLs, or converting string values from the form into the appropriate Java paradigms. Building upon the standard servlet API, Tapestry will run on any application server or servlet container.

Along with Tapestry's rich set of components, we have an evolving set of Ajax-enabled components from the Tacos library. Though still in beta, they provide robust functionality that allows us to "Ajaxify" a Tapestry application. Not only is Ajax development greatly simplified with Tacos, we even have built-in effects and complex widgets thanks to the high-quality Dojo library. Though we've only scratched the surface, it's clear that Tacos and Tapestry are a great combination for creating robust, scalable web applications based on Java.

# CHAPTER 7

■■■

# Spring and Ajax

**Y**ou can't be a Java developer and be unaware of the Spring framework (found at `www.springframework.org`). The Spring framework is a popular alternative to the Java EE architecture that is rapidly gaining widespread use throughout the industry.

In this chapter we'll explore the Spring framework and how its features can be leveraged in your Ajax applications. This chapter starts by taking a quick but detailed look at the Spring framework and explains why it has created such a buzz within the developer community recently. Two of Spring's main features, aspect-oriented programming and dependency injection, are described in plain, easy-to-understand terms. After those explanations, a basic example of a Spring-based application is shown.

But this is a book about Ajax, right? The in-depth analysis of Spring is necessary to understand how Spring's feature set can be leveraged for Ajax-style interactions. You'll see how Spring and Ajax complement each other to build highly interactive, robust, and maintainable applications.

## What Is Spring?

The Spring framework describes itself as a leading full-stack Java and Java EE application framework that helps reduce development effort and costs while improving test coverage and quality. That's all well and good, but there are two rather bold proclamations in that statement: first, that it's a leading full-stack Java EE application framework; and second, that it reduces development effort and costs while improving test coverage and quality.

Let's examine the first statement first, that Spring is a leading full-stack Java EE application framework. Isn't Java EE the leading full-stack Java EE application framework? What's wrong with Java EE?

The real answer isn't necessarily what's wrong with Java EE but rather what sets Spring apart from Java EE. The most obvious difference between Java EE and Spring is that Spring does not require a Java EE container to execute. Spring can be used in servlet containers like Tomcat or even in Java SE projects. Fundamentally, Java EE applications depend on Java EE application servers to implement Java EE functionality. In contrast, Spring implements all of its own functionality itself and only requires the standard Java runtime to execute.

This fundamental difference between Spring and Java EE feeds the second statement that Spring reduces development efforts and costs while improving test coverage and quality. Applications that utilize Java EE services must be executed within a Java EE application server. This makes unit testing much harder, because artifacts like session beans and entity beans must be compiled and deployed to the Java EE application server before they can be executed. Spring applications, on the other hand, can be unit-tested without an application server, which simplifies the code-test-repeat cycle.

## Just Another Framework?

At this point you may be thinking to yourself that Spring is just another application framework. Aren't there several different Java application frameworks out there? Don't they all claim to make application development faster, easier, and cheaper? What sets Spring apart from other solutions?

Spring has a vibrant user community that has sustained a high level of interest for the past few years, ensuring continued development and support. Spring enjoys more than 20 developers too, which is much more than the many one- or two-developer frameworks and libraries that exist today.

## Aspect-Oriented Programming and Dependency Injection

Object-oriented programming (OOP) is a programming paradigm that was hailed as the savior for all software development woes when it first began to see widespread use in the 1980s. Smalltalk was the first widely used programming language that supported OOP concepts like *classes* and *objects*. Smalltalk also pioneered the concept of *inheritance*, which enables *polymorphic behavior*.

As an experienced Java developer you are already familiar with OOP, but for consistency's sake, let's quickly review its main concepts. OOP is based on the concept of modeling real-world entities as discreet software artifacts called *classes*. A class is best described as the template for building a concrete instance of a class, which is formally known as an *object*. Developers find it much easier to extend and maintain software built using OOP techniques because the software closely models the business domain it was built to service.

As you know, a class should mimic the properties and behavior of the real-world entity that it is modeling, essentially grouping together data (properties) and the functions (behavior) that are meant to modify the data. Objects provide encapsulation, which means that the object's data is hidden from other objects and can be accessed only through well-defined interfaces on the object, which is intended to prevent misuse of the data by other objects. Encapsulation ensures that the data represented by an object can be manipulated only via certain interfaces that are defined by the object itself.

Large software systems built using OOP are composed of many objects that collaborate with other objects by sending messages to each other. Since objects hide their internal state from other objects, the only way that objects can collaborate with each other is by sending messages to one another. In concept this is all well and good, but sometimes the OOP model begins to break down a bit in large software systems. Objects are supposed to interact by sending messages to each other, but how are objects supposed to find the other objects with which they are supposed to collaborate?

You've surely seen this problem before, especially if you've worked on Java EE applications. You start by writing classes and objects that model the business domain in which you're working. You're feeling good because the classes and objects have high cohesion, meaning they do one thing and do it well. The classes and objects are what you would describe as "clean and tight" because they don't contain any extraneous code that doesn't relate to the business domain.

Then it starts. You start writing a service bean that coordinates some of the services provided by the application. Not a problem. The session bean uses multiple Data Access Objects (DAOs) to modify a relational database. The service bean is supposed to coordinate the transaction among the DAOs, so you start writing code to manage the transaction. But wait—transaction management isn't a core feature of the business domain. You then notice that your DAOs perform a lot of Java Naming and Directory Interface (JNDI) lookups to retrieve database connections from the application server. If you're using Enterprise Java Beans (EJB), then you're performing a lot of JNDI lookups to access session beans from the web tier, and the session beans are likely performing JNDI lookups to access the entity beans they're using.

OK, so you're doing a few JNDI lookups here and there. No big deal. Now you decide that logging statements need to appear in the code, and soon after that, you decide to implement performance monitoring on the most-used methods. It's not hard to do. All you have to do is copy and paste those logging statements and performance monitors from one method to another, right?

Suddenly your clean and tight application has been littered with JNDI lookups, logging statements, performance monitors, and other plumbing code that really has no relation to the business domain in which you're working. Some (or many!) of your domain objects and service objects may be littered with code that deals with low-level implementation details like transaction management and collaborating object lookup. These details don't have anything to do with the core business domain that the application is modeling, but rather they are the necessary evils of a large-scale software application. OOP is a great paradigm that looks and sounds wonderful on paper, but in the real world it begins to break down a bit as objects become cluttered with the necessary-but-evil low-level implementation details.

Certainly details like logging code and object lookups aren't the worst thing in the world, and like anything else, good coding practices can help mitigate many of the problems associated with such low-level details. So what's a developer to do?

The newest paradigms to hit the scene are aspect-oriented programming (AOP) and dependency injection (DI). AOP helps solve the problem of implementing low-level functionality that applies to many classes in a system, like logging or error handling, without cluttering the domain object. DI is an answer to the common problem of looking up collaborating objects.

While not the only solution available, Spring is definitely among the most widely used AOP and DI containers. Spring provides a wide range of functionality meant to enhance developer productivity, but much of this functionality is based on Spring's excellent support for AOP and DI. We'll take a brief look at how Spring handles AOP and DI and what it means for your applications.

## Introduction to Spring and AOP

AOP is a programming paradigm that allows us to factor common, low-level functionality known as *cross-cutting concerns* out of domain classes and encapsulate them so that they can be reused across a wide range of unrelated classes. The real trick to this is being able to reapply those cross-cutting concerns where and when they are needed in a non-invasive fashion, as in, by not changing the classes to which the cross-cutting functionality should apply.

Does that sound like a mouthful? It probably does, but consider this simple example method:

```
public int addTwoNumbers(int first, int second) {
    int sum = first + second;
    return sum;
}
```

The addTwoNumbers method, to the surprise of no one, returns the sum of two integers. But what if you want to add some logging statements to the method so that the entering and exiting of the method gets logged to the logging console? No problem—just add logging statements to the beginning and end of the method body. Doing so makes the method look like this:

```
public int addTwoNumbers(int first, int second) {
    LoggingUtil.log("entering addTwoNumbers");
    int sum = first + second;
    LoggingUtil.log("exiting addTwoNumbers");
    return sum;
}
```

The actual business logic requires only two lines of code, but the amount of code required to log the start and end of the method is also two lines long, effectively doubling the size of the method.

No big deal, one might say. The two lines required to log the entering and exiting of the method are hardly complicated, and since most methods are longer than two lines, it won't really double the size of the method.

Now consider the scenario where the same method is suspected of being a performance bottleneck. To diagnose the cause of the performance bottleneck, you decide to add performance instrumentation to this (and other) methods. The addTwoNumbers method now grows to this:

```
public int addTwoNumbers(int first, int second) {
    LoggingUtil.log("entering addTwoNumbers");
    PerformanceTimer.start("addTwoNumbers");
    int sum = first + second;
    PerformanceTimer.end("addTwoNumbers");
    LoggingUtil.log("exiting addTwoNumbers");
    return sum;
}
```

Now our previously slim, two-line method is six lines long, and only two of the lines have anything to do with actual business logic. Worse yet, the method just *looks* ugly. If software development is truly an art and science, this method clearly fails in the artistic category. The method just has a bad smell to it. There's too much going on inside the method that doesn't relate to the intended purpose of the method. To top it all off, the code that performs the logging functions and performance monitoring must be repeated in every method that requires that functionality, leading to more ugly methods and significant code bloat. Isn't there a better way?

Remember, a few paragraphs ago we defined AOP as implementing low-level functionality that applies to many classes in a system. Certainly logging and performance monitoring fit this description. Let's clean up this mess by applying AOP to the example.

The first thing we need to do is abstract the logging and performance monitoring functionality into their own discreet units, or *advice*. Advice is the term given to the code that we want to apply to the existing domain code. We need to create logging advice and performance monitoring advice that can be reused with many different domain implementations.

The point at which the advice is joined with the domain code is known as a *point cut*. For both the logging and performance monitoring advice, the point cuts are at the beginning of the domain method and the end of the domain method.

The combination of an advice with a point cut is named an *aspect*. Using the addTwoNumbers method as an example, we want to create logging and performance monitoring advices that apply at the beginning and end of the method to form logging and performance monitoring aspects. By doing so we will remove the logging and performance monitoring code from the addTwoNumbers method, yet we will still reap the benefits of having this functionality available.

Are you now sufficiently interested in what AOP can do for you? This was just an introduction and a bit of a tease. A little later you'll see how Spring implements AOP and will let us do exactly what we describe.

## Introduction to Spring and Dependency Injection

Compared to AOP, which maybe left your brain hurting a little bit as you tried to grasp its core concepts, dependency injection (DI) is a relatively simple concept. You can probably find some more in-depth explanations describing DI, but it basically boils down to this: Have you ever written EJB 2.x style beans and had to use JNDI lookups to obtain an instance of the EJB from container? You have to create an instance of the InitialContext object and then use the lookup method to obtain an instance of the desired bean. If you're using local EJBs, you then only have to cast the result of the lookup to the correct type. If you're using remote EJBs, then you have the additional step of calling PortableRemoteObject. narrow to finish accessing the bean. This process needs to be repeated for *every single bean* that is managed by the container. Not surprisingly, this led to the creation of the ServiceLocator pattern, which aims to encapsulate these steps in a single class.

The worst part of JNDI lookups is that they need to occur within a container, since the container is required to manage the bean. This means that any object that relies on JNDI lookups to find collaborating objects cannot be tested in a normal unit-testing environment. Instead, it must be tested within the confines of a container. This is certainly possible, but it slows down the development process because code must be deployed to a container before unit tests can be executed.

Enter DI. Dependency injection solves this problem by completely eliminating the need for complicated JNDI lookups. Instead of designing a class to use JNDI lookups to find collaborating objects, the class simply exposes getter and setter methods for collaborating objects. An outside component—for our purposes, this component is Spring—is responsible for *injecting* collaborating objects via the setter methods. In fact, Spring even allows collaborating objects to be injected as parameters to the target object's constructor method.

Relationships between collaborating and target objects are defined in Spring's XML configuration files. This provides a loose coupling between the collaborating objects, as objects needn't be concerned with how they obtain references to collaborating objects; Spring automatically manages these relationships. Because JNDI lookups are not involved, objects can be easily unit-tested outside of any container. In fact, since target objects expose collaborating objects as setter and getter methods, Spring isn't even necessary during unit testing, as the developer can specify collaborating objects using the setter methods.

Spring makes it easy to build applications as if individual objects are LEGO bricks that are snapped together using Spring to create fully functional applications. The loose coupling between collaborating objects makes it easy to change and update relationships between objects as requirements evolve. How successful is Spring's implementation of DI? Look no further than the new EJB 3.0 specification. EJB 3.0 supports DI out of the box, and this feature was in no doubt influenced by Spring's popularity and growing mindshare.

As we get further into this chapter you'll see exactly how Spring implements DI and how it can change the way you build web applications. Now, without further ado, let's dive headfirst into Spring to get a feel for its capabilities and features.

# Getting Started with Spring

This text won't try to be a complete tutorial on Spring. Such a tutorial can (and has) filled a complete book itself, like *Pro Spring* by Rob Harrop (Apress, 2005). Here, you'll see a simple "Hello World" example that demonstrates how to get Spring up and running in a web environment so we can build on it in future examples.

This example uses both Spring and Spring MVC. Spring MVC is, as its name suggests, a web model-view-controller framework, not unlike Struts. Spring MVC is conceptually similar to Struts but is designed to avoid many of the pitfalls associated with Struts. For example, a Spring MVC `Controller` is conceptually similar to a Struts `Action`, but unlike a Struts `Action`, a Spring MVC `Controller` is not required to extend a particular abstract class.

Figure 7-1 shows the "Hello World" page this example will create. You can see that in addition to printing the static "Hello World" text, the application also writes the current date string to the page in addition to printing the results of a simple iteration.

**Figure 7-1.** *A simple web page constructed using Spring and Spring MVC*

We'll start from the top and work our way down. The JSP that produces this page is, as you likely expect, rather simple and is shown in Listing 7-1.

**Listing 7-1.** *helloWorld.jsp*

```jsp
<%@ include file="/jsp/include/imports.jsp" %>

<!DOCTYPE html PUBLIC "-//W3C//DTD XHTML 1.0 Strict//EN"
        "http://www.w3.org/TR/xhtml1/DTD/xhtml1-strict.dtd">

<html xmlns="http://www.w3.org/1999/xhtml">
    <head>
        <title>Chapter 7: Spring MVC Hello World</title>
    </head>
    <body>
        <h1>Hello World!</h1>
        <h3>Date string: ${domain.dateString}</h3>
        <ul>
            <c:forEach var="str" items="${domain.strings}">
                <li>${str}</li>
            </c:forEach>
        </ul>
    </body>
</html>
```

The key to this JSP page is the scoped variable named domain. You can see that the domain variable has a property named dateString that holds the current date string. It also has a strings property that holds a list of strings that are rendered as an unordered list. This example uses the JSTL shorthand dollar sign for printing the values out to the page.

OK, so the JSP is easy. How do we get into the Spring stuff? Let's start with the web.xml file. Since this example uses Spring MVC, we need to configure the web.xml file just as we would as if we were using Struts. Like Struts, Spring MVC provides a servlet named DispatcherServlet that handles all incoming requests and delegates them to the appropriate controllers. This servlet needs to be defined in the application's web.xml file, and requests must be mapped to the servlet. Listing 7-2 shows the additions to the web.xml file to enable the DispatcherServlet.

**Listing 7-2.** *Additions to the web.xml File to Enable Struts MVC*

```xml
<servlet>
    <servlet-name>springdispatch</servlet-name>
    <servlet-class>
        org.springframework.web.servlet.DispatcherServlet
    </servlet-class>
    <load-on-startup>1</load-on-startup>
</servlet>
```

```
<servlet-mapping>
    <servlet-name>springdispatch</servlet-name>
    <url-pattern>*.app</url-pattern>
</servlet-mapping>
```

Again, as with the JSP shown in Listing 7-1, there's nothing here you haven't seen before. The servlet tag specifies the Spring MVC DispatcherServlet and gives it a logical name of springdispatch. The servlet-mapping tag maps all URLs ending in .app to the springdispatch servlet. The mapping can be whatever you desire it to be. Some developers choose to map everything that ends with .html to the DispatcherServlet as then all pages look like static HTML pages to users and even to search engines.

So far so good, right? So far you've seen a simple JSP and the additions to the web.xml file to activate the Spring MVC DispatcherServlet. We can now turn our attention to creating some Spring beans that perform some useful functionality.

The example web page shown in Figure 7-1 has two dynamically built sections: the current date and the list of strings that make up the unordered list. Instead of scattering the functionality to build this content amongst many classes, we're going to encapsulate it all in a single service class. Listing 7-3 shows the HelloWorldService interface, which defines the contract that the service must implement.

**Listing 7-3.** *HelloWorldService.java*

```
package com.proajax.chapt7.service;

import java.util.List;

public interface HelloWorldService {

    public String getCurrentDateString();

    public List<String> getUnorderedList();
}
```

The interface defines two public methods: getCurrentDateString, which returns the current date as a String and getUnorderedList, which returns a List of Strings that will be rendered as an unordered list. Of course, the interface doesn't define any implementation of these methods; we create a SimpleHelloWorldService class that implements HelloWorldService and provides an implementation for its methods. The source code for SimpleHelloWorldService is shown in Listing 7-4.

**Listing 7-4.** *SimpleHelloWorldService.java*

```java
package com.proajax.chapt7.service;

import java.util.Date;
import java.util.ArrayList;
import java.util.List;

public class SimpleHelloWorldService implements HelloWorldService {

    public List getStrings() {
        List strings = new ArrayList();
        for(int i = 0; i < 10; i++) {
            strings.add("The number I'm thinking of is: " + i);
        }
        return strings;
    }

    public String getCurrentDateString() {
        return new Date().toString();
    }

    public List<String> getUnorderedList() {
        List<String> strings = new ArrayList();
        for(int i = 0; i < 10; i++) {
            strings.add("The number I'm thinking of is: " + i);
        }
        return strings;
    }
}
```

The nice thing about this service is that it's implemented as a Plain Old Java Object, more commonly known as a POJO. In the traditional Java EE world, a service bean like this may have been implemented as a stateless session bean. Since this service is implemented as a POJO, it can be easily tested outside of the container and can be run in any Java runtime environment. Unlike a session bean it does not require an EJB container in which to run. Already Spring is starting to show its advantages.

The last component left to build is the controller class. This is the class that will actually handle the request and use an instance of the HelloWorldService to build the dynamic portions of the page. This class is roughly similar to a Struts Action class, except that it does not need to extend a concrete class, rather it only needs to implement an interface. Listing 7-5 shows the HelloWorldController class.

**Listing 7-5.** *HelloWorldController.java*

```java
package com.proajax.chapt7.ui;

import com.proajax.chapt7.service.HelloWorldService;
import java.util.HashMap;
import java.util.Map;
import javax.servlet.http.HttpServletRequest;
import javax.servlet.http.HttpServletResponse;
import org.springframework.web.servlet.ModelAndView;
import org.springframework.web.servlet.mvc.Controller;

public class HelloWorldController implements Controller {
    private HelloWorldService service = null;

    public ModelAndView handleRequest(HttpServletRequest request
            , HttpServletResponse response) throws Exception {

        Map domain = new HashMap();
        domain.put("dateString", service.getCurrentDateString());
        domain.put("strings", service.getUnorderedList());

        return new ModelAndView("helloWorld", "domain", domain);
    }

    public void setService(HelloWorldService service) {
        this.service = service;
    }
}
```

The HelloWorldController class implements the Spring MVC Controller interface, which defines the handleRequest method. The handleRequest method is roughly similar to the execute method in a Struts Action class. The handleRequest method takes two parameters, HttpServletRequest and HttpServletResponse, and returns an instance of the ModelAndView class. ModelAndView is a placeholder class for the model that will be rendered and the view that will render the model. The model must be an instance of a Map that holds key/value pairs.

You can see that the handleRequest method makes use of an instance of SimpleHelloService to provide the date string and a list of Strings. The date string and list of strings are added to the Map using unique keys. Fortunately the JSTL makes it easy to access the values in the Map using standard dot notation in the form map.key.

But where does the instance of HelloWorldService come from? Shouldn't there be some code that calls a factory method, or maybe an abstract factory, or maybe even a JNDI lookup to access an instance of HelloWorldService?

The answer is "none of the above." The HelloWorldController class is not responsible for creating its own instance of HelloWorldService. Instead, it relies on Spring's dependency injection feature to provide an instance of HelloWorldService.

The last item we need to look at, the item that ties everything together, is the springdispatch-servlet.xml file. In this file are the bean definitions for the HelloWorldService bean, the HelloWorldController, and the view resolver. The source code for springdispatch-servlet.xml is shown in Listing 7-6.

**Listing 7-6.** *springdispatch-servlet.xml*

```xml
<?xml version="1.0" encoding="UTF-8"?>
<!DOCTYPE beans PUBLIC "-//SPRING//DTD BEAN//EN"
    "http://www.springframework.org/dtd/spring-beans.dtd">

<beans>
    <bean id="springController"
        class="com.proajax.chapt7.ui.HelloWorldController">
        <property name="service">
            <ref bean="serviceBean"/>
        </property>
    </bean>

    <bean id="serviceBean"
        class="com.proajax.chapt7.service.SimpleHelloWorldService"/>

    <bean id="urlMapping"
        class="org.springframework.web.servlet.handler.SimpleUrlHandlerMapping">
        <property name="mappings">
            <props>
                <prop key="/hello.app">springController</prop>
            </props>
        </property>
    </bean>
```

```
<bean id="viewResolver"
    class="org.springframework.web.servlet.view.InternalResourceViewResolver">
        <property name="viewClass">
            <value>org.springframework.web.servlet.view.JstlView</value>
        </property>
        <property name="suffix"><value>.jsp</value></property>
    </bean>
</beans>
```

The naming of the file as `springdispatch-servlet.xml` was a very deliberate choice. If you refer back to Listing 7-2 you'll see that the Spring MVC dispatcher servlet was given a logical `servlet-name` of `springdispatch`. By using this name in conjunction with `-servlet.xml`, the Spring MVC dispatcher servlet will automatically load the XML file and initialize the beans specified within.

The first bean specified within `springdispatch-servlet.xml` is an instance of the `HelloWorldService` interface. The bean is given an `id` of `serviceBean`, and the concrete class is the `SimpleHelloWorldService` class.

The next specified bean is the `HelloWorldController`, which is given an `id` of `springController`. Remember a few paragraphs back when we questioned how exactly the controller created or accessed an instance of `HelloWorldService`? Here's where the magic happens. The `HelloWorldController` bean has a `property` child element, which is given the `name` of `service`. The property refers to a bean with an `id` of `serviceBean`, which of course you just read about in the previous paragraph.

Referring back to Listing 7-5, which shows the `HelloWorldController`, you'll see that there is a JavaBeans-style setter method for a property named `service`, which just so happens to be of type `HelloWorldService`. You can now see that Spring is creating an instance of the `SimpleHelloWorldService` class (which implements `HelloWorldService`) and uses the `HelloWorldController`'s `setService` method to add the service to the controller. All of this happens without you having to explicitly create an instance of `HelloWorldService` or having to use JNDI to find it. Removing this "plumbing" code from the controller keeps the code clean and uncluttered and focused on business logic.

The last two beans defined in the `springdispatch-servlet.xml` file are specific to Spring MVC. The `urlMapping` bean maps URLs matching `/hello.app` to the `springController` bean, which is an instance of the `HelloWorldController` class. The `viewResolver` bean is a helper class that resolves views to servlets and JSPs located within the web application. Note that this bean has a `property` named `suffix` that has a value of `.jsp`. In Listing 7-5, the controller creates a `ModelAndView` object, and the first parameter passed to the constructor is the string `helloWorld`, which is supposed to refer to the `helloWorld.jsp` file. Since the `viewResolver` bean automatically appends a `.jsp` to the specified view names, we don't need to include the `.jsp` in the view name.

The result of all of this is the web page shown in Figure 7-1. OK, that's not bad for a "Hello World" application, but is that all there is to it?

A discussion on Spring wouldn't be complete without highlighting how Spring reduces the cost of programming to interfaces, rather than to concrete implementations, to nearly zero. Recall that in the source code for the HelloWorldController (Listing 7-5) the code always refers to HelloWorldService, which is an interface, not a concrete class. The actual implementation, SimpleHelloWorldService, is created by Spring and injected into the controller class. If you want to change the implementation of HelloWorldService, all you need to do is write a new implementing class and change the class definition of the serviceBean bean in springdispatch-servlet.xml to use the new implementation.

Suppose you want to change the implementation of HelloWorldService to provide the date string in a different format, and that the contents of the list of strings should change. Also assume that the SimpleHelloWorldService class, the current implementation of HelloWorldService, is reused elsewhere and should not be changed. So, you write a new implementation of HelloWorldService named AdvancedHelloWorldService, which is shown in Listing 7-7.

**Listing 7-7.** *AdvancedHelloWorldService.java*

```
package com.proajax.chapt7.service;

import java.text.SimpleDateFormat;
import java.util.ArrayList;
import java.util.Date;
import java.util.List;

public class AdvancedHelloWorldService implements HelloWorldService {
    public static final String DATE_FORMAT =
            "hh:mm 'o''clock' a, zzzz ' on ' EEEEE, MMMMM d, yyyy";

    public String getCurrentDateString() {
        SimpleDateFormat formatter = new SimpleDateFormat(DATE_FORMAT);
        return formatter.format(new Date());
    }

    public List<String> getUnorderedList() {
        List<String> strings = new ArrayList();

        for(int i = 0; i < 10; i++) {
            strings.add("The square of " + i + " is: " + (i * i));
        }
        return strings;
    }

}
```

The only thing needed to make the "Hello World" application use this implementation instead of SimpleHelloWorldService is to change the serviceBean bean definition in springdispatch-servlet.xml to use the AdvancedHelloWorldService class:

```
<bean id="serviceBean"
    class="com.proajax.chapt7.service.AdvancedHelloWorldService"/>
```

Running the application using the new AdvancedHelloWorldService class renders the web page shown in Figure 7-2.

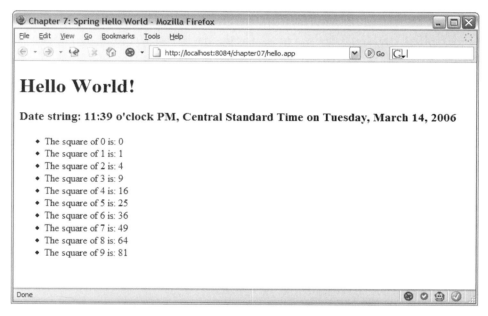

**Figure 7-2.** *Updated web page that uses a new implementation of HelloWorldService*

All you had to do to make HelloWorldController use the new AdvancedHelloWorldService class was change the bean definition. Another way to accomplish the same task would be to define a new bean of type AdvancedHelloWorldService, give it a unique bean id, and use that bean in the HelloWorldController bean definition. Either way, you were able to change an implementation without touching the HelloWorldController class. By using Spring's dependency injection, the HelloWorldController class doesn't need to concern itself with the details of actually creating an instance of HelloWorldService; all it does is supply a JavaBeans-style setter method for it and let Spring manage the creation of the bean. It may seem trivial in a small application like this, but imagine a large application where potentially hundreds of classes could be affected by a change in an implementing class. By using Spring and dependency injection and programming to an interface, such a large change could be handled easily.

# Ajax and Spring

You can see from the previous example that Spring greatly reduces the amount of effort needed to build the service layer for your application. Spring reduces the cost of programming to interfaces rather than concrete implementations to near zero, creating an environment that is flexible and robust.

That's all well and good, but what does a robust and flexible service have to do with Ajax, which is primarily a client-side concern? Most likely your first foray into Ajax will be to add Ajax interactions to an existing application. Your well-designed application likely includes a service layer that is reused by multiple views within the application. But, alas, all of those existing views rely on the tried and true request/response paradigms, and you'll want to add Ajax-powered views to those existing views. The Ajax views may interact slightly differently with the service layer than the traditional request/response views, and Spring can help make it easy to extend the service layer to accommodate Ajax views.

Chapter 4 introduced you to DWR, a Java open source library that lets developers write JavaScript that accesses Java running on a remote application server as if it were running locally in the browser. Chapter 4 explained how DWR exposes regular JavaBeans objects to JavaScript running in the browser.

Chapter 4 used regular JavaBeans objects as the exposed Java objects. In addition to this, DWR also provides the ability to use Spring beans, and by doing so the beans can be extended using AOP or DI techniques.

Configuring DWR to use Spring beans is quite easy. In the `dwr.xml` file, a Spring bean can be configured by setting the `creator` attribute of the `create` element to `spring`, instructing DWR to use the Spring creator to create the desired bean:

```
<create creator="spring" javascript="SpringBean">
    <param name="beanName" value="serviceBean"/>
</create>
```

The `value` attribute of the `param` element is the name of the desired Spring bean as defined in the `beans.xml` configuration file. That's all you need to do to configure DWR to use Spring beans. Very nice!

# The Inventory Control Application

The inventory control application is a fictitious application that lets users manage the prices of products sold by their organizations. The application uses DWR and JavaScript Templates to manage the Ajax interactions and Spring to manage the service layer objects. The application makes use of Spring's built-in support for AOP and DI to demonstrate how easy it is to apply these techniques using Spring.

## Application Security

The inventory control application, as you might expect, requires users to log in to the application by providing a user name and password. Figure 7-3 shows the application login page.

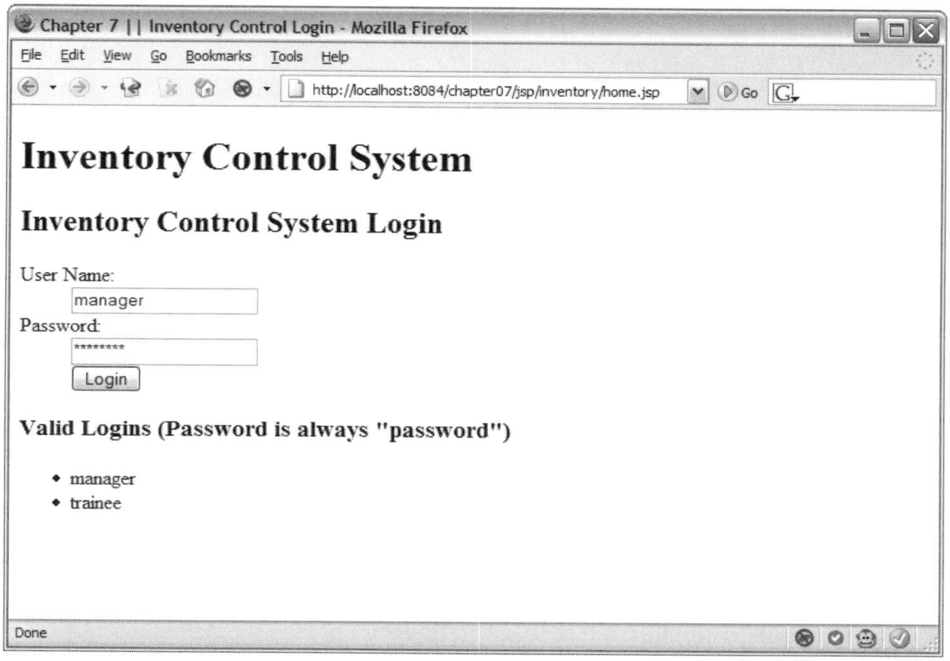

**Figure 7-3.** *The application login page*

The login page is rendered by the login.jsp file, whose source code is shown in Listing 7-8.

**Listing 7-8.** *login.jsp*

```
<!DOCTYPE html PUBLIC "-//W3C//DTD XHTML 1.0 Strict//EN"
         "http://www.w3.org/TR/xhtml1/DTD/xhtml1-strict.dtd">

<html xmlns="http://www.w3.org/1999/xhtml">

    <head>
        <title>Chapter 7 || Inventory Control Login</title>
    </head>
```

```
    <body onload="document.getElementById('j_username').focus();">
      <div id="wrapper">
          <h1>Inventory Control System</h1>
          <form name="security" id="security"
              action="j_security_check" method="post">

              <h2>Inventory Control System Login</h2>

              <dl>
                  <dt><label for="j_username">User Name:</label></dt>
                  <dd>
                      <input type="text" name="j_username" id="j_username"
                      value="" size="20" maxlength="20" />
                  </dd>

                  <dt><label for="j_password">Password:</label></dt>
                  <dd>
                      <input type="password" name="j_password" id="j_password"
                      value="" size="20" maxlength="20" />
                  </dd>
                  <dd class="button">
                      <input type="submit" value="Login"/>
                  </dd>
              </dl>
          </form>

          <h3>Valid Logins (Password is always "password")</h3>
          <ul>
              <li>manager</li>
              <li>trainee</li>
          </ul>

      </div>
    </body>

</html>
```

This example uses the built-in Java EE security model for user authentication and authorization. You can see that the form's action is j_security_check, which is the built-in keyword for the built-in Java EE security model. The user name and password fields use j_username and j_password, respectively, as the form element names, as required by the Java EE specification.

Java EE security is enabled via the `web.xml` file. Listing 7-9 shows the additions to the `web.xml` file to enable Java EE security. If you're unfamiliar with the Java EE security model, you can figure much of it out for yourself by carefully reading Listing 7-9.

**Listing 7-9.** *Additions to web.xml to Enable Java EE Security*

```
<security-constraint>
    <web-resource-collection>
        <web-resource-name>Inventory Control System</web-resource-name>
        <description>Inventory control system</description>
        <url-pattern>/jsp/inventory/*</url-pattern>
        <http-method>GET</http-method>
        <http-method>POST</http-method>
    </web-resource-collection>
    <auth-constraint>
        <role-name>manager-role</role-name>
        <role-name>trainee-role</role-name>
    </auth-constraint>
</security-constraint>

<security-constraint>
    <web-resource-collection>
        <web-resource-name>DWR Requests</web-resource-name>
        <description>DWR Requests</description>
        <url-pattern>/dwr/*</url-pattern>
        <http-method>GET</http-method>
        <http-method>POST</http-method>
    </web-resource-collection>
    <auth-constraint>
        <role-name>manager-role</role-name>
        <role-name>trainee-role</role-name>
    </auth-constraint>
</security-constraint>

<login-config>
    <auth-method>FORM</auth-method>
    <form-login-config>
        <form-login-page>/jsp/inventory/login.jsp</form-login-page>
        <form-error-page>/jsp/inventory/login_failure.jsp</form-error-page>
    </form-login-config>
</login-config>
```

```
<security-role>
    <role-name>manager-role</role-name>
</security-role>
<security-role>
    <role-name>trainee-role</role-name>
</security-role>
```

The `security-constraint` elements define a set of web resources that require authentication and authorization and the roles that are allowed to access the web resources. The `web-resource-collection` element defines the secured web resources by using the `url-pattern` element. All resources matching the `url-pattern` string are secured. In this example, the `/jsp/inventory/*` pattern secures all of the application's JSP files, while the `/dwr/*` secures any potential Ajax requests sent by DWR.

The `auth-constraint` elements define the security roles that have access to the secured resources. The security roles are declared by the `security-role` elements at the bottom of Listing 7-9. This application defines two security roles: a role for mangers called `manager-role` and a role for trainees called `trainee-role`.

The `login-config` element configures the way in which the user will log in to the application. The `auth-method` element declares that `form-based` authentication will be used, as we saw in Listing 7-8 where the form element used the `j_security_check` action. The `form-login-page` element defines the actual login page, while the `form-error-page` element defines the page that appears if the login fails.

The last piece of the security puzzle is to configure the application server to read the available user names, passwords, and security roles from some central repository. Most production applications use LDAP or something similar to store this information. This example uses Tomcat's built-in `tomcat-users.xml` file to define the list of user names, passwords, and security roles. The `tomcat-users.xml` file is found in the `${TOMCAT_BASE}/conf` directory. The following additions were made to the `tomcat-users.xml` file to declare the `manager` and `trainee` users, along with the `manager-role` and `trainee-role` roles.

```
<role rolename="manager-role"/>
<role rolename="trainee-role"/>
<user username="trainee" password="password" roles="trainee-role"/>
<user username="manager" password="password" roles="manager-role"/>
```

Finally, the `context.xml` file in the WAR file's `META-INF` directory needs to be updated to tell Tomcat to use the file-based security realm. The contents of the `context.xml` file are as follows:

```
<?xml version="1.0" encoding="UTF-8"?>
<Context path="/chapter07">
    <Realm className="org.apache.catalina.realm.MemoryRealm" />
</Context>
```

## The Manage Prices Page

The main page of the inventory control system lets the user manage the current prices of items available within the store. The main page is shown in Figure 7-4.

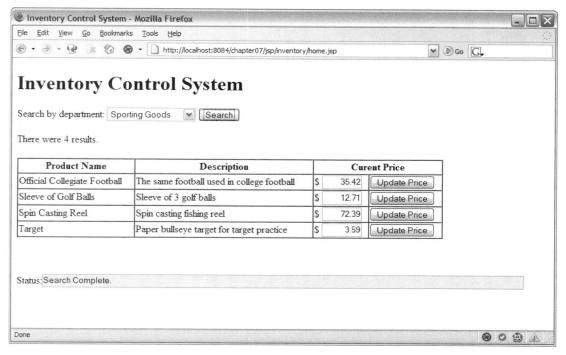

**Figure 7-4.** *This page provides functionality to update a product's price.*

The user searches for products by department and a list is returned showing the name, description, and current price for each product in the list. The user can update the product's price by changing the price and clicking the Update Price button.

Nothing too flashy happening on this page, right? That's true, but there is some Ajax magic happening behind the scenes. First, clicking the Search button invokes an Ajax request to search for the products in the specified department. Instead of refreshing the entire page for doing a search, Ajax is used to dynamically build the results table, making the application appear much snappier to the user.

Second, Ajax is once again used for updating the price. When the user enters a new price and clicks the Update Price button, an Ajax request is sent to the server with the product ID and the new price. After a (hopefully) successful update of the product's price, a response indicating the status of the update process is returned to the browser. If the update operation is successful, the Status area indicates that to the user.

## Domain Layer

The domain model for this application is quite simple. It consists of a single class, Product, that models the products sold in the store. Listing 7-10 shows the source code for the Product class.

**Listing 7-10.** *Product.java*

```java
package com.proajax.chapt7.domain;

public class Product {
    private Long id;
    private String name= "";
    private String description = "";
    private double price = 0.00;

    public Product() {}

    public Product(Long id, String name, String description, double price) {
        super();
        this.id = id;
        this.name = name;
        this.description = description;
        this.price = price;
    }

    public String getName() {
        return name;
    }

    public void setName(String name) {
        this.name = name;
    }

    public String getDescription() {
        return description;
    }

    public void setDescription(String description) {
        this.description = description;
    }
```

```
    public double getPrice() {
        return price;
    }

    public void setPrice(double price) {
        this.price = price;
    }

    public Long getId() {
        return id;
    }

    public void setId(Long id) {
        this.id = id;
    }
}
```

The Product class is implemented as a simple JavaBean with four properties: the product's id, name, description, and price. Each property has its own set of accessor and mutator methods. The class implements two constructors: one no-args constructor and another one that accepts the id, name, description, and price as method arguments.

There are a number of ways in which the Product class could have been implemented. For example, each department may have its own subclass of Product, such as a SportingGoodsProduct or a ClothingProduct. Product could also have additional domain functionality, such as an applyPercentageDiscount method that would discount the product's price by the specified percentage. For this example, the Product class was kept simple.

## Data Access Layer

Many of today's web-based applications are variations upon a common theme: reading and writing data to a database. Armed with the (simple) domain layer, the application now needs a way to access a persistent database so each Product's properties can read from and write to a database.

The Data Access Object[1] (DAO) pattern is a common Java EE pattern for accessing databases. The DAO pattern is used to abstract and encapsulate all access to the database. A well-designed DAO will completely encapsulate the inner workings of *how* it actually connects to a database, and it should only expose a public API that describes the DAO's available operations. A DAO that accesses a relational database should not expose any of the low-level details regarding the relational database to its clients; instead, it should only expose methods that describe what should be done, such as findProducts or updateProductPrice.

---

1. http://java.sun.com/blueprints/corej2eepatterns/Patterns/DataAccessObject.html

The data access layer for this example is broken down into two parts. First, a Java interface describing the operations that should be implemented by any DAO that implements the interface; and second, a concrete implementation of the interface. Listing 7-11 shows the DAO interface supporting the Product class.

**Listing 7-11.** *ProductDAO.java*

```java
package com.proajax.chapt7.dao;

import com.proajax.chapt7.domain.Product;
import java.util.List;

public interface ProductDAO {

    public List<Product> findProductsBy(String department);

    void updateProductPrice(Long productId, Double price);
}
```

The ProductDAO interface defines two methods: findProductsByDepartment and updateProductPrice. The findProductsByDepartment method, not surprisingly, searches for all products within the given department. The updateProductPrice method, as its name describes, updates the price of the product with the given productId to the specified price. This interface defines a clean API for accessing the database that stores product information. Clients of this interface don't know (and don't care!) how the underlying database is implemented.

Of course, the interface isn't particularly useful without an implementing class. Listing 7-12 lists an implementation of the ProductDAO interface named ProductDAOImpl.

**Listing 7-12.** *ProductDAOImpl.java*

```java
package com.proajax.chapt7.dao;

import com.proajax.chapt7.domain.Product;
import java.util.ArrayList;
import java.util.List;

public class ProductDAOImpl implements ProductDAO {

    public List<Product> findProductsByDepartment(String department) {
        if(department.trim().equalsIgnoreCase("grocery")) {
            return getGroceryProducts();
        }
```

```java
        else if(department.trim().equalsIgnoreCase("clothing")) {
            return getClothingProducts();
        }
        else if(department.trim().equalsIgnoreCase("sporting")) {
            return getSportingGoodsProducts();
        }
        else if(department.trim().equalsIgnoreCase("home")) {
            return getHomeFurnishingsProducts();
        }

        return getGroceryProducts();
    }

    public void updateProductPrice(Long productId, Double price) {
        // persist the new price to the database
    }

    private List getGroceryProducts() {
        List products = new ArrayList();

        products.add(new Product(new Long(1), "WonderLoad Bread",
                "Dual pack of healthy wheat bread", 1.59));
        products.add(new Product(new Long(2),"Heartland Gallon Milk",
                "One gallon of 2% milk", 2.34));
        products.add(new Product(new Long(3), "Ultra Chip Cookies",
                "Pack of chocolate chip cookies", 3.72));
        products.add(new Product(new Long(4),"Crunchy Potato Chips",
                "Bag of super crunchy potato chips", 2.51));

        return products;
    }

    private List getClothingProducts() {
        List products = new ArrayList();

        products.add(new Product(new Long(5), "Minnesota Vikings Cap",
                "Baseball cap featuring the Vikings logo", 15.99));
        products.add(new Product(new Long(6),"Jogging suit",
                "All weather jogging suit", 44.99));
        products.add(new Product(new Long(7), "Leather Jacket",
                "Leather jacket with removable liner", 115.89));
```

```
            products.add(new Product(new Long(8),"T-shirt",
                    "Cotton t-shirt in assorted colors", 9.99));

            return products;

        }

        private List getSportingGoodsProducts() {
            List products = new ArrayList();

            products.add(new Product(new Long(9), "Official Collegiate Football",
                    "The same football used in college football", 35.42));
            products.add(new Product(new Long(10),"Sleeve of Golf Balls",
                    "Sleeve of 3 golf balls", 12.71));
            products.add(new Product(new Long(11), "Spin Casting Reel",
                    "Spin casting fishing reel", 72.39));
            products.add(new Product(new Long(12),"Target",
                    "Paper bullseye target for target practice", 3.59));

            return products;
        }

        private List getHomeFurnishingsProducts() {
            List products = new ArrayList();

            products.add(new Product(new Long(13), "Coffee Table",
                    "Oak finished coffee table with glass top", 136.80));
            products.add(new Product(new Long(14),"Lamp",
                    "Single bulb lamp with brass finish", 41.65));
            products.add(new Product(new Long(15), "Glider Rocker",
                    "Glider rocker in assorted colors", 123.75));
            products.add(new Product(new Long(16),"Cordless Telephone",
                    "Cordless telephone with answering machine", 58.12));

            return products;
        }
    }
```

Looking at the source code for ProductDAOImpl, you'll likely notice something missing, like the fact that it doesn't actually access a database of any sort. Instead, all of the method calls are either empty or return hard-coded data. So what's the point?

Writing database access code is hard. Some estimates say that up to 80 percent of the time spent on a project is spent on building the data access layer. That's an awful large amount of time. To help mitigate some of that cost, why not split up to the work so that one team works on the data access layer and others work on the web and service layers? To make such an arrangement work, the web and service layers still need to interact with *some* implementation of the data access layer. By writing a DAO implementation that uses hard-coded values, the web and service layers can be developed while the full-blown DAO implementation is being built.

## Service Layer

Remember that one of the key benefits to using the Spring framework is that the cost of programming to interfaces rather than concrete classes is reduced to nearly zero. Like the data access layer you just saw, the service layer will be written as both a generic interface and a concrete class that implements the interface. Listing 7-13 shows the source code for the ProductService interface.

**Listing 7-13.** *ProductService.java*

```
package com.proajax.chapt7.service;

import com.proajax.chapt7.domain.Product;
import java.util.List;

public interface ProductService {
    public List<Product> findProductsByDepartment(String department);

    public void updatePrice(Long productId, Double newPrice);

}
```

You can see that this interface defines only two methods: findProductsByDepartment and updatePrice. The class implementing this interface is ProductServiceImpl, which is shown in Listing 7-14.

**Listing 7-14.** *ProductServiceImpl.java*

```
package com.proajax.chapt7.service;

import com.proajax.chapt7.dao.ProductDAO;
import com.proajax.chapt7.domain.Product;
import com.proajax.chapt7.ui.ProductSearchResult;
import java.util.List;
```

```
public class ProductServiceImpl implements ProductService {
    private ProductDAO productDAO = null;

    public List<Product> findProductsByDepartment(String department) {
        List<Product> products =
                productDAO.findProductsByDepartment(department);
        return products;
    }

    public ProductDAO getProductDAO() {
        return productDAO;
    }

    public void setProductDAO(ProductDAO inventoryDAO) {
        this.productDAO = inventoryDAO;
    }

    public void updatePrice(Long productId, Double newPrice) {
        productDAO.updateProductPrice(productId, newPrice);
    }
}
```

The implementation of this interface is rather simple. About all it does is access the DAO layer to provide access to the underlying database. Notice how this implementation works with an instance of ProductDAO. Remember that ProductDAO is an interface, not a concrete class, so any class that implements the ProductDAO interface can be used by this object. By using an interface, we've decreased the amount of coupling between the service object implementation and the DAO layer, and we've already taken advantage of this by writing a "dummy" implementation of the ProductDAO to help speed development.

You may be wondering why ProductServiceImpl defines getter and setter methods for the productDAO property that does not appear on the ProductService interface. This was done intentionally and with good reason. An implementation of the ProductService interface doesn't necessarily need to use a ProductDAO to do the work for which it was designed. The fact that the ProductServiceImpl class actually does use ProductDAO to do its work is merely an implementation detail and has nothing to do with the business API that should be exposed by the ProductService interface. By keeping the ProductService interface "pure" and free from implementation details you can more easily change the implementation in the future.

## AOP

Earlier in the chapter we discussed the potential benefits of AOP and how it can help remove cross-cutting concerns from application code. This example makes use of two aspects: a performance monitoring aspect and a security logging aspect.

The performance monitoring aspect is a very common application of AOP. Performance monitoring and logging is a cross-cutting concern that can be handled using AOP, and doing so will prevent the pollution of application business logic with the low-level details of monitoring the amount of time it takes to execute a method. Using AOP will greatly reduce the amount of code needed to add performance monitoring to the application, and adding it to new objects is as simple as applying the existing aspect to the new object.

Listing 7-15 lists the source code for the performance monitoring aspect. The PerformanceLoggingInterceptor class implements the MethodInterceptor interface. The MethodInterceptor interface declares a single method named invoke.

**Listing 7-15.** *PerformanceLoggingInterceptor.java*

```
package com.proajax.chapt7.aop;

import org.aopalliance.intercept.MethodInterceptor;
import org.aopalliance.intercept.MethodInvocation;

public class PerformanceLoggingInterceptor implements MethodInterceptor{

    public Object invoke(MethodInvocation methodInvocation) throws Throwable {
        // record the start and end time of the method
        long start = System.currentTimeMillis();
        Object returnValue = methodInvocation.proceed();
        long end = System.currentTimeMillis();

        // create the performance information string
        String className =
                methodInvocation.getMethod().getDeclaringClass().getName();
        StringBuffer buf = new StringBuffer("\n\n")
            .append("Method ")
            .append(className)
            .append(".")
            .append(methodInvocation.getMethod().getName())
            .append(" executed in ")
            .append(end - start)
            .append(" milliseconds");
```

```
        // log to the console for now
        System.out.println(buf.toString());

        return returnValue;
    }
}
```

The `invoke` method is an implementation of an "around" interceptor because it lets you write advice both before and after the invocation of the target method. The first thing this implementation of the `invoke` method does is record the current time from the `System` object and store it in the `start` variable. Next, the `proceed` method of the `methodInvocation` object is called, which effectively calls the target method and allows it to execute. Once that completes, the current time is recorded to the `end` variable. Armed with the target method's start and end time, all that's needed is a little arithmetic to determine the amount of time the target method needed to execute. The last part of the `invoke` method logs the results of the performance monitoring; in this example the data is simply written to the console.

Take a minute to read through the source code in Listing 7-15. Even if you're unfamiliar with the particulars, most of the details should become readily apparent and easy to follow.

The second aspect used by this application is a bit more clever than the performance monitoring aspect. Remember when we were setting up the container-managed security we created for security roles, one for mangers and one for trainees? Consider this use case: the company wants to allow trainees access to the system, but the company wants to keep closer track on what trainees are doing when they're using the system. Certainly one option would be to add logging statements to each and every important business method in the application, but wouldn't it be better to write a reusable aspect that encapsulates such functionality?

The `RoleLoggingInterceptor` shown in Listing 7-16 does just that. Like the `PerformanceLoggingInterceptor` class, this class implements the `MethodInterceptor` interface and the `invoke` method.

**Listing 7-16.** *RoleLoggingInterceptor.java*

```
package com.proajax.chapt7.aop;

import java.util.Date;
import javax.servlet.http.HttpServletRequest;
import org.aopalliance.intercept.MethodInterceptor;
import org.aopalliance.intercept.MethodInvocation;
import uk.ltd.getahead.dwr.WebContext;
import uk.ltd.getahead.dwr.WebContextFactory;
```

```java
public class RoleLoggingInterceptor implements MethodInterceptor {
    public Object invoke(MethodInvocation methodInvocation) throws Throwable {

        // get the WebContext from DWR to get the HttpServletRequest
        WebContext context = WebContextFactory.get();
        HttpServletRequest request = context.getHttpServletRequest();

        // log actions performed by "trainee-role" role
        if(request.isUserInRole("trainee-role")) {
            StringBuffer buf = new StringBuffer();
            buf.append("\nUser ")
            .append(request.getUserPrincipal().getName())
            .append(" is accessing ")
            .append(methodInvocation.getMethod()
                                        .getDeclaringClass().getName())
            .append(".")
            .append(methodInvocation.getMethod().getName())
            .append( " at ")
            .append(new Date().toString());

            System.out.println(buf.toString());
        }

        // continue by allowing the method to execute
        Object obj = methodInvocation.proceed();

        // return any return values from the method
        return obj;
    }
}
```

The key to this implementation of the invoke method is that it checks to see whether the current user is assigned to the trainee-role security role, and if so, logs a message stating the user name, the class and method being accessed, and the current time. Users who are not assigned to the trainee-role security role (like managers) will not have their actions logged.

How exactly does this method determine whether the user is assigned to the trainee-role security role? As you may remember, the HttpServletRequest class defines a method named isUserInRole that returns a boolean indicating whether the current user is assigned to the specified role. However, an instance of HttpServletRequest is not one of the method parameters to the invoke method, so how is it available for use in that method?

DWR provides the WebContext object that is specifically designed to provide access to these useful servlet parameters. An instance of the WebContext object is obtained by using the WebContextFactory's static get method. From there the getHttpServletRequest method provides access to the HttpServletRequest object.

The final thing you may be wondering is how to wire these aspects together with target objects. It's simple to do, and if you can just hold that thought for a minute you'll see how easy it is to do using the magic of Spring.

## Data Helper Objects

So far you've seen most of the service and data access layers and have learned how Spring's support for AOP and dependency injection can be leveraged to build a flexible and easily maintainable application. Before we leave the service and data access tiers and investigate the client tier, there's one more set of objects we need to investigate.

As stated earlier, this example uses DWR to handle the low-level Ajax plumbing, so we don't have to worry about writing a bunch of redundant JavaScript that uses the XMLHttpRequest object. An added bonus of DWR is that it can access Spring beans as easily as it can access any other Java object, so we'll use that capability to call the ProductService directly from the browser-side JavaScript.

The price management page of the application offers the user two actions: searching for all of the products within a department and updating the price of a product. Not coincidentally, the ProductService interface defines a method for each of these actions. So far so good, right?

The problem with this scenario is that the return values of the two ProductService methods don't exactly fit what the client needs. For example, the updatePrice method has a void return value. This is normal and expected behavior for a general-purpose API, but what if an error occurs? How will the user be notified of the error? The JavaScript client can't catch errors thrown from the service layer or data access layer. We could change the updatePrice method to return some sort of object that encapsulates the results of the method, but that's nonstandard behavior, not to mention the fact that if this were an existing service bean that was being adapted for Ajax use, changing the return type of the method would break all of the existing code that uses that method.

One simple yet robust solution to this problem is shown in Listing 7-17. Instead of interacting directly with the ProductService, the JavaScript client will work with an instance of the ProductServiceRemote class.

**Listing 7-17.** *ProductServiceRemote.java*

```
package com.proajax.chapt7.service;

import com.proajax.chapt7.domain.Product;
import com.proajax.chapt7.ui.ProductSearchResult;
import com.proajax.chapt7.ui.UpdateProductPriceResult;
```

```java
import java.util.List;

public class ProductServiceRemote {

    private ProductService productService;

    public ProductSearchResult findProductsByDepartment(String department) {
        List<Product> products = productService.findProductsByDepartment(department);
        ProductSearchResult result = new ProductSearchResult(products);
        return result;
    }

    public UpdateProductPriceResult updateProductPrice(Long productId
            , Double newPrice) {
        UpdateProductPriceResult result = new UpdateProductPriceResult();
        result.setSuccessful(true);

        try {
            productService.updatePrice(productId, newPrice);
        }
        catch(Throwable t) {
            result.setSuccessful(false);
            result.setErrorMessage(t.toString());
        }

        return result;
    }

    public ProductService getProductService() {
        return productService;
    }

    public void setProductService(ProductService productService) {
        this.productService = productService;
    }
}
```

The ProductServiceRemote class is a thin wrapper[2] around ProductService. For the most part, the methods on ProductServiceRemote simply call the equivalent methods on

---

2. Strict followers of design patterns will recognize this as the Decorator pattern.

ProductService. ProductServiceRemote adds value by creating a JavaBean object that can be serialized by DWR and sent as the return value of a method call.

For example, the updateProductPrice wraps the call to the ProductService's updatePrice method. The updateProductPrice method creates and returns an instance of the UpdateProductPriceResult (Listing 7-18) class, which encapsulates a property indicating success or failure and the error message if one occurred. The findProductsByDepartment method returns a ProductSearchResult (Listing 7-19) object which encapsulates the results of the search.

**Listing 7-18.** *UpdateProductPriceResult.java*

```java
package com.proajax.chapt7.ui;

public class UpdateProductPriceResult {

    private boolean successful;
    private String errorMessage = "";

    public boolean isSuccessful() {
        return successful;
    }

    public void setSuccessful(boolean successful) {
        this.successful = successful;
    }

    public String getErrorMessage() {
        return errorMessage;
    }

    public void setErrorMessage(String errorMessage) {
        this.errorMessage = errorMessage;
    }
}
```

The advantage of wrapping ProductService with an Ajax-specific object is that the API for ProductService remains "pure" and doesn't have to be specifically changed to accommodate Ajax functionality, maximizing ProductService's reusability and preventing a tight coupling between the service layer and Ajax functionality.

**Listing 7-19.** *ProductSearchResult.java*

```java
package com.proajax.chapt7.ui;

import com.proajax.chapt7.domain.Product;
import java.util.List;

public class ProductSearchResult {

    private List<Product> products;
    private int resultCount;

    public ProductSearchResult(List<Product> products) {
        this.products = products;
        resultCount = products.size();
    }

    public List<Product> getProducts() {
        return products;
    }

    public void setProducts(List<Product> products) {
        this.products = products;
    }

    public int getResultCount() {
        return resultCount;
    }

    public void setResultCount(int resultCount) {
        this.resultCount = resultCount;
    }

}
```

## Spring Beans Configuration

The Java code for the service and data access layers is now complete. The last thing left to do is to wire everything together using Spring's XML configuration file. Listing 7-20 shows the Spring beans.xml file for this example that wires everything together.

**Listing 7-20.** *The* beans.xml *File Configures Spring's Dependency Injection and AOP Aspects*

```xml
<?xml version="1.0" encoding="UTF-8"?>
<!DOCTYPE beans PUBLIC "-//SPRING//DTD BEAN//EN"
    "http://www.springframework.org/dtd/spring-beans.dtd">

<beans>
    <bean id="serviceBean"
    class="com.proajax.chapt7.service.AdvancedHelloWorldService"/>

    <bean id="productDAO"
    class="com.proajax.chapt7.dao.ProductDAOImpl"/>

    <bean id="productService"
    class="com.proajax.chapt7.service.ProductServiceImpl">
        <property name="productDAO" ref="productDAO"/>
    </bean>

    <bean id="productServiceRemote"
    class="com.proajax.chapt7.service.ProductServiceRemote">
        <property name="inventoryService" ref="inventoryService"/>
    </bean>

    <bean id="roleLoggingInterceptor"
    class="com.proajax.chapt7.aop.RoleLoggingInterceptor"/>

    <bean id="performanceLoggingInterceptor"
    class="com.proajax.chapt7.aop.PerformanceLoggingInterceptor"/>

    <bean id="productServiceProxy"
    class="org.springframework.aop.framework.ProxyFactoryBean">
        <property name="target">
            <ref local="inventoryServiceRemote"/>
        </property>
        <property name="interceptorNames">
            <list>
                <value>roleLoggingInterceptor</value>
                <value>performanceLoggingInterceptor</value>
            </list>
        </property>
    </bean>
</beans>
```

We'll start from the top and work our way down through the listing. As we do, you should be able to imagine that we're building the application by snapping components (Spring beans) together to form a single, functional unit. You can imagine that the individual Spring beans are LEGO bricks and the configuration done in beans.xml simply snaps the bricks together.

The first Spring bean for the application is the productDAO bean. This bean, of course, is the data access object. Note that the specified bean class is the actual concrete implementation class, not the interface definition. Most classes in the beans.xml file should be concrete implementations, not interfaces. In contrast, when you're writing the actual Java code, try to code to the interface instead of the implementation as much as possible.

The next bean is the productService bean. This bean is the actual service bean implementation. This is also the first example of dependency injection. The productService bean defines a property named productDAO that points back to the productDAO bean you saw in the preceding paragraph. All this is doing is telling Spring to inject (using the setProductDAO method) the productDAO bean into the productService bean. The productService bean did not have to use any complicated JNDI lookups to find the data access bean, and in fact it didn't even have to use the new keyword to create a new instance. All productService has to do is expose a public setter method so Spring can inject an instance directly into the productService bean. The method signature of the setProductDAO method says that it accepts an instance of ProductDAO (an interface), meaning that any class implementing the ProductDAO interface can be used. In this case, we're using the ProductDAOImpl class. Changing this implementation is as easy as changing the XML file. If you haven't seen it before you should now be realizing how Spring makes it easy to code to interfaces rather than concrete implementations.

Following the productService bean in beans.xml is the productServiceRemote bean. This is the actual object that the JavaScript client will work with through DWR. This bean also relies on dependency injection to obtain its instance of a ProductService. Here, the productService bean defined in the previous bean definition satisfies the dependency injection.

The last three bean definitions have to do with AOP, which you've no doubt been waiting on the edge of your seat to hear more about. The roleLoggingInterceptor and performanceLoggingInterceptor beans refer to the aspects we saw in a previous section. You remember that these aspects represent cross-cutting concerns that can be applied to multiple targets.

The last bean, productServiceProxy, is how the two aspects are wired together with the productServiceRemote bean. First, note that the class used to define this bean is ProxyFactoryBean, which is a special Spring class that handles the adding of aspects to target objects. The target in this instance is the productServiceRemote bean. By listing the roleLoggingInterceptor and performanceLoggingInterceptor in the list of interceptorNames, we've configured the productServiceRemote bean so that all of its method calls will be intercepted by first the roleLoggingInterceptor and then the performanceLoggingInterceptor.

This is a very powerful concept. Without polluting the core business functionality of the productServiceRemote bean, we've been able to add two aspects to the bean's functionality. All we had to do was some simple configuration in an XML file. Adding or removing aspects in the future is as easy as editing the XML file. You can also see how easy it would be to reuse these aspects across multiple target beans.

Remember the example at the beginning of the chapter that introduced AOP concepts, where the simple method was polluted with code for logging and performance monitoring? You can now see how the logging and performance monitoring code could be removed from the method and placed in their own aspects. They could then be reused across multiple classes by adding entries to the XML configuration file. The application code stays clean and free of such low-level code not related to business functions.

### The Web Tier

Before we start writing the client-side JSPs and JavaScript, we should configure DWR through the dwr.xml file, which is placed in the WAR file's WEB-INF directory. The dwr.xml file is shown in Listing 7-21.

**Listing 7-21.** *dwr.xml*

```
<!DOCTYPE dwr PUBLIC
    "-//GetAhead Limited//DTD Direct Web Remoting 1.0//EN"
    "http://www.getahead.ltd.uk/dwr/dwr10.dtd">

<dwr>
    <allow>
        <create creator="spring" javascript="SpringBean">
            <param name="beanName" value="serviceBean"/>
        </create>

        <create creator="spring" javascript="ProductService">
            <param name="beanName" value="productServiceProxy"/>
        </create>

        <convert converter="bean" match="com.proajax.chapt7.domain.Product">
            <param name="include" value="id, name, description, price"/>
        </convert>

        <convert converter="bean"
            match="com.proajax.chapt7.ui.ProductSearchResult">
            <param name="products, resultCount"/>
        </convert>
```

```
        <convert converter="bean"
            match="com.proajax.chapt7.ui.UpdateProductPriceResult">
            <param name="successful, errorMessages"/>
        </convert>
    </allow>
</dwr>
```

The big news in this file is the `ProductService` bean. Note how the `creator` for this bean is `spring` as opposed to `new`. This instructs DWR to retrieve the bean as a Spring bean rather than create a new instance using the `new` keyword. The rest of the beans in `dwr.xml` are classes that DWR must serialize to equivalent JavaScript objects. The `Product` class is the `Product` domain object, while the `ProductSearchResult` and `UpdateProductPriceResult` classes are the return objects of the `ProductServiceRemote` class's `findProductsByDepartment` and `updateProductPrice` methods, respectively.

With the service and data access tiers complete, we can now turn our attention to the web tier. The search and update price functionality all occurs on a single JSP page named `home.jsp`, which you saw in Figure 7-4. The source code for `home.jsp` is shown in Listing 7-22.

**Listing 7-22.** *home.jsp*

```
<!DOCTYPE html PUBLIC "-//W3C//DTD XHTML 1.0 Strict//EN"
            "http://www.w3.org/TR/xhtml1/DTD/xhtml1-strict.dtd">
<%@page pageEncoding="UTF-8"%>

<html xmlns="http://www.w3.org/1999/xhtml">

    <head>
        <title>Inventory Control System</title>
        <script type="text/javascript"
        src="/chapter07/dwr/interface/ProductService.js"></script>
        <script type="text/javascript" src="/chapter07/dwr/engine.js"></script>
        <script type="text/javascript"
        src="/chapter07/js/inventory.js"></script>
        <script type="text/javascript"
        src="/chapter07/js/template.js"></script>


    </head>

    <body>
        <div id="wrapper">
            <h1>Inventory Control System</h1>
```

```
            Search by department:
            <select id="selectDepartment">
                <option value="home">Home Furnishings</option>
                <option value="clothing">Clothing</option>
                <option value="sporting">Sporting Goods</option>
                <option value="grocery">Grocery</option>
            </select>

            <button onclick="findProductsByDepartment();">Search</button>

            <br /><br />
            <div id="products">

            </div>
        </div>

        <br /><br /><br />
        Status:<input type="text" id="status"
        readonly="readonly" style="width:90%;"/>

        <div id="jstTemplates" style="display:none;">
            <textarea id="searchResultsTemplate">
                <jsp:include page="searchResultsTemplate.jst"/>
            </textarea>
        </div>
    </body>

</html>
```

You should recognize the engine.js and ProductService.js files as DWR JavaScript files, and template.js is the JavaScript Templates file that will render new content from the Ajax request. At the bottom of the page is the textarea that holds the JavaScript Templates file, which is split out into its own file and included using the jsp:include tag.

All of the custom JavaScript for this application resides in the product.js JavaScript file, which is shown in Listing 7-23. The product.js file is only 40 lines long, including validation code, and since we covered DWR in depth in Chapter 4, most of it should seem pretty familiar to you.

**Listing 7-23.** *product.js*

```
function findProductsByDepartment() {
    document.getElementById("status").value = "Searching...";
    var department = document.getElementById("selectDepartment").value;
    ProductService.findProductsByDepartment(department, handleFindProducts);
}

function handleFindProducts(searchResult) {
    var result = TrimPath.processDOMTemplate("searchResultsTemplate"
                                                , searchResult);
    document.getElementById("inventory").innerHTML = result;
    document.getElementById("status").value = "Search Complete.";
}

function updatePrice(productId, price) {
    if(!isValidDollarAmount(price)) {
        alert("Not a valid dollar amount.");
        return;
    }

    document.getElementById("status").value = "Updating...";
    ProductService.updateProductPrice(productId, price, handleUpdatePrice);
}

function handleUpdatePrice(result) {
    if(result.successful) {
        document.getElementById("status").value = "Update Successful.";
    }
    else {
        var errorMessage = "Updated failed. Error message: ";
        var errorMessge = errorMessage + result.errorMessage;
        document.getElementById("status").value = errorMessage;
    }
}

function isValidDollarAmount(amount) {
    var isValid =
    RegExp(/^\$?\d+(\.\d{2})?$/)
    .test(String(amount).replace(/^\s+|\s+$/g, ""));
    return isValid;
}
```

Clicking the Search button calls the findProductsByDepartment function. The first thing this function does is update the text of the status bar at the bottom of the page to indicate that the application is busy searching. Next, it retrieves the value of the selected department from the select box. Finally, it uses DWR to call the findProductsByDepartment method on the ProductServiceRemote bean, passing the selected department to it. The handleFindProducts function is specified as the function that will handle the server response.

The handleFindProducts function is responsible for rendering the table that lists all of the products that exist for the selected department. The argument named searchResult that is passed to the function is the DWR JavaScript representation of the ProductSearchResult object. The function uses JavaScript Templates to parse the searchResult object into HTML that is inserted into the page as the innerHTML of the products element. The JavaScript Templates markup syntax is stored in the searchResultsTemplate.jst file, which is shown in Listing 7-24. The handleFindProducts function concludes by updating the status text at the bottom of the page.

**Listing 7-24.** *searchResultsTemplate.jst*

```
There were ${resultCount} results.

<br /><br />
<table border="1" cellspacing="0" width="80%">
    <thead>
        <th>Product Name</th>
        <th>Description</th>
        <th colspan="2">Current Price</th>
    </thead>
    <tbody>
        {for p in products}
            <tr>
                <td>${p.name}</td>
                <td>${p.description}</td>
                <td>$
                    <input type="text" id="id-${p.id}"
                        value="${p.price}" size="6" style="text-align:right;"/>
                </td>
                <td>
                    <button onclick="updatePrice(${p.id}
                        , document.getElementById('id-${p.id}').value);">
                        Update Price
                    </button>
                </td>
            </tr>
```

```
    {/for}
  </tbody>
</table>
```

The template first retrieves the number of products in the result list and prints that to the page. Then, the template builds a table of the products found in the search, including placing the price in an input box so it can be edited and saved by clicking the Update Price button.

Clicking an Update Price button calls the updatePrice function, passing to it the id of the selected product and the price appearing in the text box. The updatePrice function first calls the isValidDollarAmount function to verify that the text entered by the user is a valid dollar amount. If it's not, updatePrice displays an error message in the alert box and exits.

Assuming the entered dollar amount is valid, updatePrice updates the status text and uses DWR to call the updateProductPrice method on the ProductServiceRemote Spring bean, passing to it the product id and the new price. The handleUpdatePrice function is specified as the function that handles the server response.

A JavaScript object named result, representing the UpdateProductPriceResult object, is passed to the handleUpdatePrice function. The result object has two attributes: a boolean named successful, indicating whether the update operation was successful, and a string named errorMessage that holds the text of any errors that may have occurred during the update operation. The handleUpdate price function checks the success attribute, and if it's true, updates the status text and exits. If the success attribute is false then the status text is updated to indicate that the update operation failed, and the errorMessage attribute is included in the status text.

# Summary

This chapter introduced you to the power and flexibility that Spring can bring to your Java applications. Spring is a lightweight container that makes it easy to program to interfaces rather than concrete implementations and promotes the use of simple JavaBeans-style objects rather than complex container-managed objects like EJBs.

Aspect-oriented programming (AOP) is a new programming technique that complements the more traditional object-oriented programming (OOP) paradigm. AOP allows developers to dynamically add nonbusiness-oriented functionality to objects without polluting the business-related code with secondary requirements like logging or performance monitoring. These secondary requirements can be refactored into their own classes called aspects and reused across multiple objects. Spring supports AOP by allowing aspects to be added to objects through an XML configuration file.

Dependency injection (DI) is a method by which objects are not responsible for looking up their own collaborating objects. Instead of using complicated JNDI lookups or even using the new keyword to create a new collaborating object, an object can simply expose JavaBeans-style getter and setter methods for collaborating objects. An object relying on DI is easy to unit-test outside of any type of container because it doesn't rely on the JNDI services provided by the container. Spring provides DI functionality through XML configuration files. An object's collaborators can be specified via XML, and Spring will automatically inject the collaborators into the target object.

DWR, which we explored in depth in Chapter 4, provides seamless integration with Spring beans. By simply specifying the correct bean in the dwr.xml file, DWR allows a Spring bean to be accessed directly from client-side JavaScript. By doing so, Ajax requests via DWR can take advantage of all of Spring's features like AOP and DI.

In this chapter you saw how DWR and Spring can be combined to build a robust and flexible application that can easily change to meet evolving business requirements. Spring lets us build the service and data access layers as simple, discreet objects that are snapped together like LEGO bricks to build the application.

In the next chapter you'll take a look at the only true Java standard for web frameworks, JavaServer Faces (JSF), and how JSF supports Ajax-style interactions.

# CHAPTER 8

■■■

# JavaServer Faces

**A**ll of the frameworks we've discussed so far all share a common trait—though based heavily on standard Java technology, none are backed by a specification from Sun. Each rose from shortcomings (real or perceived) in the way Sun chose to approach the task of building dynamic web applications. While servlets were better than using CGI scripts and JavaServer Pages were considerably easier to work with than servlets, a number of frameworks have been developed to simplify development. It was in this light that Sun announced the JavaServer Faces (JSF) specification at the 2001 edition of the JavaOne conference (in no small part as an answer to Microsoft's .NET platform).

Alas, it wasn't until March 2004 that the JSF working group released a 1.0 edition of the spec. During this time a number of new frameworks were created, while others were significantly enhanced. Both JSPs and servlets evolved by closing many of the gaps reported by early adopters. Though initial experiences with JSF weren't always very positive, things are certainly changing today. A number of companies have taken a long, hard look at JSF and found it to be a well-executed framework with a thriving component marketplace. Consultants in the JSF space have indicated that interest in training and mentoring in JSF has picked up considerably. As organizations look for answers in the post-Struts world, many are giving the nod to JSF. In this chapter, we will provide a high-level overview of JSF, show how you can add Ajax into the mix, and give you a glimpse of the power of using prebuilt Ajax components.

## What Is JSF?

Much like servlets and JSPs, JavaServer Faces is simply a specification (JSR 127) from Sun. There is a reference implementation (`http://java.sun.com/javaee/javaserverfaces/download.html`) and an open source implementation backed by Apache called MyFaces (`http://myfaces.apache.org`). So what exactly is JSF? Essentially, JSF is Swing for the web, or to put it another way, Swing and Struts merged. (Struts founder Craig McClanahan and early Struts committer David Geary were on the JSF Expert Group.) Relying on an architecture similar to Struts, JSF handles most of the plumbing code that encumbers standard JSP development.

At its core, JSF provides the following three things:

- Prebuilt user-interface components

- An event-driven programming model

- A component model that facilitates creation of new components

Out of the box, JSF is configured to work with JSP technology, though this isn't a requirement. (In fact, JSF has no knowledge of JSP, so forget about using page scope.)

# Getting Started with JSF

First things first. We need to download an implementation of JSF (we'll use the reference implementation in our examples) and install the appropriate JARs per the installation instructions. Once you have the requisite JAR files in place, you need to configure the special servlet that processes every JSF page. We need to associate a URL pattern with this servlet so that our JSF pages are handled appropriately. See Listing 8-1; here we are defining a prefix pattern.[1] For example, let's say the URL is http://www.apress.com/faces/view.jsp. The JSF servlet will strip off the faces prefix and load the view.jsp file.

**Listing 8-1.** *Configuring the JSF Servlet*

```
<servlet>
    <servlet-name>Faces Servlet</servlet-name>
    <servlet-class>javax.faces.webapp.FacesServlet</servlet-class>
    <load-on-startup>1</load-on-startup>
</servlet>
<servlet-mapping>
    <servlet-name>Faces Servlet</servlet-name>
    <url-pattern>/faces/*</url-pattern>
</servlet-mapping>
```

Believe it or not, that's all there is to it.[2] Let's write a simple JSF page to make sure we've got everything set up properly. Our first example really won't do much, but we'll build on top of it (see Listing 8-2). If you've worked with JSPs before, this really doesn't look all that interesting. We have included a couple of tag libraries, and for some reason we've wrapped

---

1. Of course, you aren't limited to using the prefix notation. You could just as easily use a special extension like *.faces or *.jsf.
2. With Java EE 5, JSF becomes part of the container, meaning that the configuration is rendered unnecessary.

most of the HTML in an `<f:view>` tag. Without this wrapper tag, the JSF tags wouldn't work as we expect them to.

**Listing 8-2.** *The First JSF Example*

```
<%@taglib uri="http://java.sun.com/jsf/core" prefix="f"%>
<%@taglib uri="http://java.sun.com/jsf/html" prefix="h"%>

<html>
    <f:view>
        <head>
            <title>Hello JSF</title>
        </head>
        <body>

        <h1>A Simple JSF Example</h1>
        Hello There!

        </body>
    </f:view>
</html>
```

Deploying this to your servlet container and pointing your browser at this file results in the output shown in Figure 8-1. (Notice that the URL includes the `faces` prefix.)

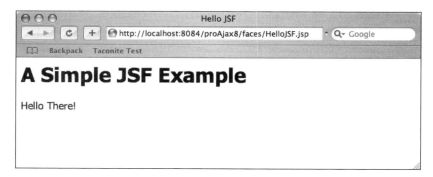

**Figure 8-1.** *A simple JSF example*

Let's tweak this example a bit. Let's allow a user to enter their name, and then we'll just echo it back to them. We'll need to do four things: create a new JSP, create a bean to hold the user name, add some configuration information, and tweak our original JSP. Our new JSP will need a form and a button (see Listing 8-3).

**Listing 8-3.** *The Echo.jsp File*

```
<%@taglib uri="http://java.sun.com/jsf/core" prefix="f"%>
<%@taglib uri="http://java.sun.com/jsf/html" prefix="h"%>

<html>
    <f:view>
        <head>
            <title>A Simple JSF Example</title>
        </head>
        <body>
        <h:form>
            <h1>Please Enter Your Name</h1>
            Name: <h:inputText value="#{user.name}"/>
            <p>
            <h:commandButton value="Say Hello" action="hello"/>
        </h:form>
        </body>
    </f:view>
</html>
```

This page will look something like Figure 8-2. Frankly, this doesn't look too different from a regular JSP, does it? We've got a form, an input field, and a button. There are three key things in this code. First, we have the <h:form> tag. Obviously, this creates a form element to hold our input field. Second, we have the <h:inputText> tag, which creates a text input element. The interesting thing here is the value attribute. We're saying this field is wired to a user bean and its name attribute. Third, we've created a button using the <h:commandButton> tag. In this instance, the value attribute represents the label on the button. More interesting than the label, though, is the action attribute. This has to do with JSF's navigation rules. (We'll get to that in just a second.)

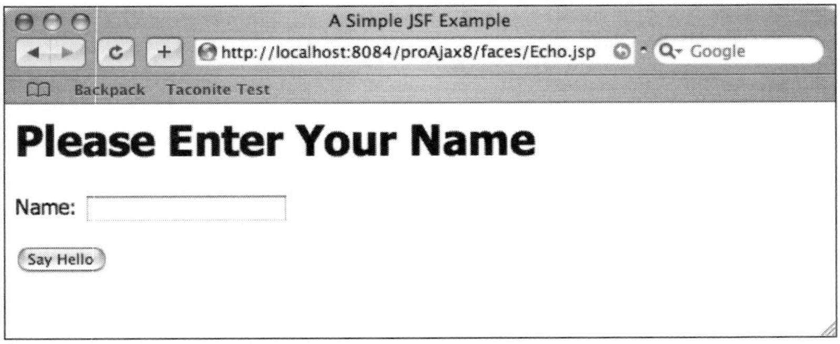

**Figure 8-2.** *Handling user input*

Now that we can collect input from the user, we need someplace for it to go, so we'll create a simple User class. Our User class will follow the standard Java bean paradigm, meaning that we have properties with getters and setters. With JSF, we use beans as the glue between our front-end presentation and our back-end data logic. (And like Tapestry, we won't have to do much to wire them together.) The User class will look something like Listing 8-4.

**Listing 8-4.** *The User Class*

```
package com.proajax.chap8;

public class User {

    private String name = "";

    public User() {
    }

    public String getName() {
        return name;
    }

    public void setName(String name) {
        this.name = name;
    }
}
```

OK, so we've got a bean and the form, but how do we connect the two? At this point, we need to create a configuration file for JSF. Create a new file called faces-config.xml and place it in your web application's WEB-INF folder. The configuration file tells JSF about the navigation rules for your application, and it also manages the beans. For this example, our faces-config.xml looks like Listing 8-5.

**Listing 8-5.** *The faces-config.xml File*

```
<?xml version='1.0' encoding='UTF-8'?>

<!DOCTYPE faces-config PUBLIC
    "-//Sun Microsystems, Inc.//DTD JavaServer Faces Config 1.1//EN"
    "http://java.sun.com/dtd/web-facesconfig_1_1.dtd">
```

```
<faces-config>
    <navigation-rule>
        <from-view-id>/Echo.jsp</from-view-id>
        <navigation-case>
            <from-outcome>hello</from-outcome>
            <to-view-id>/HelloJSF.jsp</to-view-id>
        </navigation-case>
    </navigation-rule>

    <managed-bean>
        <managed-bean-name>user</managed-bean-name>
        <managed-bean-class>com.proajax.chap8.User</managed-bean-class>
        <managed-bean-scope>session</managed-bean-scope>
    </managed-bean>

</faces-config>
```

What's going on here? First, we're defining a navigation rule. JSF has a built-in navigation handler that figures out where to go next. In this case, we're specifying whether the hello action from the Echo.jsp file takes us to the HelloJSF.jsp page. You'll notice that this outcome matches the action attribute from the button we created in the Echo.jsp file; if an outcome wasn't mapped in the configuration file, the current page just refreshes. Next, we've created a managed bean. Essentially, we are telling the framework to instantiate an instance of the User class (written earlier) and bind it to the session scope under the name user. We have other scopes at our disposal. We could have used "none" if we didn't want the bean cached at all. We could have used request scope for short-lived data, or we even could have used application scope if we wanted this bean to last for the lifetime of the application. Here we've used the session scope, meaning that we'll associate an instance of the bean with a specific user session.

OK, so we've got our form, our bean, and we've wired them together. Now we have to tweak our original JSP a bit to output the user name. We'll add <h:outputText value="#{user.name}"/> between the There and the ! in the JSP source from our HelloJSF.jsp file. If we put a name into the input field and click the button, we'll see something like Figure 8-3.

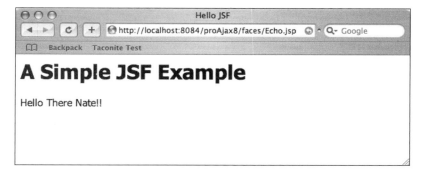

**Figure 8-3.** *Echoing a name*

# Dynamic Navigation

Of course, hard-coding navigation rules isn't the most robust solution. After all, the flow of a web application often depends on more than just what button or link was pressed; it typically is based on what a user entered on the page. JSF easily meets this need by allowing you to associate a method with a *user action*. Let's modify our Echo.jsp example a bit to demonstrate what this might look like.

For starters, we'll add a new method to our User class. If the user enters the name "Nate," we will head to our familiar Hello page, but if they don't, we'll send them someplace else. Let's start by adding the code from Listing 8-6 to the User class. We now need to make a call to this method from our button, so we'll replace the hard-coded action of "hello" with action="#{user.isNate}". This is a *method expression*—we are telling JSF to fire the isNate method on the user bean when this button is selected. Keep in mind that in this instance, the method expression doesn't take parameters and return a String value. (The actual signature is enforced by the JSF component. Some methods may take a parameter and return void, for instance.) The JSF navigation handler uses the returned String in conjunction with the navigation rules to determine the flow of the application. Finally, we need to add the configuration from Listing 8-7 to your faces-config.xml file so that JSF knows what page each outcome maps to.

**Listing 8-6.** *The isNate Method*

```
public String isNate() {
    String result = "notNate";
    if (name.equalsIgnoreCase("Nate")) {
        result = "nate";
    }
    return result;
}
```

**Listing 8-7.** *The Navigation Rules*

```
<navigation-rule>
    <from-view-id>/Echo3.jsp</from-view-id>
    <navigation-case>
        <from-outcome>nate</from-outcome>
        <to-view-id>/HelloJSF.jsp</to-view-id>
    </navigation-case>
    <navigation-case>
        <from-outcome>notNate</from-outcome>
        <to-view-id>/NotNate.jsp</to-view-id>
    </navigation-case>
</navigation-rule>
```

Now, when we enter something other than "Nate" (like "Ryan"), we see something like
Figure 8-4.

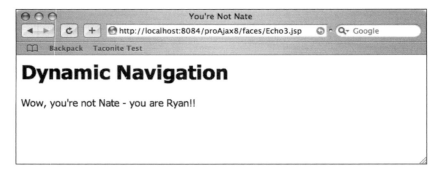

**Figure 8-4.** *Dynamic navigation*

# JSF Taglibs

As you can see, creating JSF applications involves utilizing the two tag libraries: core and
HTML. So far, we've touched on only a few of them. In practice, there are more than 40
that provide for a variety of needs. In general, the core tags are simply helpers to the HTML,
and they include

- actionListener

- attribute

- convertDateTime

- converter

- convertNumber

- facet

- loadBundle

- param

- selectItem

- selectItems

- subview

- validateDoubleRange

- validateLength

- validateLongRange

- validator

- valueChangeListener

- verbatim

- view

Essentially, these tags are all things you would "add" to a component—special validators, listeners, converters, parameters, and attributes. The HTML tags are familiar to web developers and give us the components we need to build our applications, including inputs, outputs, buttons, and links. The HTML tags are

- column

- commandButton

- commandLink

- dataTable

- form

- graphicImage

- inputHidden

- inputSecret

- inputText

- inputTextArea

- message

- messages

- outputFormat

- outputLabel

- outputLink

- outputText

- panelGrid

- panelGroup

- selectBooleanCheckbox

- selectManyCheckbox

- selectManyListbox

- selectManyMenu

- selectOneListbox

- selectOneMenu

- selectOneRadio

Tag libraries are nothing special; chances are you've probably created your own custom tags or used those from another library. But unlike other libraries, the JSF tags represent both a component (output) and a specific renderer (link). This explains the apparent wordiness of the HTML tags. The first part of the tag name (for example, selectMany) is the specific behavioral component, while the second part (for example, Checkbox) represents the specific renderer. This approach allows us to easily swap rendering technology in and out if we need to extend or modify our application.

These tags have a number of useful attributes. For example, you can apply CSS using inline styles with the `style` attribute or via classes with the `styleClass` attribute. Most tags have pass-through attributes for common HTML attributes such as `maxlength`, `size`, and `disabled`, and most tags support common DHTML attributes like `onchange`, `onkeypress`, and `onblur`. For a complete list, consult the documentation.

In the Ajax arena, we are particularly interested in these attributes. But before you run off to take advantage of all those change events by coding a whole bunch of JavaScript, you need to understand how components are named by JSF. For fun, let's say you want to display the value of the textbox in an alert when it loses focus. You might write some code like that in Listing 8-8. Of course, we'd take advantage of the pass-through attributes of the `inputText` tag, and you'd probably provide your own ID (like "name").

**Listing 8-8.** *A Simple Alert*

```
function showValue() {
    var value = document.getElementById("name").value;
    alert("The value is: " + value);
}
```

Surprisingly, running this code results in Figure 8-5. The value is "null." Hmm, what went wrong?

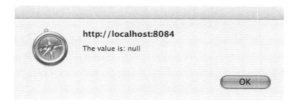

**Figure 8-5.** *An unexpected result*

The answer lies hidden in the HTML generated by JSF. First, if you don't supply an `id` attribute to your tags (as we didn't in our previous example), JSF will automatically generate them for us. So, if we look at the source produced from the `Echo.jsp` file, we see something like Listing 8-9. As you can see, JSF kindly named our form and our button (and inserted a hidden field that is used to save state on the client). Looking more closely, we can also see that JSF modified the `name` attribute of our input field. Instead of simply being "name" as our JavaScript was expecting, the form name and a colon have been prepended to the name value of our field. All form components that JSF generates will be named `formName:componentName`, meaning that our JavaScript needs to reference the element with this compound name. With this in mind, we'll add an `id` to our form and modify our function to take into account the JSF naming pattern. These changes result in Figure 8-6.

**Listing 8-9.** *The Echo.jsp HTML*

```html
<html>
    <head>
        <title>A Simple JSF Example</title>
        <script type="text/javascript">
            function showValue() {
                var value = document.getElementById("name");
                alert("The value is: " + value);
            }
        </script>

    </head>
    <body>
        <form id="_id0" method="post" action="/proAjax8/faces/Echo2.jsp"
            enctype="application/x-www-form-urlencoded">

        <h1>Please Enter Your Name</h1>
        Name: <input id="_id0:name" type="text" name="_id0:name"
            onblur="showValue()" />
        <p>
        <input type="submit" name="_id0:_id1" value="Say Hello" />
        <input type="hidden" name="_id0" value="_id0" />
        </form>
    </body>

</html>
```

**Figure 8-6.** *Displaying the name*

# Validating and Converting

So far, we've seen how to set basic String properties, and while it's great that we don't have to deal with session or request objects, eventually any web application worth its salt will have other data types. Unlike other frameworks that force us to convert from the strings of the web to the data types we store on the back end, JSF can handle most of the common conversions for us. We can always create our own converter if we need something more complicated. Of course, it's also pretty likely that we'll want to validate our input, too. Luckily JSF can help us out quite a bit in that regard. While we can certainly build our own converters and validators, JSF has a pretty decent set of built-in helpers that we can leverage out of the box.

Let's start by showing how we can use JSF to convert properties for us by looking at the standard converters: f:convertDateTime and f:convertNumber. (You can also set a converter on a component by supplying the ID of a given converter via the converter attribute.) Both tags have a number of attributes that let you specify the maximum numbers of digits, date patterns, locales, currency codes, and so on. JSF also supplies a standard error message (that can be overridden) and redisplays the page if a conversion fails. Let's take a look at some code that puts this into action by examining a very simplified bill pay system (see Listing 8-10). Our form will allow the user to input a "Pay to" value, an amount to pay, and a date to pay the bill on.

**Listing 8-10.** *ConvertAndValidate.jsp*

```
<%@taglib uri="http://java.sun.com/jsf/core" prefix="f"%>
<%@taglib uri="http://java.sun.com/jsf/html" prefix="h"%>

<html>
    <f:view>
        <head>
            <title>Converters and Validators</title>
        </head>
        <body>
            <h1>Not Really Bill Pay</h1>
            <h:form id="form">
                <h:panelGrid columns="3">
                    <h:outputText value="Pay to:"/>
                    <h:inputText value="#{billpay.payTo}" id="payTo"/>
                    <h:message for="payTo" style="color:red"/>
                    <h:outputText value="Amount:"/>
                    <h:inputText value="#{billpay.amount}" id="amount">
                        <f:convertNumber minFractionDigits="2"/>
                    </h:inputText>
                    <h:message for="amount" style="color:red"/>
                    <h:outputText value="Date:"/>
                    <h:inputText value="#{billpay.payDate}" id="payDate">
                        <f:convertDateTime pattern="MM/dd/yyyy"/>
                    </h:inputText>
```

```
                    <h:message for="payDate" style="color:red"/>
                </h:panelGrid>
                <h:commandButton value="Pay Bill" action="paybill"/>
            </h:form>
        </body>
    </f:view>
</html>
```

Much of this should look pretty familiar by now. We've got a form, some inputs, and a button. However, there are a few new elements here. First, we see an h:panelGrid tag. This tag creates a table (defined with three columns in this example) behind the scenes, saving us from the effort of having to manually lay out the page.[3] If you've ever programmed in Swing before, you've probably worked with concepts similar to the h:panelGrid. As you can see from Figure 8-7, JSF figures out when a new row is needed.

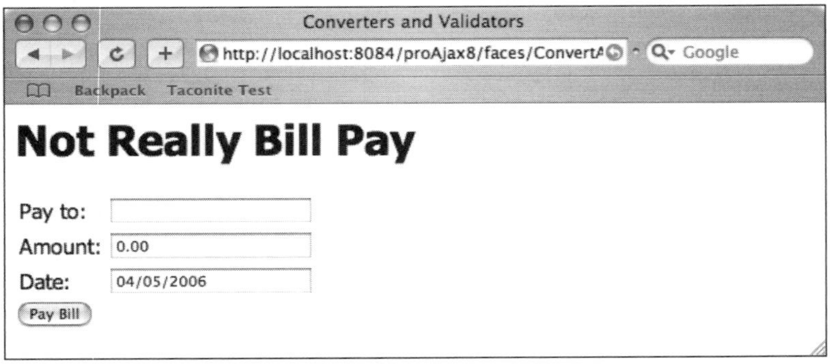

**Figure 8-7.** *Bill pay system in action*

The next thing you might notice are the h:message tags, which, as you might have guessed, display messages. Many first-time JSF developers are surprised when their pages are simply redisplayed on a validation or conversion error. Without including a message component, you won't see any messages. So, before you point the finger at a malfunctioning button or navigation rule, make sure there aren't some missing message components. You'll also notice that we've used the style attribute to change the message color to red. In a production system, you would want to use a style class instead. We've also taken advantage of f:convertDateTime and f:convertNumber to help us with our conversions. Now, if the properties we're binding our components to are primitives, Strings, BigInteger, or BigDecimal, JSF will automatically pick the proper converter for us. However, we're on our own with date values, and here we've chosen to say that our Amount field must have two decimal places since it represents a currency. You can see from the code that we want our Date field

---

3. Yes, we know that tables aren't ideal for page layout, but this is just an example!

to be displayed in month/day/year format, and JSF happily obliges. So what happens when we input some garbage into these fields? See Figure 8-8. Though these aren't exactly the best messages in the world, that's not bad for almost no effort on our part.

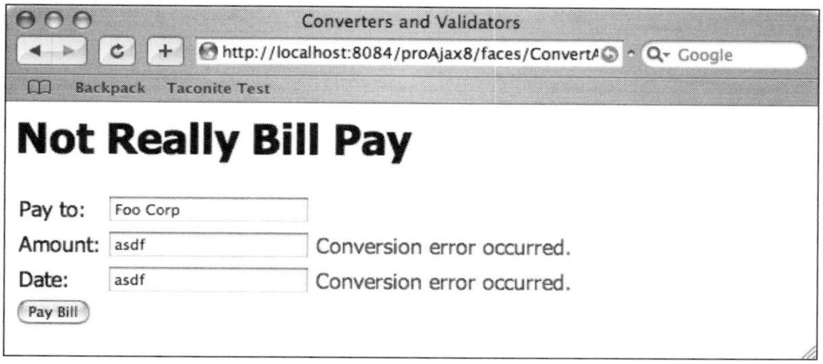

**Figure 8-8.** *Showing conversion errors*

Let's tweak this example a bit to add one of JSF's built-in validators to our "Pay to" and Amount fields. First, let's say for some arbitrary reason we want to cap the length of the "Pay to" field to 25 characters. To do this, we'll add an f:validateLength tag to our existing input tag, and we'll set a value of 25 to the maximum attribute. Next, we'll add a constraint to our "Pay to" field that says you must pay at least $5 but no more than $5,000. We accomplish this by adding an f:validateDoubleRange tag and supplying our minimum and maximum values. When we're done, our code should look something like Listing 8-11.

**Listing 8-11.** *Adding Validations*

```
<h:outputText value="Pay to:"/>
<h:inputText value="#{billpay.payTo}" id="payTo">
    <f:validateLength maximum="25"/>
</h:inputText>
<h:message for="payTo" style="color:red"/>
<h:outputText value="Amount:"/>
<h:inputText value="#{billpay.amount}" id="amount">
    <f:convertNumber minFractionDigits="2"/>
    <f:validateDoubleRange minimum="5" maximum="5000"/>
</h:inputText>
<h:message for="amount" style="color:red"/>
```

If our user inputs values that cause these validations to fail, you'll see something like Figure 8-9. Again, in a production environment you would probably want to supply different error messages, but considering that all we did was add a simple tag to our page, this is pretty slick.

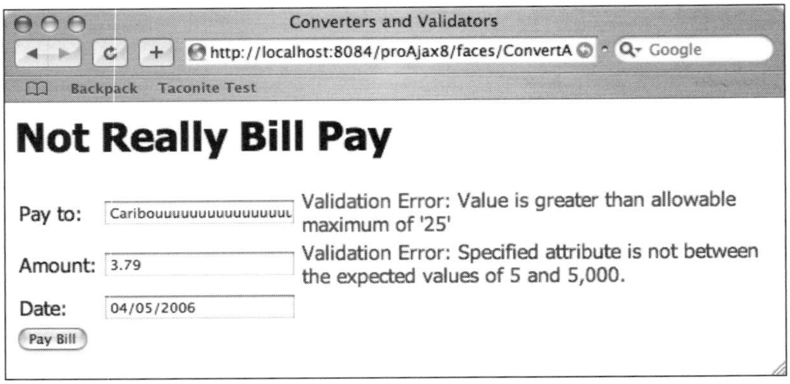

**Figure 8-9.** *Showing validation errors*

JSF makes it pretty easy to create your own validator or converter. For example, let's say our business rules require that the "Pay to" name cannot contain an "x." Obviously we need our own validator to do this. The first thing we need to do is create a new class that implements the javax.faces.validator.Validator interface. The Validator interface defines one method:

```
public void validate(FacesContext context, UIComponent component, Object value)
```

If a validation fails, this method throws a ValidatorException that contains a message; otherwise, it just returns. Our validator will look like Listing 8-12. (The isInvalidName method uses default access control for testing purposes.) As you can see, if the validation fails, we create a new FacesMessage (in a production environment, we'd most likely grab our messages from a resource bundle), and we throw the expected ValidatorException.

**Listing 8-12.** *A Custom Validator*

```
public class CustomValidator implements Validator {

    /** Creates a new instance of CustomValidator */
    public CustomValidator() {
    }

    public void validate(FacesContext context, UIComponent component,
            Object value) {
        if(null==value) {
            return;
        }
```

```
        if (isInvalidName(value.toString())) {
            FacesMessage message = new FacesMessage(FacesMessage.SEVERITY_ERROR,
                    "Summary Message", "Invalid Pay To Name!");
            throw new ValidatorException(message);
        }
    }

    boolean isInvalidName(String value) {
        boolean valid = false;
        if(value.indexOf("x") > -1) {
            valid = true;
        }
        return valid;
    }
}
```

Once we have our validation class, we need to register it with JSF. To do this, we add the lines shown in Listing 8-13 to our `faces-config.xml` file. Now that we have this validation registered, we can add a `validator` tag to our input field: `<f:validator validatorId="nameValidator"/>`. Entering an invalid name will result in the output shown in Figure 8-10.

**Listing 8-13.** *Registering a Validator*

```
<validator>
    <validator-id>nameValidator</validator-id>
    <validator-class>com.proajax.chap8.CustomValidator</validator-class>
</validator>
```

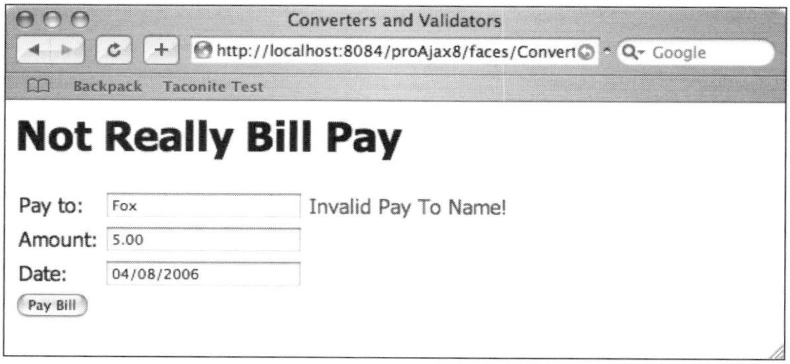

**Figure 8-10.** *A custom validator in action*

# Developing JSF Applications with an IDE

All of these examples were simple enough that writing them without the aid of a visual development environment was not a challenge. However, JSF was specifically designed with tool support in mind, and on any decent-sized production application, this can greatly improve developer productivity. For example, using tools like Oracle JDeveloper and Java Studio Creator, you can graphically lay out the page by using a palette of available components (see Figure 8-11). We can just drag and drop our way to an application (see Figure 8-12). We can also graphically define our navigation (see Figure 8-13). It is widely expected that developers will use tools like Java Studio Creator to simplify the development process.

**Figure 8-11.** *The Components palette*

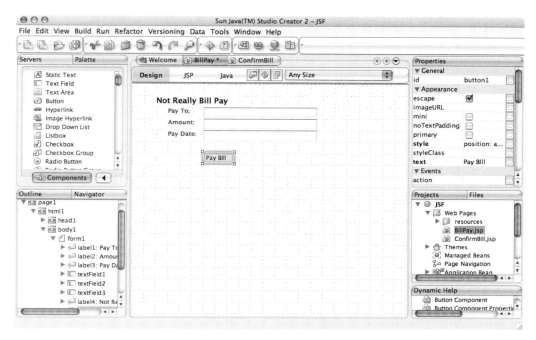

**Figure 8-12.** *Using an IDE to graphically lay out a JSF page*

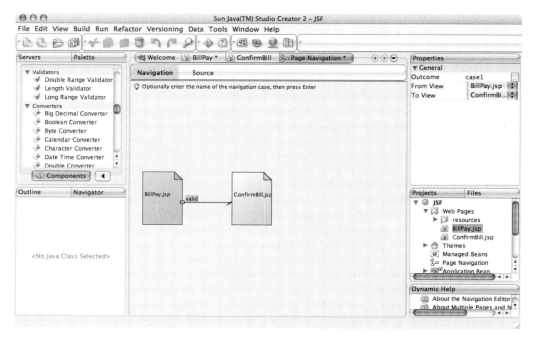

**Figure 8-13.** *Defining navigation graphically*

# Other JSF Technologies

As we've mentioned, JSF is simply a specification, and there are a number of add-ons and extensions that you should be aware of. While it's possible to develop an entire JSF application without using any of these technologies, you should have an awareness of what's available. Of course, this isn't an exhaustive list (more are started regularly), and as JSF evolves, so too will these projects.

### THE IMPORTANCE OF CHOICE

As mentioned, JSF is simply a specification from Sun, one that can be implemented by any number of vendors. While some people may not appreciate the nuances of this approach, in practice it means that we developers are free to choose the best implementation. We aren't forced to accept whatever a specific company feels is appropriate. Choice also forces companies to innovate. With a thriving open source community, commercial entities must present demonstrably better products. While there might be some initial confusion when dealing with a number of options, when all is said and done, our users ultimately benefit.

## Apache Tomahawk

In these examples, we're working with the JSF reference implementation. However, it has some limitations—most notably, the lack of components. Thanks to the nature of Java, we aren't limited to using Sun's standard components; we can turn to third parties like the open source MyFaces project (http://myfaces.apache.org). MyFaces includes the Apache Tomahawk project (http://myfaces.apache.org/tomahawk/index.html), which includes dozens of components. There is a fair amount of overlap, especially now that Oracle has donated its ADF Faces to the Apache Software Foundation. It can be confusing, such as when you have to decide whether to use Tree, Tree Table, or Tree2, but the competition is good for developers and good for JSF. Like many open source projects, documentation is not a priority. Still, with JSF, you aren't limited to one vendor's view of what you need to build your applications.

## Facelets

Another interesting extension to JSF is the java.net Facelets project. Facelets is essentially a Tapestry-like framework on top of JSF. It provides a lightweight templating framework and brings Tapestry-like views to the picture. It provides very precise error handling and also provides Tiles-like composition, allowing developers to reuse layouts by combining pages from separate files. For better or worse, it does not use the JSP runtime, but it does make use of JSP syntax. Also, your component library of choice needs to support Facelets.

(The standard JSF tag libraries, Apache MyFaces, and ADF Faces are all supported.) One caveat: Facelets doesn't work terribly well with the JSF 1.1 Reference Implementation.

## Shale

Shale is the next generation of the wildly popular (though now essentially legacy) Struts application framework. Essentially Shale is a set of services built on top of JSF. Shale adds Spring and Apache Commons Validator integration, annotation support for configuring managed beans, converters, renderers, Ajax extensions, Tapestry-like views via Clay, and also Web Flow. Shale's Web Flow is modeled after Spring's Web Flow, which allows you to configure wizard-like dialogs. You can define states, transitions, and subdialogs to quickly and easily create thick, client-like wizards.

## Seam

In many circles, EJB is a four-letter word, though EJB 3.0 may change this impression. EJB expert group member and Hibernate creator Gavin King, inspired by Ruby on Rails, has created Seam, a unified component model for JSF and EJB 3.0. Seam ties JSF and EJB 3.0 (or Hibernate 3.0) together by making heavy use of annotations. JBoss, now owned by Red Hat, stands behind Seam (which is both a pro and a con), and it has very good documentation. However, as of this writing, it is still in beta. Still, with the power of two important specifications combined with a leading application server vendor behind it, expect to see more on this in the future.

# The JSF Life Cycle

Before we can fully explore the use of Ajax in JSF, we need to understand the JSF life cycle. There are six phases to the JSF life cycle (see Figure 8-14):

1. Restore View

2. Apply Request Values

3. Process Validation

4. Update Model

5. Invoke Application

6. Render Response

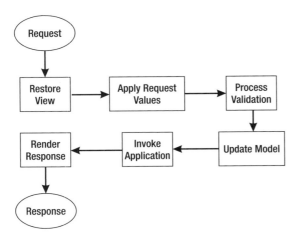

**Figure 8-14.** *The JSF life cycle*

The life cycle isn't set in stone; it's possible to skip certain phases based on what you're trying to do. Depending on exactly what you are focusing on (creating custom components, application development issues, and so on), you might concern yourself with only certain aspects of the life cycle.

## Restore View

JSF is a component-based framework; each page is made up of a hierarchy of components with UIViewRoot at the top. On the server, these hierarchies are identified by a view ID that is managed by the server. When a request comes through the Faces servlet, the view ID is extracted from the URL and used to look up the view. (If the view doesn't exist, it's created.) The first time a user loads a page, a new UIViewRoot is created, and JSF moves directly to the Render Response phase, where the component hierarchy is filled out. The component hierarchy will either be saved on the server (in session) or on the client (in a hidden form field). If the view already exists, JSF reconstructs the state and moves on to the Apply Request Values phase.

## Apply Request Values

Once JSF has retrieved the view, the values from the request parameters (or cookie or header values) can be retrieved. During this phase, the component hierarchy is traversed, and the values are stored.

## Process Validation

At this point, our data is converted using either the default converters or any special ones we've built. Once our values have been converted, JSF will fire the validation associated with a given component again using either a built-in JSF validator or a custom one. If a validation fails, a message is added to the `FacesContext`, and JSF jumps to the Render Response phase, where the current view is redisplayed with the error messages (assuming the developer included a message component). If there are no validation errors, JSF moves on to the Update Model phase.

## Update Model

At this point, we have strongly typed and converted valid data, so JSF can go ahead and update the model. (Of course, it is possible that additional field-level validation will be invoked on the model.) It is at this point that the managed beans we've associated with our components get invoked. While we know that the individual form fields contain valid data, it is likely that we will have to apply cross-field validation.

## Invoke Application

JSF has taken care of the plumbing. The form values have been converted and validated, and our model has been populated. At this point, our code takes over, and we run our business logic. It's at this point that we can change the navigation flow of our application by returning various outcomes (discussed previously in the Dynamic Navigation section).

## Render Response

At this point, JSF renders the response. The view and its current state are displayed to the user.

# JSF and Ajax

JSF is actually quite Ajax-friendly provided that you remember how elements are named. (See the earlier discussion on the `name` attribute in the "JSF Taglibs" section.) When it comes to talking to the server, we have a couple of options. First, we could go outside of the JSF life cycle completely by using a servlet or servlet `Filter`. Ajax is commonly used to fill in parts of the form based on previously entered data. To demonstrate this, let's fill in the Amount field based on the "Pay to" field by creating a `Filter` that will examine the value and return an appropriate amount. Our `Filter` might look something like Listing 8-14.

**Listing 8-14.** *A Simple Filter*

```java
package com.proajax.chap8;

import javax.servlet.*;
import javax.servlet.http.HttpServletRequest;
import javax.servlet.http.HttpServletResponse;
import java.io.IOException;

public class AjaxFilter implements Filter {
    public void init(FilterConfig filterConfig) throws ServletException {
    }

    public void doFilter(ServletRequest servletRequest,
                ServletResponse servletResponse,
                FilterChain filterChain)
                throws IOException, ServletException {
        HttpServletRequest  request = (HttpServletRequest) servletRequest;
        HttpServletResponse response = (HttpServletResponse)servletResponse;
        String value = request.getParameter("payTo");

        response.setContentType("text/xml");
        response.setHeader("Cache-Control", "no-cache");
        response.setStatus(HttpServletResponse.SC_OK);
        response.getWriter().write(getResponseForValue(value));

        filterChain.doFilter(request, response);
    }

    public void destroy() {
    }

    private String getResponseForValue(String value) {
        String response = "";
        if("Foo".equals(value)) {
            response = "<value><amount>40.92</amount></value>";
        }
        return response;
    }
}
```

Obviously, in a production environment, our getResponseForValue method would probably go off to a database and retrieve the value, but it's not key for our purposes. Now that we have the filter created, we need to configure it in our web.xml file (see Listing 8-15).

**Listing 8-15.** *Configuring the Servlet Filter*

```
<filter>
    <description>processes ajax requests</description>
    <filter-name>AjaxFilter</filter-name>
    <filter-class>com.proajax.chap8.AjaxFilter</filter-class>
</filter>
<filter-mapping>
    <filter-name>AjaxFilter</filter-name>
    <url-pattern>*.ajax</url-pattern>
</filter-mapping>
```

Now that we have the server side ready, we can go ahead and create our form. Basically, this will be the same JSP we've been using thus far, however there's a little more JavaScript in this one (see Listing 8-16). We're coding most of the Ajax by hand; chances are you'd use an existing library or extract this code into your own toolkit.

**Listing 8-16.** *The FormComplete JSP*

```
<%@taglib uri="http://java.sun.com/jsf/core" prefix="f"%>
<%@taglib uri="http://java.sun.com/jsf/html" prefix="h"%>

<html>
    <f:view>
        <head>
            <title>JSF Ajaxian Form Complete</title>
            <script type="text/javascript">
                var xmlHttp;

                function getValue() {
                    var value = document.getElementById("form:payTo").value;
                    var url = "foo.ajax";
                    startRequest(url, value);
                }

                function createXMLHttpRequest() {
                    if (window.ActiveXObject) {
                        xmlHttp = new ActiveXObject("Microsoft.XMLHTTP");
                    }
```

```
                else if (window.XMLHttpRequest) {
                    xmlHttp = new XMLHttpRequest();
                }
            }

            function startRequest(url, value) {
                createXMLHttpRequest();
                xmlHttp.onreadystatechange = processValue;
                xmlHttp.open("POST", url, true);
                xmlHttp.setRequestHeader("Content-Type",
                    "application/x-www-form-urlencoded");
                xmlHttp.send("ajax=true&payTo=" + value);
            }

            function processValue() {
                if(xmlHttp.readyState == 4) {
                    if(xmlHttp.status == 200) {
                        var xmlDoc = xmlHttp.responseXML;
                        var node = xmlDoc.getElementsByTagName("amount")[0];
                        var amount = node.childNodes[0].nodeValue;
                        var element = document.getElementById("form:amount");
                        element.value = amount;
                    }
                }
            }
        </script>
    </head>
    <body>
        <h1>Not Really Bill Pay</h1>
        <h:form id="form">
            <h:panelGrid columns="3">
                <h:outputText value="Pay to:"/>
                <h:inputText value="#{billpay.payTo}" id="payTo"
                    onblur="getValue()">
                    <f:validateLength maximum="25"/>
                    <f:validator validatorId="nameValidator"/>
                </h:inputText>
                <h:message for="payTo" style="color:red"/>
                <h:outputText value="Amount:"/>
```

```
            <h:inputText value="#{billpay.amount}" id="amount">
                <f:convertNumber minFractionDigits="2"/>
                <f:validateDoubleRange minimum="5" maximum="5000"/>
            </h:inputText>
            <h:message for="amount" style="color:red"/>
            <h:outputText value="Date:"/>
            <h:inputText value="#{billpay.payDate}" id="payDate">
                <f:convertDateTime pattern="MM/dd/yyyy"/>
            </h:inputText>
            <h:message for="payDate" style="color:red"/>
          </h:panelGrid>
          <h:commandButton value="Pay Bill" action="paybill"/>
        </h:form>
      </body>
    </f:view>
</html>
```

There are a few key things in this code. First, the URL we set on the XHR object has to be one that will trigger our filter (hence `foo.ajax`). Second, you'll notice that we're calling the server with the POST method, though we certainly could have used GET—it really doesn't matter. Third, you'll notice that we have to take JSF's component naming into account with our JavaScript. That's why we say `document.getElementById("form:amount")` instead of `document.getElementById("amount")`. The result of this call looks something like Figure 8-15.

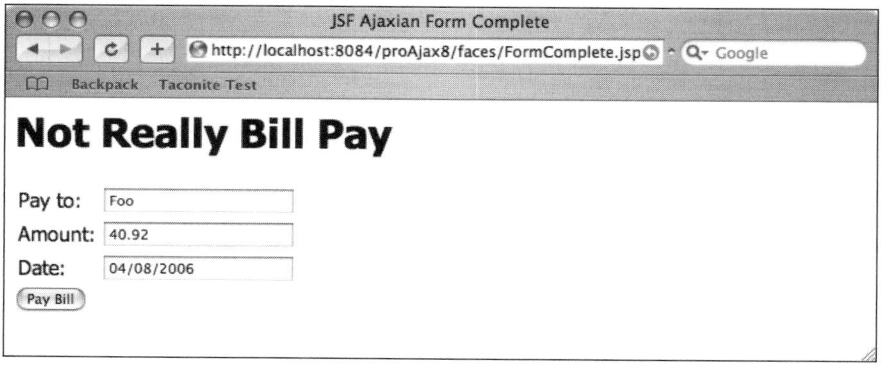

**Figure 8-15.** *JSF* `FormComplete` *with a servlet* `Filter`

This takes us completely outside of the JSF life cycle, meaning that we haven't fired any of the validation or converters that we've configured for this page. JSF has an alternative route, the `PhaseListener` interface. Let's redo our example, replacing the servlet `Filter` with a class that implements the `PhaseListener` interface (see Listing 8-17).

**Listing 8-17.** *An Ajax* PhaseListener

```
package com.proajax.chap8;

import javax.faces.event.PhaseListener;
import javax.faces.event.PhaseEvent;
import javax.faces.event.PhaseId;
import javax.faces.context.FacesContext;
import javax.faces.component.UIViewRoot;
import javax.faces.component.UIInput;
import javax.faces.validator.Validator;
import javax.faces.validator.ValidatorException;
import javax.servlet.http.HttpServletResponse;
import java.io.PrintWriter;
import java.util.Map;

public class AjaxPhaseListener implements PhaseListener {
    private static final String
            ERROR_MESSAGE = "Invalid Pay To Name.";

    public PhaseId getPhaseId() {
        return PhaseId.RESTORE_VIEW;
    }

    public void beforePhase(PhaseEvent phaseEvent) {
    }

    public void afterPhase(PhaseEvent phaseEvent) {
        FacesContext context = FacesContext.getCurrentInstance();
        Map requestParams =
            context.getExternalContext().getRequestParameterMap();
        String ajaxParam = (String)requestParams.get("ajax");

        if("true".equals(ajaxParam)) {
            UIViewRoot viewRoot = context.getViewRoot();
            UIInput payTo = (UIInput)viewRoot.findComponent("form:payTo");
            int children = viewRoot.getChildCount();
            boolean valid = true;
```

```java
            if(payTo != null) {
                HttpServletResponse response =
                        (HttpServletResponse)context.getExternalContext()
                            .getResponse();
                Validator[] validators = payTo.getValidators();
                String value = (String)requestParams.get("payTo");

                PrintWriter writer = null;
                try {
                    writer = response.getWriter();
                }
                catch (java.io.IOException ex) {
                    ex.printStackTrace();
                }

                // fire all validators and catch exceptions
                for (int i = 0; i < validators.length; i++) {
                    Validator validator = validators[i];
                    try {
                        validator.validate(context, payTo, value);
                    }
                    catch (ValidatorException ve) {
                        writer.write(ERROR_MESSAGE);
                        valid = false;
                        break;
                    }
                }
                if(valid) {
                    writer.write(getResponseForValue(value));
                }
            }
            context.responseComplete();
        }
    }

    private String getResponseForValue(String value) {
        String response = "";
        if("Foo".equals(value)) {
            response = "<value><amount>40.92</amount></value>";
        }
        return response;
    }
}
```

Obviously, this looks an awful lot like our previous example. We can use largely the same JSP; however, we need to change the URL that we're calling via the XHR object. (We can use an empty string.) Entering "Foo" for the "Pay to" value results in Figure 8-16.

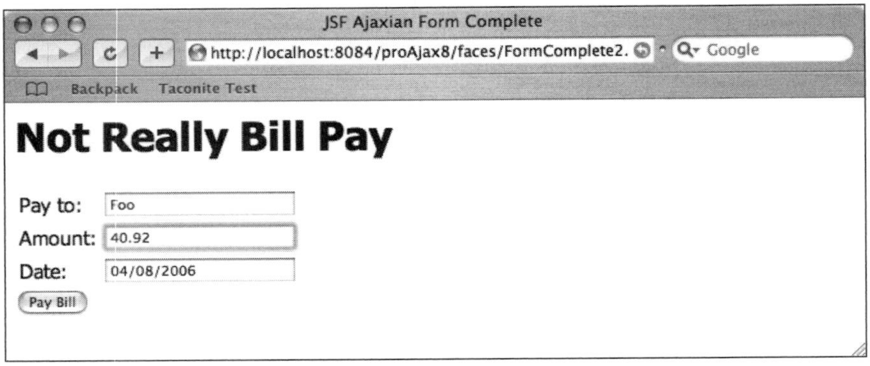

**Figure 8-16.** *JSF FormComplete with a PhaseListener*

In a production application, it is much more likely that you would create a custom JSF component. However, that is beyond the scope of this book.

# JSF Ajax Components

While you might create your own component or two, chances are you'll take advantage of something that's prebuilt. The Apache Tomahawk project mentioned earlier in this chapter contains a number of Ajax components, such as

- `InputSuggestAjax`

- `InputTextAjax`

- `HtmlCommandButtonAjax`

- `HtmlSelectManyCheckboxAjax`

- `HtmlSelectOneRadioAjax`

Chances are that this list will grow over the coming months and that other library providers will step in to fill the gap. As of this writing, all of these components are still in the "sandbox." However, we expect them to move beyond that stage soon. In the meantime, you can try the autocomplete widget that's available in Sun's Java Studio Creator 2.

Working with the Completion Text Field component could not be simpler. If you've read our previous book *Foundations of Ajax* (Apress, 2005), you know that we actually built an autocomplete widget like that in Google Suggest. While it isn't rocket science, there's quite a bit of code involved. However, with a prebuilt component, we can focus on the place we add value—business logic. First of all, you need to install the Ajax component library via the Component Library Manager. (See http://developers.sun.com/prodtech/javatools/ jscreator/reference/fi/2/ajax.html for complete instructions.) Once installed, the library will appear on your palette like any other component set.

At this point, we can simply create a new page and drop a Completion Text Field on it. While this may not look like much in the Design view (see Figure 8-17), take a look at what is generated on our behalf (see Listing 8-18). As you can see, dragging and dropping saves us a few keystrokes!

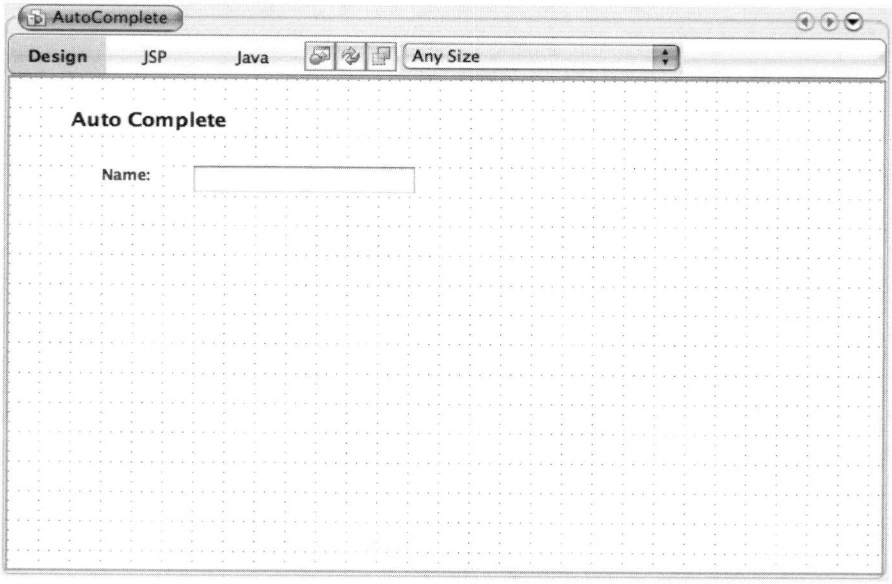

**Figure 8-17.** *Java Studio Creator's Design view*

**Listing 8-18.** *The Generated Code*

```
<?xml version="1.0" encoding="UTF-8"?>
<jsp:root version="1.2" xmlns:ajaxTags=http://java.sun.com/blueprints/
ajaxtextfield
    xmlns:bp="http://java.sun.com/blueprints/ui/14"
    xmlns:f="http://java.sun.com/jsf/core" xmlns:h=http://java.sun.com/jsf/html
    xmlns:jsp="http://java.sun.com/JSP/Page" xmlns:ui="http://www.sun.com/web/ui">
<jsp:directive.page contentType="text/html;charset=UTF-8" pageEncoding="UTF-8"/>
```

```
<f:view>
    <ui:page binding="#{AutoComplete.page1}" id="page1">
        <ui:html binding="#{AutoComplete.html1}" id="html1">
            <ui:head binding="#{AutoComplete.head1}" id="head1">
                <ui:link binding="#{AutoComplete.link1}" id="link1"
                    url="/resources/stylesheet.css"/>
            </ui:head>
            <ui:body binding="#{AutoComplete.body1}" id="body1"
                    style="-rave-layout: grid">
                <ui:form binding="#{AutoComplete.form1}" id="form1">
                    <ui:label binding="#{AutoComplete.label1}"
                            id="label1" labelLevel="1"
                        style="left: 48px;
                        top: 24px; position: absolute" text="Auto Complete"/>
                    <ui:label binding="#{AutoComplete.label2}"
                            id="label2" style="left: 72px;
                        top: 72px;
                        position: absolute" text="Name:"/>
                    <ajaxTags:completionField binding="#{AutoComplete.ajaxTextField1}"
                        completionMethod="#{AutoComplete.ajaxTextField1_complete}"
                        id="ajaxTextField1"
                            style="left: 144px; top: 72px; position: absolute"/>
                </ui:form>
            </ui:body>
        </ui:html>
    </ui:page>
</f:view>
</jsp:root>
```

By looking closely at the generated code, you can probably guess what our next
step is. One of the attributes of the completionField is the completionMethod—called
ajaxTextField1_complete. We need to add our business logic to this method. If we double-
click on the component in the Design view, we'll be automatically taken to this method
(which has a TODO label and some sample code to help us along). For our simple example,
we'll borrow some code from the autocomplete example from *Foundations of Ajax* (see
Listing 8-19). The names variable refers to a List that is created during the init method.
Obviously in production code you'd likely go off to a database instead. All we're doing here
is returning a set of names that matches the prefix. Running this code looks something like
Figure 8-18.

**Listing 8-19.** *A Simple Complete Method*

```
public void ajaxTextField1_complete(FacesContext context, String prefix,
        CompletionResult result) {
    String prefix_upper = prefix.toUpperCase();
    Iterator iter = names.iterator();
    while(iter.hasNext()) {
        String name = (String) iter.next();
        String name_upper_case = name.toUpperCase();
        if(name_upper_case.startsWith(prefix_upper)){
            result.addItem(name);
        }
    }
}
```

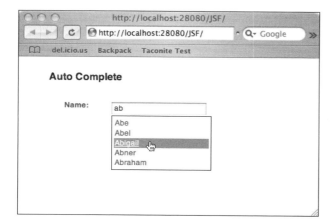

**Figure 8-18.** *The autocomplete widget in action*

As you can see, working with existing components makes our jobs a whole lot easier.

# Summary

As the one web framework that's actually a Sun specification, Java developers cannot simply ignore JSF. With new frameworks like Seam based upon its foundations, it's clear that JSF has much to offer. Though it's taken some time for JSF to take off, with the availability of books like *Pro JSF and Ajax* by John R. Fallows and Jonas Jacobi (Apress, 2006), it is clear that the momentum is there. Using existing components and leveraging integrated tools can slash implementation time and allow developers to focus on the business needs instead of the plumbing of a web application. While we've only scratched the surface of what can be done in JSF and Ajax, hopefully we've given you the tools to try it out for yourself.

# Index

## ■Symbols

$() function
    DWR, 125, 136, 140
    Prototype library, 76

## ■A

abort() method (XMLHttpRequest), 12–13
accel attribute (animations), 103
action attribute (button), 266, 268
Action class
    design considerations, 180
    SaveReservationAction class and, 177
    Struts support, 153, 155–156, 225, 229
    struts-config.xml file and, 168
    ValidateReservationAction class and, 174, 176
action element (path attribute), 168
ActionForm object
    context object and, 138
    design considerations, 180
    form-bean element, 165
    Struts design, 154–155, 181
    validate method, 155–156, 174
action-mappings element, 165, 168
ActionMessages object, 156
actions
    Selenium tests and, 59
    Taconite library and, 112
ActiveX controls, 10–11
Adaptive Path, 8

addClassName() method (Element), 80
addFormElements() method (Taconite), 112
addFormElementsById() method (Taconite), 111–112
addNamedFormElements() method (Taconite), 112
AddPodcast class, 198–199, 201, 216
addPodcast method (AddPodcast), 201, 216
Address class, 128–131, 133–137, 140
addToCounter method, 192
addTwoNumbers method, 222–223
advice, 223
afterFinish callback function, 91
afterUpdate callback function, 91
Ajax
    about, 3, 5–9
    AjaxAnywhere and, 149
    avoiding common gotchas, 16, 18–20
    debugging requests, 40–41, 43, 45
    design considerations, 179–180
    JSF and, 285, 287–289, 291–292
    prebuilt components, 292, 294–295
    Prototype support, 86–89
    Spring framework and, 233–234
    and Struts integration, 157–161
    Struts support, 155–156, 161–163
    Tapestry support, 204–209, 211–212, 214–216
    typical interaction, 13–15

Ajax patterns
    Auto Refresh, 22
    Draggable DOM, 23
    Fade Anything Technique, 18, 21
    Partial Page Paint, 22
    website for, 20
AjaxAnywhere, 149
Ajax.Autocompleter, 99–101
AjaxDirectLink component (Tacos), 205
AjaxEventSubmit component (Tacos), 205
AjaxForm component (Tacos), 205, 215
AjaxLinkSubmit component (Tacos), 205
AjaxRequest object (Taconite), 111, 113–115
ajax-response tag, 146
AjaxSubmit component (Tacos), 205, 215
AjaxTags library, 141–148
ajaxtags.css file, 144–145
alert class, 46
alert statement, 46
Amazon.com, 5–6
animations, Dojo Toolkit and, 103–105
annotations, 190
AOP (aspect-oriented programming)
    about, 221–223
    inventory control application, 234,
        247–249, 255
Apache Tomahawk, 282, 292
Appear effect (script.aculo.us), 98
appendChild() method (DOM), 111
Apply Request Values phase (JSF), 284
aspect, 223
aspect-oriented programming. See AOP
assertions, 59
assertValue() command (Selenium), 59
asynchronous communications
    Ajax support, 18
    common gotchas, 18

debugging Ajax requests, 40–41, 43, 45
    dojo.io.bind, 107
    Prototype library and, 87
    script.aculo.us and, 94–95
auth-constraint element, 238
authentication, 236, 238
auth-method element, 238
authorization, 236
Auto Refresh (pattern), 22
autocomplete
    AjaxTags library, 142–148
    Google Suggest and, 19
    Java Studio Creator, 292
    script.aculo.us, 98–101
autocomplete tag (JSP), 144–146
AutoCompleter component (Tacos), 205

■B

Back button, 18, 109
Backpack, 80–81
Basecamp, 21
BasePage class, 190
baseURL attribute (autocomplete tag), 145
bean:write tag, 169
Before() method (Insertion), 82
beforeStart callback function, 91
beforeUpdate callback function, 91
bind() method (dojo.io.bind), 110
BlindDown effect (script.aculo.us), 98
BlindUp effect (script.aculo.us), 98
BlockView feature (A9), 23
blogging, 16
BluePrints Solutions Catalog, 5
Body component (Tapestry), 197, 210
bookmarking, 110
breakpoints, 54–55

browsers
    Ajax support, 5
    DWR support, 122–123
    graceful degradation and, 198
    JavaScript Templates, 138
    POST method and, 127
    Selenium test tool, 58
    simplified detection, 84–85
    Taconite support, 111
    View Source feature, 39
    XMLHttpRequest object and, 5, 10
builder.js file, 90

■**C**

calculateCharacterSum method
    (RemoteBean), 126
callback function
    about, 15
    DWR and, 122
    Prototype library and, 87
Chain of Responsibility design pattern, 181
changeURL parameter (dojo.io.bind), 110
childNodes() method, 38
classes
    cohesion in, 221
    Smalltalk support, 220
    Spring framework, 228
    Tapestry support, 202
className attribute
    autocomplete tag, 145
    Prototype library and, 76
cleanWhitespace() method (Element), 80
click() command (Selenium), 59, 65, 70
clickAndWait() command (Selenium), 59,
    63, 65
client-side processing, 111–113
closure (JavaScript), 127
code completion, intelligent, 30

COL element, 90
COLGROUP element, 90
colorFadeIn() method (Dojo), 106
colorFadeOut() method (Dojo), 107
commands, Selenium tests and, 59
Commons Logging library (Tapestry), 185
Commons Validator
    design considerations, 180
    Struts Shale, 283
    Struts validation, 155–156, 170–172, 174
    validation errors, 174
Completion Text Field component, 292–294
completionMethod attribute
    (CompletionField), 294
components
    JSF converters, 275
    JSF taglibs, 272–273
    prebuilt Ajax, 292, 294–295
    Tacos support, 205–209
    Tapestry and, 184
Components palette (Java Studio Creator), 280
compression tools, JavaScript, 35–38
configuration files, 267
console class, 46
content option (dojo.io.bind), 109
Content-Type response header, 113, 115
context node
    actions and, 112–113
    Taconite and, 115
context objects, 138
contextNodeID attribute, 115
Continue option (Venkman), 55
Controller class (Spring MVC), 225, 229
controls.js file, 90
convert tag (DWR), 130
converter attribute (convert tag), 130, 275
converting JSF, 274, 276–279, 285

core tags (JSF), 270

create tag (DWR), 119, 122–123, 130, 234

createElement() method (DOM), 111

createSaveButtonCell function, 136

createTextNode method (document), 123

createXMLHttpRequest method, 11

creator attribute (create tag), 119, 234

cross-cutting concerns, 222, 247

CSS

    AjaxTags and, 144

    Firebug extension and, 45

    Firefox error console and, 43

    JSF taglibs and, 273

Ctrl+Shift+F key combination, 33

Ctrl+Space key combination, 33

curly braces, 36

currentFrame variable (Effect), 92

curve attribute (animations), 103

custom_rhino.jar file, 37

■D

DAOs (Data Access Objects), 221, 241, 246

data helper objects, 250–252

data object, 109

Date class

    code completion for, 30

    DWR and, 118

    Tapestry and, 189

DatePicker component (Tacos), 205

debugging

    Ajax requests, 40–41, 43, 45

    with alert statements, 46

    DWR and, 122

    JavaScript tools, 52–54, 56

    Tacos support, 211

debug() method (Logger), 50

dependency injection (DI)

    about, 220–222

    inventory control application, 234

    Spring framework and, 224

Désy, Nicolas, 32

development tools

    debugging Ajax requests, 40–41, 43, 45

    inspecting DOM structures, 38, 40

    JavaScript compression tools, 35–38

    JavaScript debugging tools, 52–54, 56

    JavaScript Source Code Editor, 27–28

    JSEclipse, 28–29, 31

    JsUnit testing framework, 56–57

    NetBeans JavaScript plug-in, 32–33

    Selenium test tool, 58–61, 63, 65–68, 70

DI. *See* dependency injection

Dialog component (Tacos), 205

Digg news site, 22

Direct Web Remoting. *See* DWR

DirectLink component

    about, 188

    resetting counters, 191

    Tacos support, 205

DirtyFormWarning component (Tacos), 205

disable() method (Form), 77

disabled attribute (JSF), 273

DispatcherServlet, 226–227

div element

    id attribute, 168

    innerHTML property, 141, 162

    Taconite and, 114–115

document object

    code completion for, 30

    createTextNode method, 123

    getElementByID() method, 125

    NetBeans plug-in and, 33

Document Object Model. *See* DOM

doGet method (AjaxTags), 146

doHelloWorld function (Taconite), 114

Dojo Toolkit

about, 37–38, 102

animations, 103–105

dojo.io.bind, 107, 109–110

effects, 105, 215

methods for effects, 106–107

Tacos support, 206, 212

dojo.graphics.htmlEffects module, 105

dojo.io.bind, 107, 109

DOM (Document Object Model)

context node and, 112

Draggable DOM pattern, 23

DWR support, 124, 137

inspecting structures, 38, 40

JavaScript Templates, 137

JSON-RPC-Java framework and, 149

manipulating, 78, 80, 82, 84

Mouseover DOM Inspector, 39–40

Partial Page Paint pattern, 23

Taconite library and, 110–113

XMLHttpRequest object and, 5, 10

dot notation

DWR support, 125

JavaScript and, 122–123

JavaScript Templates and, 138

dragdrop.js file, 90

Draggable DOM pattern, 23

DropOut effect (script.aculo.us), 98

DropTarget component (Tacos), 205

dumpObject function (Log), 49

duration attribute (animations), 103

duration option (Effect), 91

DWR (Direct Web Remoting)

about, 117, 234

browser scripting, 122–123

installing, 118–119

inventory control application, 234, 250, 255–256

JavaScript Templates, 137–141

passing multiple parameters, 126–127

passing object parameters, 128–131, 133–134

sending single parameter, 124–125

verifying installation, 120–121

WebContext object, 250

DWREngine object, 127

dwr.jar library, 118

DWRUtil object, 124–126

dwr.xml file, 119, 122, 130, 234

dynamic navigation, JSF, 269–270, 285

## E

Editor tab (Selenium IDE), 68

Effect (script.aculo.us)

Effect.Appear, 98

Effect.BlindDown, 98

Effect.BlindUp, 98

Effect.Dropout, 98

Effect.Fade, 98

Effect.Fold, 98

Effect.Grow, 98

Effect.Highlight, 91, 94

Effect.MoveBy, 91

Effect.Opacity, 91–93, 98

Effect.Parallel, 91–92, 95–96

Effect.Puff, 98

Effect.Pulsate, 98

Effect.Scale, 91, 93–94

Effect.Shake, 98

Effect.Shrink, 98

Effect.SlideDown, 98

Effect.SlideUp, 98

Effect.Squish, 98

Effect.SwitchOff, 98

options arguments, 91

syntax for, 90

variables, 92

Effect.Appear, 98

Effect.BlindDown, 98

Effect.BlindUp, 98

Effect.Dropout, 98

Effect.Fade, 98

Effect.Fold, 98

Effect.Grow, 98

Effect.Highlight, 91, 94

Effect.MoveBy, 91

Effect.Opacity, 91–93, 98

Effect.Parallel, 91, 95–96

Effect.Puff, 98

Effect.Pulsate, 98

Effect.Scale, 91, 93–94

Effect.Shake, 98

Effect.Shrink, 98

Effect.SlideDown, 98

Effect.SlideUp, 98

Effect.Squish, 98

Effect.SwitchOff, 98

effects[] array (Effect), 92

effects.js file, 90, 93

EJB (Enterprise Java Beans), 221, 224, 283

element attribute, 91

Element class (Prototype), 78, 80, 92

element variable (Effect), 92

elements. *See also* Effect (script.aculo.us)

combination effects, 97

hiding/showing, 78–79

opacity of, 92

enable() method (Form), 77

encapsulation, 220

endcolor parameter (Effect.Highlight), 94

engine (Tapestry), 184

engine.js file, 120, 124

Enterprise Java Beans (EJB), 221, 224, 283

Enumerable component (Prototype), 89

error() method

Log4JS logging utility, 46

Logger class, 50

errors tag, 157, 169

eval() function, 87

Event object, 89

evt object, 109

execute method (Action), 229

explode effect (Dojo), 215

Extensible Application Markup Language (XAML), 4

## ■F

FaceContext component, 285

Facelets project, 282

Fade Anything Technique (FAT) pattern, 18, 21

fade effect

Dojo Toolkit, 215

script.aculo.us, 98

fade() method (Dojo), 106

fadeHide() method (Dojo), 106, 215

fadeIn() method (Dojo), 105–106

fadeOut() method (Dojo), 106

fadeShow() method (Dojo), 106, 215

Fallows, John R., 295

fatal() method (Log4JS), 46

favelets, 39

f:convertDateTime tag, 275–276

f:convertNumber tag, 275–276

Field class (Prototype), 82

filters, JSF, 285, 287, 289

finishOn variable (Effect), 92

FireBug extension (Firefox), 43–45

firewalls, 131

first() method (Dojo_, 104

FishEyeList component (Tacos), 205

Flickr, 16

focusFirstElement() method (Form), 77

Fold effect (script.aculo.us), 98

For component (Tapestry), 205

Form class (Prototype), 77, 162

Form component (Tapestry), 197, 205

form element

    h:form tag, 266

    name attribute, 172

form-beans element, 165, 168

form-error-page element, 238

form-login-page element, 238

forms

    dojo.io.bind and, 109

    JSF example, 287

    Prototype and, 77

    Prototype library, 77

    Tacos support, 212–216

    Tapestry and, 183, 193–201, 203

    validating input, 173

Forward button, 109

forward element, 169

fps option (Effect), 91

FRAMESET element, 90

from option (Effect), 91

Fuchs, Thomas, 90

functions, breakpoints within, 54–55

future breakpoint, 54

f:validateDoubleRange tag, 277

f:validateLength tag, 277

f:validator tag, 279

f:view tag, 264

**G**

Garnier, Jean-Michel, 154

Garrett, Jesse James, 8

Geary, David, 263

GET method (HTTP), 87, 127, 154

get method (WebContextFactory), 250

getAllResponseHeaders() method
    (XMLHttpRequest), 12–13

getCurrentDateString method, 227

getDocumentById() method, 76

getElementByID() method, 38, 125, 289

getElements() method (Form), 77

getElementsByClassName() method, 76

getElementsByTagName() method, 76

getHeight() method (Element), 80

getHttpServletRequest method, 250

getInputs() method (Form), 77

getLuckyNumber function, 127

getPerson function, 141

getPerson() method (RemoteBean), 131, 133,
    138, 141

getPersonUsingJst function, 141

getResponseHeader() method
    (XMLHttpRequest), 12–13

getServerDate() method (RemoteBean), 119,
    121–122

getServerDateTime function, 123

getSumOfCharactersInString function, 125

getUnorderedList method, 227

getValue() method, 103

getXMLHttpRequestObject() method
    (Taconite), 112

Ginda, Robert, 52

Global object, 184

Gmail, 18

Google Earth, 3

Google Maps, 3, 5, 16

Google Suggest
Ajax support, 5, 142
autocomplete and, 19
XMLHttpRequest object and, 5
graceful degradation, 198
Gross, Christian, 20
Grow effect (script.aculo.us), 98

### ■H

handleGetLuckyNumber function, 127
handleGetPerson function, 133–134
handleGetServerDateTime function, 123
handleGetSumOfCharactersInString
function, 125–126
handleRequest method, 229
handleResponse function, 162, 168
handleSaveAddress function, 136
handleSaveAddressUsingJst function, 141
hard breakpoint, 54
Harrop, Rob, 225
hasClassName() method (Element), 80
hasEntry function, 162
h:commandButton tag, 266
h:form tag, 266
Hibernate, 283
hide() method (Element), 80, 92
Hieatt, Edward, 57
highlight effect
Dojo Toolkit, 215
script.aculo.us, 91, 94
h:inputText tag, 266
HiveMind library (Tapestry), 185
h:message tag, 276
h:outputText tag, 268
h:panelGrid tag, 276

HTML
Insertion class and, 82
JavaScript Templates and, 138
Prototype library and, 88
HTML element, 90
html node (Mouseover DOM Inspector), 40
HTML tags (JSF), 271–272
html:errors tag, 169
html:messages tag, 169
HTTP sniffers, 41–43
HttpServletRequest object
access to, 249–250
handleRequest method, 229
Tapestry and, 183
HttpServletResponse object, 229
HttpSession object, 183–184

### ■I

IComponent interface, 202
id attribute
div element, 168
DOM support, 59, 114–115
JSF and, 273
textarea element, 141
IDE (integrated development environment)
debugging and, 52
Java and, 27–28
JSF applications, 280
Selenium test tool, 67–68, 70
IDEA (IntelliJ), 28
IEngine interface, 202
IMarkupWriter interface, 202
implementing Struts, 153–155, 163–172,
174–179
implode effect (Dojo), 215
incrementCounter method (DirectLink),
189–190

info() method
   Log4JS logging utility, 46
   Logger class, 50
inheritance, 220
InitialContext object, 224
InlineEditBox component (Tacos),
   205–206, 208
innerHTML property
   Ajax support, 88
   handleResponse method, 162
   issues with, 90
   processDOMTemplate method, 141
   setting HTML with, 134
   span element, 123
   Taconite library and, 111, 115
input attribute (validateReservation),
   168–169
Insert component (Tapestry), 186–188, 200
Insertion class (Prototype), 80, 82, 84
installation
   DWR, 118–121
   JavaScript Templates, 138
integration, Ajax and Struts, 157–161
intelligent code completion, 30
InterAKT, 28–29, 31
Internet Explorer browser, 5, 10, 39
inventory control application
   AOP and, 247–249
   application security, 235–236, 238
   data access layer, 241–245
   data helper objects, 250–252
   domain layer, 240–241
   main page, 239
   service layer, 245–246
   Spring beans configuration, 253, 255–256
   web tier, 256–258, 260–261
Invoke Application phase (JSF), 285

invoke method, 248–249
IPage interface, 202
IRequestCycle interface, 202
isReadForValidation function, 162
item tag, 146

**J**

Jacobi, Jonas, 295
Java
   annotations, 190
   DAO pattern, 241
   DWR and, 117
   Model 2 MVC pattern and, 153
   obfuscation and, 36
   security model, 237
   Spring framework and, 219
Java Naming and Directory Interface (JNDI),
   221, 224
Java Studio Creator, 280–281
JavaBeans
   DWR and, 118–119, 130, 234
   Taconite library and, 111
JavaScript
   Ajax and, 5
   closure, 127
   compression tools, 35–38
   creating source files, 29
   curly braces, 36
   debugging tools, 52–54, 56
   DWR and, 118
   Firefox error console and, 43
   getSumOfCharactersInString function, 125
   input validation and, 155
   inspecting objects, 52
   line feed characters, 36
   logging utilities, 45–46, 48–50, 52
   Prototype library, 50
   security and, 36

Selenium test tool, 58

semicolon and, 36

validation logic and, 9

XMLHttpRequest object and, 10

javascript attribute (create tag), 119, 122–123

JavaScript Object Notation (JSON), 149

JavaScript Source Code Editor

about, 27–28

JSEclipse, 28–29, 31

NetBeans JavaScript plug-in, 32–33

JavaScript Templates (JST)

DWR support, 137–141

inventory control application, 234, 258, 260

JavaServer Faces. *See* JSF

JavaServer Pages Standard Tag Library (JSTL), 207

JBoss, 283

JDeveloper (Oracle), 280

JNDI (Java Naming and Directory Interface), 221, 224

j_password keyword, 236

JSEclipse, 28–29, 31

j_security_check action, 236, 238

JSF (JavaServer Faces)

about, 263

Ajax and, 285, 287–289, 291–292

Ajax components, 292, 294–295

background, 263

dynamic navigation, 269–270, 285

getting started with, 264–268

IDE, 280

life cycle, 283–285

other technologies, 282–283

Struts Shale, 283

taglibs, 270–273

validating and converting, 274, 276–279

JSF Reference Implementation, 282

js/jsd API, 52

JSLint utility, 36

JSON (JavaScript Object Notation), 149

JSP

AjaxAnywhere and, 149

AjaxTags library and, 141–144

autocomplete tag, 144–146

Struts and Ajax integration, 157

JSTL (JavaServer Pages Standard Tag Library), 207

JsUnit testing framework, 57–58, 71

JUnit testing framework, 56–57

j_username keyword, 236

**■K**

key combinations

Lumberjack utility, 49, 51

Mouseover DOM Inspector, 40

NetBeans plug-in, 33

King, Gavin, 283

Konqueror browser, 10

**■L**

li tags, 82

line feed characters, 36

LinkSubmit component (Tapestry), 205

listener methods, 184, 193

Loaded Scripts pane (Venkman), 54

Local Variables pane (Venkman), 53, 55–56

Log class, 49

log() method (Logger), 50

Log4JS logging utility, 46, 48–49

Logger class, 50

logging utilities, 45–46, 48–50, 52

logic:messagesPresent tag, 169

login-config element, 238

Lumberjack logging utility, 49–50, 52

## M

Map class, 229

maxlength attribute (JSF), 273

McClanahan, Craig R., 153, 263

MessageResources properties file, 174

messages tag, 169

messagesPresent tag, 169

META-INF directory, 238

method expressions, 269

method option (dojo.io.bind), 109

minimumCharacters attribute
    (autocomplete tag), 145

Model 2 MVC (model-view-controller)
    pattern, 153, 157

ModelAndView class, 229, 231

Mouseover DOM Inspector, 39–40

MoveBy effect (script.aculo.us), 91

Mozilla/Firefox browser

    FireBug extension, 43–45

    Mouseover DOM Inspector, 39

    Selenium IDE and, 68

    Venkman JavaScript debugger, 52

    XMLHttpRequest object and, 5, 10

MyFaces project, 263, 282

## N

name attribute

    DOM support, 59

    form element, 172

    form-beans element, 168

    JSF and, 273

    param tag, 119, 131

name tag (AjaxTags), 146

NameService class, 142, 144–146

NetBeans HTTP Monitor, 41–43

NetBeans JavaScript plug-in, 32–33

Netflix, 6–7, 20

Netscape browser, 39, 52

## O

obfuscation, 36

Object Graph Navigation Language (OGNL),
    184–185

object-oriented programming (OOP),
    220–222

objects

    cohesion in, 221

    dependency injection and, 224

    DWR support, 128–131, 133–134, 137

    sending to remote methods, 135–137

    Smalltalk support, 220

object.xml file, 31

OGNL (Object Graph Navigation Language),
    184–185

onblur attribute (DHTML), 273

onblur event handler, 162, 180

onchange attribute (DHTML), 273

onclick event handler, 136

onComplete attribute, 87

onkeypress attribute (DHTML), 273

onreadystatechange property
    (XMLHttpRequest), 13, 108

OOP (object-oriented programming),
    220–222

Opacity effect (script.aculo.us), 91–93, 98

open() command (Selenium), 59, 63, 65, 69

open() method (XMLHttpRequest), 12–14

Opera browser, 5, 10, 39

options variable (Effect), 91–92

Oracle JDeveloper, 280

O'Reilly, Tim, 16

## P

p element

    JavaScript Templates, 140

    Mouseover DOM Inspector, 40

page (Tapestry), 184

PageBeginRender event, 198

PageBeginRenderListener interface, 198

PageLink component (Tapestry), 193, 196

Parallel effect (script.aculo.us), 91–92, 95–96

param tag (DWR), 119, 131, 234

parameters

    passing multiple parameters with DWR, 126–127

    passing object parameters with DWR, 128–131, 133–134

    sending single parameter with DWR, 124–125

    Tapestry and, 184

parameters attribute

    addToCounter method, 192

    autocomplete tag, 145

parseInBrowser attribute, 115

Partial Page Paint pattern, 22

PartialFor component (Tacos), 205

path attribute (action element), 168

patterns. *See* Ajax patterns

pause() command (Selenium), 59, 65, 67

Persist annotation, 190

Person class

    DWR example, 128–131, 133–134

    JavaScript Templates, 138, 140

PhaseListener interface, 289

Plain Old Java Object (POJO), 228

Podcast class, 194–195, 198

point cuts, 223

POJO (Plain Old Java Object), 228

polymorphic behavior, 220

popup class, 46, 49

portals, 23

POST method (HTTP), 87, 109, 127, 154, 289

postContent option (dojo.io.bind), 109

println statement, 141

Process Validation phase (JSF), 285

processDOMTemplate() method (TrimPath), 141

ProgressBar component (Tacos), 205

Prototype library (JavaScript), 50

    $() shortcut, 76

    about, 75

    Ajax support, 86, 88

    AjaxTags and, 144

    browser detection, 84–85

    forms and, 77

    manipulating the DOM, 78, 80, 82, 84

    XMLHttpRequest object and, 161

prototype.js file, 75, 90, 93

Puff effect (script.aculo.us), 98

Pulsate effect (script.aculo.us), 98

■**R**

RAM (random access memory), 18

readyState property (XMLHttpRequest), 13, 87, 108

Refresh component (Tacos), 205

regular expressions, 174

remote methods, 135–137

RemoteBean class

    calculateCharacterSum method, 126

    configuring object, 119

    getPerson() method, 131, 133, 138

    getServerDate() method, 119, 121–122

    saveAddress() method, 135–136

    script tag, 120

remove() method (Element), 80

removeClassName() method (Element), 80

Render Response phase (JSF), 284–285

renderers, 272

repeatCount attribute (animations), 103

Request class (Ajax), 86–87, 162

RequestProcessor class, 155

request/response paradigm, 8

reservationErrors.jsp file, 169

ReservationForm class, 165–168, 172

ReservationNotAvailableException, 177

ReservationService class, 176–177

reset() method (Form), 77

resetCounter method (DirectLink), 191

responseText property (XMLHttpRequest), 13

responseXML property (XMLHttpRequest), 13

Restore View phase (JSF), 284

restorecolor parameter (Effect.Highlight), 94

Rhino JavaScript engine, 37

Ruby on Rails framework, 75, 89, 283

■**S**

Safari browser, 5, 10, 109

saveAddress function, 136

saveAddress() method (RemoteBean),
     135–136

saveReservation method, 177

SaveReservationAction class, 177

Scale effect (script.aculo.us), 91, 93–94

scaleContent parameter (Effect.Scale), 94

scaleFrom parameter (Effect.Scale), 94

scaleFromCenter parameter (Effect.Scale), 94

scaleMode parameter (Effect.Scale), 94

scaleX parameter (Effect.Scale), 94

scaleY parameter (Effect.Scale), 94

script tag

    DWR and, 120

    Lumberjack utility and, 50

    src attribute, 35

script.aculo.us

    about, 90

    autocomplete widget, 98–101

    Effect syntax, 90

    Effect.Appear, 98

    Effect.BlindDown, 98

    Effect.BlindUp, 98

    Effect.Dropout, 98

    Effect.Fade, 98

    Effect.Fold, 98

    Effect.Grow, 98

    Effect.Highlight, 91, 94

    Effect.MoveBy, 91

    Effect.Opacity, 91–93, 98

    Effect.Parallel, 91–92, 95–96

    Effect.Puff, 98

    Effect.Pulsate, 98

    Effect.Scale, 91, 93–94

    Effect.Shake, 98

    Effect.Shrink, 98

    Effect.SlideDown, 98

    Effect.SlideUp, 98

    Effect.Squish, 98

    Effect.SwitchOff, 98

scriptaculous.js file, 90

scripting, browser, 122–123

Seam, 283

second() method (animations), 104

security

    Ajax and, 19

    application, 235–236, 238

    JavaScript and, 36

    white-listing and, 131

security-constraint element, 238

security-role element, 238

Selenium test tool

    about, 58–59

    example tests, 60–61, 63, 65–67

    IDE, 67–68, 70

    JavaScript and, 36

    JsUnit framework and, 71

semicolon (;), 36

send() method (XMLHttpRequest), 12–13

sendFormforValidation function, 162

sendRequest() method (Taconite), 111–112, 114

serialize() method (Form), 77, 162

server-side processing, 112–113, 118

servlet-mapping tag, 227

servlets

JSF, 285

Spring support, 219

Tapestry and, 183–184

setEchoDebugInfo() method (Taconite), 112

setPostRequest() method (Taconite), 112

setRequestHeader() method (XMLHttpRequest), 12–13

setUp() function (JsUnit), 57

setUp() method (JUnit), 57

setValue function (DWRUtil), 124, 126

setVerb function (DWREngine), 127

Shake effect (script.aculo.us), 98

Shell component (Tapestry), 193

Ship, Howard Lewis, 183

show() method (Element), 80, 92

Shrink effect (script.aculo.us), 98

size attribute (JSF), 273

slide effect (Dojo), 215

slideBy() method (Dojo), 106, 215

SlideDown effect (script.aculo.us), 98

slide() method (Dojo), 106

slider.js file, 90

slideTo() method (Dojo), 106, 215

SlideUp effect (script.aculo.us), 98

Smalltalk, 220

source attribute (autocomplete tag), 145

Source Code pane (Venkman), 54

Source tab (Selenium IDE), 70

span element, 123–124

Spring framework

about, 219–220

Ajax support, 233–234

application security, 235–236, 238

aspect-oriented programming and, 221–223, 247–249

data access layer, 241–245

data helper objects, 250–252

dependency injection and, 224

domain layer, 240–241

getting started, 225–231, 233

manages prices page, 239

service layer, 245–246

Spring beans configuration, 253, 255–256

Struts Shale, 283

web tier, 256–258, 260–261

Spring MVC, 225–227, 229, 231

springdispatch-servlet.xml file, 230–231, 233

Squish effect (script.aculo.us), 98

src attribute (script tag), 35

Standard Widget Toolkit (SWT), 4

Star Tribune, 7–8

startcolor parameter (Effect.Highlight), 94

startOn variable (Effect), 92

status property (XMLHttpRequest), 13

statusText property (XMLHttpRequest), 13

Step Into option (Venkman), 55

Step Over option (Venkman), 55

Stephenson, Sam, 75

String class

code completion for, 30

DWR and, 118

Prototype library and, 89

Struts
Ajax integration and, 157–161
background, 153
designing, 153–155, 179–180
future of, 180–182
implementing, 153–155, 163–172,
174–177, 179
Spring MVC and, 225–226
validation, 153, 155–156, 161–163,
170–172, 174
Struts Shale, 181, 283
Struts Ti, 182
struts-config.xml file
action-mappings section, 168
example, 165
explanation of, 163
MessageResources.properties file, 174
SaveReservationAction class, 177
style attribute
JSF taglibs, 273, 276
p element, 40
STYLE element, 90
styleClass attribute (JSF), 273
Submit component (Tapestry), 205
Sun Microsystems, 5
SwitchOff effect (script.aculo.us), 98
synch option
dojo.io.bind, 109
Effect, 91

### ▪T

TABLE element, 90
Taconite library
about, 110
client-side processing, 111–113
installing, 113–115
server-side processing, 112–113

taconite-append-as-children tag, 112, 115
taconite-append-as-first-child tag, 112
taconite-client.js file, 113
taconite-delete tag, 112
taconite-insert-after tag, 112
taconite-insert-before tag, 113
taconite-parser.js file, 113
taconite-replace tag, 113
taconite-replace-children tag, 113
taconite-root tag, 115–116
taconite-set-attributes tag, 113
Tacos
components, 205–209
debugging support, 211
form support, 212–216
setting up, 206
tag libraries, JSF, 270–273
tag library descriptor (TLD), 207
tagging, Web 2.0 and, 16
Tapestry
about, 183–184
Ajax support, 204–209, 211–212, 214–216
annotations in, 190
class support, 202
exception support, 203
Facelets project and, 282
forms support, 193–201, 203
getting started, 185–188
target attribute (autocomplete tag), 145
TBODY element, 90
TDD (test-driven development), 56
tearDown() function (JsUnit), 57
tearDown() method (JUnit), 57
template.js file, 138

templates
    AddPodcast example, 213–214
    Facelets project, 282
    JavaScript Templates, 137–141
    Tapestry and, 184
Test Runner, 57, 60, 67
test-driven development (TDD), 56
testing tools
    DWR and, 122
    JsUnit testing framework, 57
    JUnit testing framework, 56
    Selenium test tool, 58–61, 63, 65–68, 70
text tag (Struts), 157
textarea element (Struts), 138, 140–141, 157
TFOOT element, 90
THEAD element, 90
TITLE element, 90
TLD (tag library descriptor), 207
to option (Effect), 91
toDescriptiveString function, 136
toggle() method (Prototype), 79
Tomcat, 238
Top() method (Insertion), 82
TR element, 90
transition option (Effect), 91
Tree component (Tacos), 205
TrimPath object, 141
Try class (Prototype), 84
type object, 109
type() command (Selenium), 59, 63

■U

UIViewRoot component (JSF), 284
Update Center Wizard, 32
Update Model phase (JSF), 285
Updater() method (Ajax), 88–89
url-pattern element, 238

useCache option (dojo.io.bind), 109
useLoadingMessage() method (DWRUtil), 125
util.js file, 124

■V

validate attribute (validateReservation), 168
validate method
    ActionForm class, 155–156, 174
    Validator interface, 278
validateForm method, 162
validateReservation action, 168–169, 172
ValidateReservationAction class, 174–175
validation
    JSF, 274, 276–279, 285
    Struts, 153, 155–156, 161–163, 170–172, 174
    of user input, 173
validation.xml file, 155–156, 168, 180
Validator interface, 278
ValidatorActionForm class, 165, 168, 172
ValidatorException, 278
ValidatorForm class, 168
value attribute (param tag), 119, 234
value tag (AjaxTags), 146
Venkman JavaScript debugger, 52–54, 56
verifyTextPresent() command (Selenium), 59, 63, 65, 70–71
View Source feature (browsers), 39
Visit object (Tapestry), 184
visual cues, 18
visual effects, 105

■W

W3C standards
    innerHTML property and, 90, 111
    JavaScript Templates, 137
    XMLHttpRequest object and, 10
warn() method (Log4JS), 46
warning() method (Logger), 50

Web 2.0, 16

web applications

AjaxTags library, 141

autocomplete feature, 98

dynamic navigation, 269–270

forms and, 77

graceful degradation and, 198

rise of, 3–4

Selenium test tool, 58–61, 63, 65–68, 70

Tapestry and, 184, 188

Web Flow, 283

web pages

Fade Anything Technique pattern, 21

FireBug extension and, 45

inspecting DOM structures, 38–40

Partial Page Paint pattern, 22

Test Runner and, 60

unlinkable, 17

WebContext object, 250

WEB-INF folder

application specifications, 190

configuration files, 267

inventory control application, 256

Tacos support, 206

WebObjects framework (Apple), 183

web-resource-collection element, 238

WebWork, 182

web.xml file, 118, 122, 180, 226, 237

white-listing, 131

Wikipedia, 16

window object, 30, 33

wipeIn() method (Dojo), 107, 215

wipeOut() method (Dojo), 107, 215

wobble() function, 93

write class (Log4JS), 46

write tag, 169

## ■X

XAML (Extensible Application Markup Language), 4

XHR. See XMLHttpRequest object

XHTML, 111–112, 115–116

XML User Interface Language (XUL), 4

xmlHttp variable, 11

XMLHttpRequest object (XHR)

about, 9–11

AjaxRequest object and, 114

browser support, 5

creating, 10–11

dojo.io.bind and, 107

methods and properties, 12–13

POST method and, 127

Prototype library and, 86, 161

Taconite support, 112

unlinkable pages and, 17

XMLHttpRequest Spy feature, 43–44

XMLHttpRequest Spy feature, 43–44

XUL (XML User Interface Language), 4

## ■Y

Yahoo!, 5

Yellow Fade Technique (YFT), 21, 215

# You Need the Companion eBook

## Your purchase of this book entitles you to its companion eBook for only $10.

**W**e believe this Apress title will prove so indispensable that you'll want to carry it with you everywhere, which is why we are offering the companion eBook for $10 to customers who purchase this book now. Convenient and fully searchable, the eBook version of any content-rich, page-heavy Apress book makes a valuable addition to your programming library. You can easily find, copy, and apply code—and then perform examples by quickly toggling between instructions and the application. Even simultaneously tackling a donut, diet soda, and complex code becomes simplified with hands-free eBooks!

Once you purchase this book, getting the $10 companion eBook is simple:

❶ Visit **www.apress.com/promo/tendollars/**.

❷ Complete a basic registration form to receive a randomly generated question about this title.

❸ Answer the question correctly in 60 seconds and you will receive a promotional code to redeem for the $10 eBook.

2560 Ninth Street • Suite 219 • Berkeley, CA 94710

**eBookshop**

THE EXPERT'S VOICE™

**Offer valid through 12/20/06.**